Tennyson Echoing Wordsworth

Tennyson Echoing Wordsworth

Jayne Thomas

EDINBURGH
University Press

Edinburgh University Press is one of the leading university presses in the UK. We publish academic books and journals in our selected subject areas across the humanities and social sciences, combining cutting-edge scholarship with high editorial and production values to produce academic works of lasting importance. For more information visit our website: edinburghuniversitypress.com

Edinburgh University Press Ltd
The Tun – Holyrood Road
12(2f) Jackson's Entry
Edinburgh EH8 8PJ

Typeset in 11/13 Adobe Sabon by
IDSUK (DataConnection) Ltd, and
printed and bound in Great Britain.

A CIP record for this book is available from the British Library

ISBN 978 1 4744 3687 8 (hardback)
ISBN 978 1 4744 3689 2 (webready PDF)
ISBN 978 1 4744 3690 8 (epub)

Contents

Acknowledgements

I am grateful to the British Association for Victorian Studies for the award of a Research Funding Grant in January 2017. The Award has enabled me to carry out vital archival research on the Tennyson manuscripts, papers and letters held at the Tennyson Research Centre, Lincoln, the Fitzwilliam Museum, Cambridge, Trinity College, Cambridge and the University Library Cambridge. I thank staff at the Tennyson Research Centre for helping me to locate material relevant to my work; I thank the Centre too for allowing me to quote from John Churton Collins, 'A New Study of Tennyson', 241 (January 1880), pp. 36–50. My thanks also go to the Syndics of the Fitzwilliam Museum for allowing me to consult, and quote from, Tennyson's *Poems* (1833), with autograph additions and corrections. I have drawn throughout the book from the editions of Wordsworth's poems to which Tennyson himself would have had access; these include *The Poetical Works of William Wordsworth in Five Volumes* (1827), which Tennyson is known to have owned, and I am grateful to the staff at the London Library for giving me access to the 1827 volumes, as well as *Poems, in Two Volumes* (1807), *The Miscellaneous Poems of William Wordsworth: In Four Volumes* (1820), and *The Prelude; or, Growth of a Poet's Mind: An Autobiographical Poem* (1850). Likewise, I am grateful to the staff at Special Collections and Archives, Cardiff University, for access to *Lyrical Ballads, with Other Poems, in Two Volumes* (1800), and *Yarrow Revisited; and Other Poems* (1835). A 7,000-word version of Chapter 5 appears in *Connotations: A Journal for Critical Debate*, 11 (November 2017), pp. 139–62; my thanks go to the editor of *Connotations*, Professor Matthias Bauer, for his permission to publish material from the article in a book chapter. Lastly, the anonymous readers at Edinburgh University Press have provided valuable support in shaping and refining the book for publication, and I would like to acknowledge that support here.

Introduction

Alfred, Lord Tennyson responded with exasperation to claims by critics that he 'borrowed' 'similes and expressions' from other writers,[1] which he saw as an attack upon both his powers of observation and his originality as a poet.[2] The poet, according to Tennyson, should be allowed 'some power of imagination of his own':[3] '"They allow me nothing"', he says of his critics to H. D. Rawnsley, furnishing a line or two from 'Ulysses' (1842) as evidence of the kind of critical attack to which he felt he was subject:[4] '"The deep moans round with many voices". "The deep", Byron; "moans", Horace; "many voices", Homer; and so on.'[5] Tennyson's quizzical and defensive response to John Churton Collins' provocative article, 'A New Study of Tennyson', published in the *Cornhill Magazine* in January 1880, also attests to his irritation when confronted by examples of his supposed 'borrowings': in a copy of the article annotated by the poet himself, Churton Collins' claims of imitation are marked off by Tennyson with inkily indignant protestations of 'not known to me', 'no – close at it seems', 'I read this for the first time', or simply a blistering 'nonsense' or 'no!'[6] By the close of the article, almost as if worn down by the process of defending himself, Tennyson takes a more measured tone, however, writing: 'I will answer for it that no modern poet can write a single line but among the innumerable authors of this world you will somewhere find a striking parallelism. It is the unimaginative man who thinks everything borrowed.'[7] He goes on to make a similar point in a letter of 1882, written in response to suggestions of influence in *The Princess* (1847), his first long narrative poem, although the general defence of 'parallel' passages narrows to a direct refutation of Wordsworth or Shelley's influence in his own work:

> It is scarcely possible for anyone to say or write anything in this late time of the world to which, in the rest of the literature of the world, a parallel could not somewhere be found. But when you say that this

passage or that was suggested by Wordsworth or Shelley or another, I demur; and more, I wholly disagree.[8]

In the first major study of Tennyson and Wordsworth, this book makes Tennyson's echoes and borrowings from Wordsworth its focus, operating at what was thus for the later poet a site of critical contention. The book alleges that the site of contention, however, is also a thrilling fault line, where creativity and verbal dexterity flourish and form is consolidated. Focusing on some of the most emblematic poems of Tennyson's career, including 'The Lady of Shalott' (1832; 1842), 'Ulysses' (1833; 1842) and *In Memoriam* (1850), the study examines in a series of close readings the echoes or borrowings from Wordsworth that these poems contain and the transformative part they play in his poetry. It moves beyond existing accounts of Wordsworthian influence in the selected texts to uncover new and revealing connections and interactions that shed a penetrating light on Tennyson's poetic relationship with Wordsworth. The echoes and borrowings at times nourish and inform his poetry, feeding his discussion of art, gender, faith, death, loss and poetry itself, while at others act as a constraining or defining force, augmenting his development as a poet, but also complicating and problematising his work. Wordsworth has been described as Tennyson's 'poetic father-figure';[9] like nearly all parental relationships, this involves both dependency and the desire for independence, a pattern clearly reflected in the echoes and borrowings that scatter the texts. By focusing on 'parallel' passages, the study thus re-evaluates Tennyson's poetic relationship with Wordsworth and recalibrates current critical estimates of Tennyson as a poet and indeed Poet Laureate. It also, by association, reinflects established readings of Tennyson as a post-Romantic poet, with Wordsworth revealed as the lynchpin of some of Tennyson's greatest poetry.

The book uses the term 'echo' to track the sometimes loud, sometimes faint, yet always audible Wordsworthian resonances within Tennyson's poetry. 'Echo' has affinities with the term 'allusion', but is often separated from it on the basis of authorial intentionality or agency. Stephen Hinds, for instance, describes a process 'whereby alluding poets exert themselves to draw attention to the fact that they are alluding, and to reflect upon the nature of their allusive activity'.[10] Sarah Annes Brown states the case more explicitly, arguing that allusion

> strongly implies agency; it suggests that a later writer has deliberately referenced an earlier work, inviting the reader to notice and reflect on the connection. Sometimes the echo is so unmistakable, so distinctive, that we experience no doubt in identifying a deliberate allusion.[11]

Brown recognises here how echo, if sufficiently distinctive, translates into a deliberate allusion, going on to note that 'echo is a more neutral word' than allusion,[12] which does not rule out the possibility of conscious borrowing, 'but implies that the connection isn't strong enough to prove deliberate agency or to ensure recognition in the majority of attentive readers'.[13] John Hollander gives a useful summary of the duality of echo: poets, according to Hollander, seem to echo earlier voices 'with full or suppressed consciousness',[14] 'by accident or by plan',[15] but 'with the same shaping spirit that gives form to tropes of thought and feeling'.[16] Although I use the term 'echo' throughout the book, I also therefore use the term 'allusion' on occasion as a synonym in recognition of this duality. I also use the term 'borrowing', however, as an alternative to both terms. Crucially, the overhearing of echoes also includes that of single words; Hollander again, for instance, notices how the 'fragmentations and breakings-off of intertextual echo can result in pieces of voice as small as single words, and as elusive as particular cadences' being transmitted through texts;[17] as he goes on to say, 'A single word or phrase . . . amplified or not by a phonetic scheme, may easily carry rumors of its resounding cave'.[18]

I nevertheless acknowledge that Tennyson's poetry participates in an intertextual web of literature. Intertextuality is dependent on the figure of the web or weave, a concept born out of the word 'text' itself, whose etymological base is 'a tissue, a woven fabric'.[19] In Roland Barthes' terms, the text is 'woven entirely with citations, references, echoes, cultural languages (what language is not?) antecedent or contemporary, which cut across it through and through in a vast stereophony',[20] but where 'the citations which go to make up a text are anonymous, untraceable, and yet *already read*: they are quotations without inverted commas'.[21] Intertextuality has a comprehensive theoretical background, which I am not going to rehearse here, although readers can find more information on the formation of intertextuality as a theoretical school by consulting the works of Julia Kristeva, from whom the term itself derives.[22] The book does not make claims as to whether the 'centre of intertextuality [resides] in the author, the reader or the text itself?',[23] although it acknowledges that the reader in a sense also creates,[24] as well as perceives, meaning, and that the reading of poetry is itself an imaginative and aesthetic experience.

Harold Bloom's powerful account of intra-poetic rivalry hovers over the close readings, but the processes the readings locate largely fall outside the fraught relationships that Bloom maintains exist between poets, where 'poetic history . . . is held to be indistinguishable from poetic influence, since strong poets make that history by misreading one another, so as to clear imaginative space for themselves'.[25] In Bloom's terms, an

> anxiety [is] achieved in and by the story, novel, play, poem, or essay. The anxiety may or may not be internalized by the later writer, depending upon temperament and circumstances, yet that hardly matters: the strong poem is the achieved anxiety.[26]

Bloom steps upon the 'dark and daemonic ground' that is the anxiety of influence,[27] rejecting the 'wearisome industry of source-hunting, of allusion-counting'[28] and the 'patterning of images',[29] to centre 'upon intra-poetic relationships as parallels of family romance'.[30] The book does not work on the premise that Tennyson enters upon such melancholy territory in his echoing and borrowing of Wordsworth's language and phrasing, or that his revisions of his predecessor are always operating at the level of deep, psychic impulse. Likewise, the study works primarily at the surface level, at the level of language and echo, of cadence and rhythm, the very level that Bloom eschews. It nevertheless recognises that Tennyson may at times be driven by impulse: the fact that Tennyson repeatedly and irritably defends his work against charges of plagiarism itself implies his borrowing or echoing of other poets' words and phrases is working at a psychic level, for instance; and in calling Wordsworth Tennyson's 'poetic father-figure', the book itself invokes the familial poetic relationships that Bloom describes. The readings are also a manifestation of Bloom's 'assertion that the meaning of a poem can only be a poem, but *another poem – a poem not itself*'.[31] Wordsworth's poems are the 'meaning' of the poems of Tennyson explored in the chapters that follow. The book too can be seen as Bloomian in that it privileges male rather than female authors; Tennyson and Wordsworth are two of Bloom's 'strong' poets in this sense.[32] Unlike Bloom, however, the study does not find an analogue for creativity in anxiety, in the 'symbiotic life of the poet's imagination',[33] although it accepts that anxiety surrounds the creative act. It also recognises that Bloom's model allows the reader to ask profound questions about where in the mind the creative process is located.[34] Tennyson was notoriously insecure about his creative abilities. Both Christopher Decker and Christopher Ricks remark upon Tennyson's anxiety over his own powers of composition; Decker observes how 'intertextual manoeuvres are symptoms of Tennyson's unsettling doubts and debts';[35] Ricks describes how Tennyson relies on the 'support of another poet's words'.[36] It is possible therefore that Tennyson's compositional anxiety informs and fans his borrowing or echoing of Wordsworth's language and phrasing. The book generally finds some affinity with Ricks' supportive model of influence,[37] but the model does not fully account for the processes at work in Tennyson. Tennyson is at times in productive coalition with Wordsworth, finding strength, comfort and support in the earlier poet's language and phrasing, but at other times Wordsworth has an unforeseen and constricting effect in Tennyson's work, although this can also sometimes be productive.

I draw from Ricks' 1987 comprehensive three-volume edition of *The Poems of Tennyson* in the book for reference. I accept that Wordsworth does not have connotative ownership of all of the words and phrases in Tennyson, and, where appropriate, I allow for the harmonising or discordancy of other poetic voices, including those cited by Ricks in his glosses to Tennyson's work in *The Poems of Tennyson*. The book also draws on the editions of Wordsworth's poems to which Tennyson would himself have had access, thus ensuring that the Wordsworthian words, phrases and echoes on which it focuses are drawn from texts that Tennyson himself could have or would have read, or indeed owned such as *The Poetical Works of William Wordsworth in Five Volumes* (1827). Other texts on which I draw include *Yarrow Revisited; and Other Poems* (1835), and Wordsworth's *Poems, in Two Volumes* (1807). I have added line numbers to the original material, and where appropriate volume numbers, to facilitate reading. I use shortened titles for some poems such as 'Tintern Abbey'.

Tennyson's recorded relationship with the earlier poet is respectful, and at times reverential, though not uncritical. Hallam Tennyson notes his father as saying in 1883 that Wordsworth was '"at his best on the whole the greatest English poet since Milton"'.[38] Qualified praise often turned to blunt and often derisive criticism, however, particularly in relation to Wordsworth's prosaic poetic style: Wordsworth, Tennyson claims, is '"*thick-ankled*"',[39] his work unequal, with a 'heaviness of style seen somewhat too often in poems, the subjects of which more or less defied successful treatment'.[40] It is a critical appraisal of Wordsworth's use of 'prosaic' poetic language that Tennyson makes throughout his career: Hallam Tennyson again reports how, on a visit to James Spedding and his family at Mirehouse on Bassenthwaite in 1835, his father held a contest with Edward Fitzgerald 'as to who could invent the weakest Wordsworthian line imaginable. Although Fitzgerald claimed this line, my father declared that he had composed it – A Mr Wilkinson, a Clergyman'.[41] Yet, Tennyson's criticism of Wordsworth is more often than not balanced by corresponding admiration and respect, as his comparison of Wordsworth to Milton suggests. Fitzgerald's comments from 1835 go on to note how Tennyson read 'a great deal of Wordsworth' at the Mirehouse gathering:[42] '"The Yews of Borrowdale," "The Simplon Pass," the sonnet beginning "Two Voices," "The Solitary Reaper," "Peele Castle," the "Ode on Intimations of Immortality," "The Fountain," were among his favourites'.[43] An appreciation of Wordsworth comes with time, love and not a little effort, it seems, although the admiration could at times be fleeting. Fitzgerald notes how

> A.T. . . . remembered the time when he could see nothing in 'Michael' which he now read us in admiration; though he thought Wordsworth often clumsy and diffuse. There was no end of 'This Thorn' in the piece that bears the name: 'such hammering to set a scene for so small a drama'.[44]

It comes too with an acknowledgement of the later poet's especial gifts, particularly in relation to favourite poems such as 'Tintern Abbey' and 'Yarrow Unvisited'. On a short tour of Europe in 1869 Frederick Locker-Lampson remembers Tennyson as saying:

> You must not think because I speak plainly of Wordsworth's defects as a poet that I have not a very high admiration of him. I shall never forget my deep emotion the first time I had speech with him. I have a profound admiration for 'Tintern Abbey'.[45]

And yet, Locker-Lampson notes how 'even in that poem [Tennyson] considered the old poet had shown a want of literary instinct';[46] he thought the poem, for instance, 'too long' and too repetitive, a poetic trait to which he himself is not averse.[47] Tennyson nevertheless 'greatly praised the famous line "Whose dwelling is the light of setting suns" – "the permanent in the transitory"',[48] a praise he would reiterate in 1883, calling the line '"almost the grandest in the English language, giving the sense of the abiding in the transient"'.[49] Admiration indeed turned to love,[50] with Tennyson claiming on the same tour of Europe that a love of Wordsworth is a necessary requirement for a true appreciation of his worth: '"Byron's merits are on the surface. This is not the case with Wordsworth. You must love Wordsworth ere he will seem worthy of your love"'.[51]

Tennyson's first meeting with Wordsworth was strained, however. Aubrey de Vere, an unreliable witness, perhaps,[52] describes how Tennyson was brought '"murmuring sore"' to a meeting with Wordsworth in Hampstead in 1845 set up by de Vere himself.[53] Tennyson came away from the meeting disappointed at Wordsworth's 'coldness'[54] and his own signal failure to 'inflame' the older poet's imagination with a description of a 'tropical island where the trees, when they first came into leaf, were a vivid scarlet'.[55] De Vere records a second meeting between the two poets shortly afterwards at a dinner given by Edward Moxon, Tennyson and Wordsworth's publisher. Speaking 'in a low voice, and with a perceptible emotion',[56] it was painful for Tennyson to leave the house without expressing to 'the Old Bard his sense of the obligation which all Englishmen owed to him', de Vere writes.[57] Wordsworth for his part was very much pleased at the meeting,[58] recording later in a letter to a friend:

> I saw Tennyson when I was in London several times. He is decidedly the first of our living poets, and I hope will live to give the world still better things. You will be pleased to hear that he expressed in the strongest terms his gratitude to my writings. To this I was far from indifferent.[59]

Gratitude blends with an implicit recognition here perhaps that a poetic transition is taking place: Tennyson is 'decidedly' the first of our living poets. In his 1879 essay on Wordsworth, Matthew Arnold maintains that by the publication of Tennyson's 1842 volume of poetry, 'the ear and applause of the great body of poetry-readers' turn decisively towards Tennyson and away from Wordsworth.[60] De Vere blunts the point, but marks the same shift, nonetheless: Wordsworth is the 'Poet whose great work was all but finished',[61] and Tennyson 'the youthful compeer whose chief labours were yet to come'.[62]

De Vere gives another version of Tennyson's meeting with the 'old poet' at the Moxon dinner.[63] Tennyson, he writes:

> came in and smoked his pipe. He told us with pleasure of his dinner with Wordsworth – was pleased as well as amused by Wordsworth saying to him, 'Come, brother bard, to dinner,' and taking his arm; said that he was ashamed of paying Mr. Wordsworth compliments, but that he had at last, in the dark, said something about the pleasure he had had from Mr. Wordsworth's writings, and that the old poet had taken his hand, and replied with some expressions equally kind and complimentary. Tennyson was evidently much pleased with the old man, and glad of having learned to know him.[64]

Something of Tennyson's amusement at Wordsworth and his plea-sure at being given due recognition by the older poet comes through here, as well as his pleasure at being taken as Wordsworth's equal – a brother bard, as it were. But de Vere's anecdote hints at something more profound: if Wordsworth can acknowledge that Tennyson is destined to be his poetic successor, then this acknowledgement, albeit at a fledgling stage, can be extended to include Tennyson himself.

When the offer of the Laureateship came Tennyson spent a day deciding whether to accept it.[65] There was also the question of formal dress for the occasion. Emily Tennyson reveals how Samuel Rogers, upon learning of the Tennysons' inability to find a court dress for the Levée, 'offer'd his own dress, which had been also worn by Wordsworth and had been promised to the Wordsworth family as an heirloom'.[66] Tennyson took over the mantle of the Laureateship from Wordsworth in 1850, then, by wearing robes 'borrowed' from Wordsworth. On becoming Laureate, Tennyson was keen to pay Wordsworth his due respect, the borrowed robes notwithstanding. Meditating on his first Laureate poem, 'To the Queen' (1851), Hallam Tennyson records his father as 'especially thinking of a stanza in which "the empire of Wordsworth should be asserted: for he was a representative Poet Laureate, such a poet as kings should honour, and such an one as would do honour to kings"'.[67]

Tennyson's membership of the Cambridge Apostles, the exclusive intellectual 'Platonico-Wordsworthian-Coleridgean' society formed in 1820,[68] played heavily into Tennyson's appreciation of Wordsworth's poetic gifts. Tennyson was a non-compliant, essentially 'eccentric'[69] member of the group, attending no more than five regular meetings and failing to fulfil the obligations of the society by reading a paper to assembled members; overcome with nervousness he tore up an invited paper (on '"Ghosts"') and threw it in the fire.[70] Yet, Tennyson's poetry was, for the Apostles, 'the voice of the new era',[71] and despite his extraordinary status the former Poet Laureate always remained 'in some special sense an Apostle'.[72] The society's literary taste was formed by two of its members, Frederick Denison Maurice and John Sterling. In series of articles for the *Athenaeum* between 6 January and 30 July 1828 Maurice offers his views on Wordsworth's literary merit: Wordsworth, he writes, could make us feel that '"we have all of us one human heart"',[73] although he coupled this with a pronounced regard for Percy Bysshe Shelley. Sterling too admired both Wordsworth and Shelley. He and Maurice together inspired the Apostles of Tennyson and Hallam's generation with an enthusiasm for Shelley and Wordsworth not so much as two very different poets but as one imaginary compound poet, a chimera invented by Maurice and Sterling as necessary to their own imaginative requirements'.[74] The result was the composition of a number of poems in which Wordsworthian and Shelleyan influences 'rather uncomfortably jostle against one another',[75] such as Arthur Henry Hallam's 'Timbuctoo' (1829), his entry for the Chancellor's Gold Medal at Cambridge University, and Tennyson's 'The Poet' (1830).[76] The Apostles' influence continued into the following decade as Tennyson's work begins to edge towards the kind of decorative Wordsworthianism that Sterling espoused.[77] The English or Domestic 'Idyls' of 1842, for instance, whose number include 'Dora', 'The Gardener's Daughter' and 'Audley Court', openly embrace a Wordsworthian pastoral paradigm. Sterling, comparing the poems with Wordsworth's great narrative poems such as 'Michael: A Pastoral Poem',[78] praises Tennyson for the way in which he domesticates and makes decorative the Wordsworthian English idyll.[79]

Tennyson's poetic relationship with Wordsworth has been explored in a number of articles and book chapters, and is often read through the prism of Tennyson's most iconic poems, such as 'Tears, Idle Tears', 'Ulysses', *In Memoriam* and *Maud*, or through the early poetry and the late ballads. In his compendious book on Tennyson, *Alfred Tennyson*, Seamus Perry explores Tennyson's fascination with Wordsworth's trope of recurrence or revisiting the past, most famously exemplified in 'Tintern Abbey'. Perry reveals how Tennyson revisits Wordsworth's own trope of revisiting in 'Tears, Idle Tears', concluding that

> The hesitancy of the poem's eloquence emulates the reticence of its spiritual claim: 'Tintern Abbey' works with heroic strenuousness to affirm a sense of continuity between past and present ('*Therefore* am I still / A lover of the meadows and the woods, / And mountains' (emphasis added)); 'Tears, Idle Tears' has to make do with much less hope than that (even).[80]

'Tithonus', meanwhile, 'works a remarkable variation on the theme' of changefulness.[81] Stephen Gill, in the most influential account of Wordsworth's influence on the Victorians to date, argues that what distinguishes Tennyson from Wordsworth is 'the different degrees of intellectual turbulence their knowledge caused in their confrontation, as artists, with the greatest mysteries of life – change, loss, and death'.[82] Wordsworth's 'greatest poetry pre-dates the impact of science on religion and philosophy; Tennyson's registers it'.[83] Thus, according to Gill, in Tennyson's *In Memoriam* 'almost all of the declarations that make up the affirmatory movement of that poem voice a confident faith that Tennyson could not share'.[84] In a closely read, allusive, yet socially and culturally contextualised study of Tennyson's poetry, Herbert F. Tucker, Jr charts how the poet perfects 'a consummate art through the themes, the images, and the very words that the Romantics left him';[85] Tucker reveals Wordsworth, along with Coleridge, Shelley and Keats, as significant presences in poems ranging from the juvenilia through to *Maud*, as the poet acculturates the 'doom' that is his Romantic inheritance.[86] More recently, Michael J. Sullivan explores via the hitherto unseen *Lincoln Revision Copy* of *The Golden Treasury* (1861), held in the dome at Lincoln Central Library, how Tennyson's involvement in the compilation of the anthology refutes the idea that a poet as important as Wordsworth to the young Tennyson, and so significant in adulthood, could come entirely to be rejected in old age.[87]

This book moves on from Perry and others to examine how standard affinities between Tennyson and Wordsworth are complicated and expanded in the later poet's work. Despite his many recorded comments on Wordsworth, Tennyson's poetry is the place where the real relationship with Wordsworth is played out. Tennyson is not a critic 'except in his art', as Ricks points out,[88] and this remains the underlying principle of the book. In arguing for Wordsworth's influence on Tennyson, the book acknowledges nonetheless that Wordsworth is not regarded as Tennyson's primary poetic precursor; John Keats is accorded that title. As George Saintsbury puts it: '"Keats begat Tennyson and Tennyson begat all the rest"'.[89] Margaret A. Lourie notes how 'Tennyson [like Keats] anchors his poetic world to concrete sense impressions described in meticulous detail, although for him more than for Keats visual and aural perception predominate over the other senses'.[90] Hallam, in his 1831 review of Tennyson's 1830 *Poems, Chiefly Lyrical*, 'On Some of the Characteristics of Modern Poetry, And on the Lyrical Poems of Alfred Tennyson', aligns Tennyson with poets of 'sensation' like Keats and Shelley.[91] But in Lourie's terms, Shelley forms as great an influence on Tennyson as Keats, largely giving him the poetic resources to utter 'what he found within' in 'The Kraken', for instance;[92] as she says, Shelley's 'first important successor was Tennyson'.[93] In echoing Wordsworth, Tennyson thus challenges and reinflects the Keats–Shelley identification that has stood for well over a century.

Chapter 1 examines Tennyson's 'The Lady of Shalott', arguing that the poem prefigures the movement Tennyson is to make in the English 'Idyls' towards a simplicity of diction and gaining the sympathies of a wide audience. In so doing, the poem absorbs a Wordsworthian language and poetics from which Hallam somewhat artificially separates it in his review of Tennyson's *Poems, Chiefly Lyrical*. Wordsworth's presence is clearly felt in the 1832 version of 'The Lady of Shalott', feeding Tennyson's discussion of some of the poem's major themes, although the level of borrowing from Wordsworth increases in the 1842 version of the poem, suggesting that Tennyson draws even more deeply from Wordsworth in 1842, both to assuage the critics and to search for a new poetic. Tennyson's borrowings from Wordsworth play directly into his poetic insecurities, scaffolding the poem with the earlier poet's language, yet stabilising his poetic voice and reputation. But the echoes and borrowings in the poem do more than stream into Tennyson's critical insecurities, both complicating and clarifying the poem's discussion of art, life and gender. The second part of the chapter briefly explores the linguistic and thematic connections between 'The Lady of Shalott' and the English 'Idyls', specifically 'Dora' and 'The Gardener's Daughter'.

Chapter 2 examines Tennyson's 1842 monologue, 'Ulysses'. As in 'The Lady of Shalott' the poem liberally absorbs Wordsworth's language; but here there are different effects, different consequences: if Tennyson borrows from Wordsworth in 'The Lady of Shalott' in order to loosen the restrictive epistemology in which he has been placed through his designation as a poet of 'sensation', in 'Ulysses' his borrowings allow him to distance the Romantic lyric's focus on self and to consolidate a 'new' poetic form – the dramatic monologue. In revising Wordsworth, Tennyson thus establishes his poetic difference from Wordsworth, or at least positions his poetry in relation to the poetry that precedes it. The study of Tennyson's borrowing in the poem seemingly evokes Bloom's revisionary model, yet Tennyson's 'consumption' of Wordsworth differentiates itself from Bloom's intra-poetic methodology in several ways, not least because it reveals Tennyson as seeking to reaffiliate himself with Wordsworth rather than defensively protecting himself against him.

Chapter 3 examines Tennyson's *In Memoriam*. The poem, published in the year in which Tennyson took over the Laureateship, combines private grief with public expression, as it explores faith, God and science in its attempt to come to terms with the loss of Hallam at the age of twenty-two from a brain haemorrhage, and ends with the speaker's ostensible accommodation with all three. Tennyson was open about the difficulties he sustained in writing the poem, and this chapter argues that Tennyson borrows Wordsworth's words and phrases as an aid to the writing of the poem. It explores how the Wordsworthian borrowings in the poem help the later poet to work towards finding his own form of consolation, however tenuous this consolation subsequently proves to be, and therefore to make his accommodations with his faith and with the claims of nineteenth-century science and religion, but also with the loss of Hallam himself. It also examines how the Wordsworthian language in *In Memoriam* helps Tennyson both to stabilise his 'public' voice and to develop the pastoral elements of elegy. Tennyson borrows the gifts that Wordsworth's language has to offer, and in drawing on Wordsworth in this way, Tennyson draws on a poet who is able to articulate his grief and to move towards finding his own form of consolation. The borrowings from Wordsworth form a chamber of echoes that Tennyson harnesses, reworks, reconfigures, replays in a different context and in a different time. At times the later poet is unable fully to transfigure and rework Wordsworth's language, but is constrained, limited, inhibited by it, and these effects make themselves manifest in the poem too.

Chapter 4 examines Tennyson's *Maud*, published just five years after *In Memoriam*, in 1855. The poem was met with sustained criticism, not least because of its 'innovatory' form, a 'drama in lyrics' as Tennyson himself terms it.[94] *Maud* displays a variety of influences, including, most conspicuously, *Hamlet*. It also displays a variety of metrical forms, in its attempt to render the speaker's successive phases of passion; these include ballad, heroic couplet, alexandrines and epithalamion. It has also been claimed that *Maud*, Tennyson's first non-occasional poem as Laureate, is the result of an Oedipal rivalry with Wordsworth, largely as a result of his inheritance of the Laureateship in 1850.[95] However, Wordsworth's presence in *Maud* is more complex than Bloom's somewhat unwieldy model would allow. The presence of Wordsworth's language creates a multiplicity of effects: some borrowings allow Tennyson to remodulate Wordsworth, allowing him to define himself in relation to his predecessor; others define him in turn, underlining the trajectory of the poem and questioning its narrative form; others allow Tennyson to address issues which the poem ostensibly avoids; yet others allow Tennyson to question his role as a public poet and as a poet of 'sensation'.

Chapter 5 examines the Wordsworthian echoes and borrowings in the 1860 'Tithonus'. Critics have drawn attention to the many allusions to Wordsworth in the poem, as well as to the influence of Shelley and Keats. But my reading of previously untracked Wordsworthian language and phrasing opens up hitherto unexplored aspects of the text, revealing 'Tithonus', and, in part, the earlier 'Tithon' on which it is based, as a rewriting of 'Tintern Abbey', these effects being achieved through borrowings from 'Tintern

Abbey' itself, but also through the assimilation of words and phrases from *An Evening Walk* (1793) and 'Resolution and Independence' (1807). The rewriting of 'Tithon' in 1860 in dramatic form comes after the publication of *In Memoriam* and *Maud*, both of which see Tennyson grappling with the complexities of religion, science, psychology and nature. Through the borrowing of Wordsworth's language in 'Tithonus', however, Tennyson is able to rewrite the relationship between mind and nature, of the self re-encountering itself in time, as it appears in 'Tintern Abbey'. As a result, the later poet seemingly releases himself from a Wordsworthian trope that privileges a psychologised relationship with nature. The revision of Wordsworth's pantheistic nature is evident in the earlier 'Tithon' (1833), on which the 1860 'Tithonus' is based, but its effects gain in intensity in the later monologue. The monologue as a form is already establishing a difference from Wordsworth in its rejection of Romantic universal subjectivity and its adoption of a fictional and performative persona. Thus in reworking Wordsworth's interaction between mind and nature, 'Tithonus' is consolidating a new poetic alongside revising what has ostensibly become an outdated poetic trope. The revisions, in part, free Tennyson from the universal sub-jectivity of the lyric speaker, thereby strengthening the strategies of the monologue. Yet, Tennyson's borrowings and echoes create effects that the poet cannot fully control, feeding, compromising, directing and, ultimately, supporting the poem.

I end with an analysis of Tennyson's late poem, 'Crossing the Bar' (1889); in ending with Tennyson's valedictory lyric, the book substantiates the claim that Tennyson did not move away from Wordsworth in his later years. The Conclusion also draws out the literary-historical implications of Tennyson's echoing of Words-worth's language and phrasing. In studying the echoes that sound through poems, the book validates the notion that historical and cultural context cannot fully account for the author's poetic and literary associations, as 'literature itself has a history . . . and mani-fests authors' own histories of reading and writing'.[96] Implicit in the summary is an acknowledgement of the dangers inherent in lim-iting the study of Tennyson's Romantic influences simply to one, albeit toweringly important, poet. Yet the Conclusion also implicitly acknowledges how the book's concentration on Tennyson's echo-ing of Wordsworth reveals compelling things about the later poet's poetic relationship with Wordsworth, making a timely intervention in the field of Romantic and Victorian literary continuities and dis-continuities, and expanding critical understanding of Tennyson's poetic relationship with Wordsworth and with his own poetry. Gill describes Tennyson's reverence for Wordsworth as not a 'disabling' one;[97] 'seeing the thick ankles enabled him to know the more confidently his own place as Wordsworth's proper successor as great poet, as Poet Laureate, and as Victorian cultural icon'.[98] It is this book's contention, rather, that it is Wordsworth's strengths as well as his apparent weaknesses that allow Tennyson to know his own place. In this way, the borrowed Levée robes are an indicator of Tennyson's relationship with Wordsworth and how he achieves his own sense of poetic place.

Notes

1. Page, *Tennyson: Interviews and Recollections*, p. 71.
2. Page, *Tennyson: Interviews and Recollections*, p. 71.
3. Page, *Tennyson: Interviews and Recollections*, p. 71.
4. Page, *Tennyson: Interviews and Recollections*, p. 71.
5. Page, *Tennyson: Interviews and Recollections*, p. 71. 'Many voices' is from 'Ulysses', in Tennyson, *The Poems of Tennyson*, I, l. 56 (p. 619).
6. Churton Collins, 'A New Study of Tennyson', pp. 36–50.
7. Churton Collins, 'A New Study of Tennyson', pp. 49–51 (Tennyson's annotation here runs into the next article in the January 1880 edition of the *Cornhill Magazine*, 'The Countess Adelcrantz', pp. 51–81).
8. Tennyson, *Alfred Lord Tennyson: A Memoir*, I, pp. 256–7.
9. Padel, 'Tennyson: Echo and Harmony', p. 327.
10. Hinds, *Allusion and Intertext*, p. 1.
11. Brown, *A Familiar Compound Ghost*, pp. 7–8.
12. Brown, *A Familiar Compound Ghost*, p. 8.
13. Brown, *A Familiar Compound Ghost*, p. 8.
14. Hollander, *The Figure of Echo*, p. ix.
15. Hollander, *The Figure of Echo*, p. ix.
16. Hollander, *The Figure of Echo*, p. ix.
17. Hollander, *The Figure of Echo*, p. 88.
18. Hollander, *The Figure of Echo*, p. 95.
19. Barthes, *Image-Music-Text*, p. 159.
20. Barthes, *Image-Music-Text*, p. 160.
21. Barthes, *Image-Music-Text*, p. 160.
22. The term intertextuality itself derives from Julia Kristeva's concept, based on the work of Ferdinand de Saussure and Mikhail Bakhtin, of the dialogic text, where 'any text is the absorption and transformation of another. The notion of *intertextuality* replaces that of intersubjectivity, and poetic language is read as at least *double*'. Bakhtin's notion of the social nature of language is defined by Kristeva in terms of the

horizontal and vertical: in the former, 'the word in the text belongs to both writing subject and addressee'; in the latter, 'the text is oriented toward an anterior or synchronic literary corpus'. In Kristeva's terms, these axes 'coincide' in any given text, resulting in a 'mosaic of quotations'. See Kristeva, *Desire in Language*, p. 66.

23. Allen, *Intertextuality*, p. 59.
24. Wolfgang Iser confirms that 'the literary text activates our own faculties, enabling us to recreate the world it presents. The product of this creative activity is what we might call the virtual dimension of the text, which endows it with its reality. This virtual dimension is not the text itself, nor is it the imagination of the reader: it is the coming together of text and imagination'. See Iser, 'The Reading Process', p. 215.
25. Bloom, *The Anxiety of Influence*, p. 5.
26. Bloom, *The Anxiety of Influence*, p. xxiii.
27. Bloom, *The Anxiety of Influence*, p. 25.
28. Bloom, *The Anxiety of Influence*, p. 31.
29. Bloom, *The Anxiety of Influence*, p. 7.
30. Bloom, *The Anxiety of Influence*, p. 8.
31. Bloom, *The Anxiety of Influence*, p. 70.
32. Intertextuality's gendered status has been challenged by feminist critics: Kathy Psomiades in her overview of 'The Lady of Shalott' confirms how 'Gilbert, Gubar, and Homans combined Bloom, Freud, and feminism to disclose how thoroughly gender was written into ideas about poetry, imagery, form, and intertextual reference, and thus how gendered poetry itself was'. See Psomiades, '"The Lady of Shalott"', pp. 40–1.
33. Hollander, 'The Anxiety of Influence'.
34. Hollander, 'The Anxiety of Influence'.
35. Decker, 'Tennyson's Limitations', p. 58.
36. Ricks, *Allusion to the Poets*, p. 189.
37. For more on Ricks' model, see *Allusion to the Poets*.
38. Tennyson, *Alfred Lord Tennyson: A Memoir*, II, p. 288.
39. Tennyson, *Alfred Lord Tennyson: A Memoir*, II, p. 505.
40. Tennyson, *Alfred Lord Tennyson: A Memoir*, II, pp. 504–5.
41. Tennyson, *Alfred Lord Tennyson: A Memoir*, I, p. 153.
42. Tennyson, *Alfred Lord Tennyson: A Memoir*, I, p. 151.
43. Tennyson, *Alfred Lord Tennyson: A Memoir*, I, p. 151.
44. Tennyson, *Alfred Lord Tennyson: A Memoir*, I, pp. 151–2.
45. Tennyson, *Alfred Lord Tennyson: A Memoir*, II, p. 70.
46. Tennyson, *Alfred Lord Tennyson: A Memoir*, II, p. 70.
47. Tennyson, *Alfred Lord Tennyson: A Memoir*, II, p. 70. Seamus Perry suggests that repetition is 'one of [Tennyson's] own most distinctive poetic resources', noting how 'repeating the word "again", in particular, served him superbly well on several occasions'. See Perry, *Alfred Tennyson*, p. 46.
48. Tennyson, *Alfred Lord Tennyson: A Memoir*, II, p. 70.

49. Tennyson, *Alfred Lord Tennyson: A Memoir*, II, p. 288.
50. Tennyson, *Alfred Lord Tennyson: A Memoir*, I, p. 72.
51. Tennyson, *Alfred Lord Tennyson: A Memoir*, II, p. 69.
52. Stephen Gill points out that de Vere shaped his memories for Hallam Tennyson's *Memoir*, incorrectly dating the meeting at Hampstead as taking place in 1841 or 1842. See Gill, *Wordsworth and the Victorians*, p. 190.
53. Gill, *Wordsworth and the Victorians*, p. 190, quoting from de Vere's diary for 4 May 1845.
54. Tennyson, *Alfred Lord Tennyson: A Memoir*, I, p. 209.
55. Tennyson, *Alfred Lord Tennyson: A Memoir*, I, p. 209.
56. Tennyson, *Alfred Lord Tennyson: A Memoir*, I, p. 210.
57. Tennyson, *Alfred Lord Tennyson: A Memoir*, I, p. 210.
58. Tennyson, *Alfred Lord Tennyson: A Memoir*, I, p. 210.
59. Tennyson, *Alfred Lord Tennyson: A Memoir*, I, p. 210.
60. Arnold, 'Wordsworth', p. 699.
61. Tennyson, *Alfred Lord Tennyson: A Memoir*, I, p. 210.
62. Tennyson, *Alfred Lord Tennyson: A Memoir*, I, p. 210.
63. Tennyson, *Alfred Lord Tennyson: A Memoir*, I, p. 155.
64. Tennyson, *The Letters of Alfred Lord Tennyson*, p. 238.
65. Tennyson, *Alfred Lord Tennyson: A Memoir*, I, p. 336.
66. Tennyson, *Alfred Lord Tennyson: A Memoir*, I, p. 338.
67. Tennyson, *Alfred Lord Tennyson: A Memoir*, I, p. 338.
68. Allen, *The Cambridge Apostles*, pp. 76, 1.
69. Allen, *The Cambridge Apostles*, p. 135.
70. Allen, *The Cambridge Apostles*, p. 133.
71. Allen, *The Cambridge Apostles*, p. 132.
72. Allen, *The Cambridge Apostles*, p. 133.
73. Cronin, *Romantic Victorians*, p. 149.
74. Cronin, *Romantic Victorians*, p. 150.
75. Cronin, *Romantic Victorians*, p. 150.
76. Cronin, *Romantic Victorians*, pp. 150–1.
77. Armstrong, *Victorian Poetry*, p. 107.
78. Armstrong, *Victorian Poetry*, p. 107.
79. Armstrong, *Victorian Poetry*, p. 108.
80. Perry, *Alfred Tennyson*, p. 50.
81. Perry, *Alfred Tennyson*, p. 50.
82. Gill, *Wordsworth and the Victorians*, p. 201.
83. Gill, *Wordsworth and the Victorians*, p. 200.
84. Gill, *Wordsworth and the Victorians*, p. 203.
85. Tucker, *Tennyson and the Doom of Romanticism*, p. 29.
86. Tucker, *Tennyson and the Doom of Romanticism*, p. 29.
87. Sullivan, 'Tennyson and *The Golden Treasury*', p. 236.
88. Ricks, 'Preface', in *Tennyson among the Poets*, p. viii.
89. Quoted in Lourie, 'Below the Thunders of the Upper Deep', p. 3.

90. Lourie, 'Below the Thunders of the Upper Deep', p. 4.
91. Hallam, 'On Some of the Characteristics of Modern Poetry', p. 93.
92. Lourie, 'Below the Thunders of the Upper Deep', p. 11.
93. Lourie, 'Below the Thunders of the Upper Deep', p. 7.
94. Tennyson, *The Poems of Tennyson*, II, p. 517.
95. Pease, '*Maud* and its Discontents', p. 102, drawing from Shires, '*Maud*, Masculinity and Poetic Identity', p. 280.
96. Bruster, *Quoting Shakespeare*, p. 3, quoted in Brown, *A Familiar Compound Ghost*, p. 16.
97. Gill, *Wordsworth and the Victorians*, p. 195.
98. Gill, *Wordsworth and the Victorians*, p. 195.

Chapter 1

'"She has a lovely face"':[1] Tennyson and 'The Lady of Shalott'

Tennyson turned to the Arthurian legend in 'The Lady of Shalott' (1832; revised 1842), although, characteristically, he declined to acknowledge the poem's sources, claiming that the poem was influenced by '"an Italian novelette, *Donna di Scalotta*"' rather than Malory's *Morte D'Arthur*,[2] even though the story has 'no Arthur, and no Queen . . . no mirror, weaving, curse, song, river, or island'.[3] F. J. Furnivall quotes Tennyson in January 1868 as saying:

> I met the story first in some Italian *novelle*: but the web, mirror, island, etc., were my own. Indeed, I doubt whether I should ever have put it in that shape if I had been then aware of the Maid of Astolat in *Mort Arthur*.[4]

J. M. Gray suggests, however, that Tennyson may have 'forgotten' that Malory influenced the poem.[5]

The poem, published in 1832, met with intense criticism from its first reviewers, most notably and famously in 1833 from John Wilson Croker in the *Quarterly Review*.[6] Tennyson was stung by the reviews, especially Croker's, and reworked the poem for publication in 1842. The reworked poem 'has acted as a barometer to chart the changing cultural pressures which have acted upon it at different times',[7] provoking a succession of critical responses, from New Critical readings

> in which the Lady's fate represents the life of the imagination being destroyed by a desire to enter active public life, to the playful post-structuralism of Geoffrey Hartman, for whom the Lady's barge is a 'floating signifier' forever slipping beyond our interpretative grasp.[8]

As Robert Douglas-Fairhurst confirms, the poem naturally gives rise to such a varied critical response, delighting in 'half-revealing and half-concealing'[9] and confessing 'the inadequacy of our drive to make sense of the world even as it is laying tempting clues for us to follow'.[10] Tennyson himself anticipated something of the poem's ongoing critical appeal, a calculation he bases on the poem's compact and exquisitely honed form: '"A small vessel, built on fine lines, is likely to float further down the stream of time than a big raft."'[11]

The 'fine lines' of the poem to which Tennyson refers owe much to their rich visual detail, a feature of the language of sensation. 'The Lady of Shalott' is described as a poem of sensation and Tennyson, likewise, a poet of sensation. Arthur Henry Hallam, in his 1831 essay, 'On Some of the Characteristics of Modern Poetry, And on the Lyrical Poems of Alfred Tennyson', written in response to Tennyson's 1830 collection, *Poems, Chiefly Lyrical*, first defined the poetry of sensation, differentiating the poems of Shelley and Keats, whom he describes as writing a poetry of 'sensation', from those of Wordsworth, whom he describes as writing a 'reflective' poetry,[12] in which he piles 'his thoughts in a rhetorical battery, that they may convince, instead of letting them glow in the natural course of contemplation, that they may enrapture'.[13] For the 'poet of sensation', by contrast, the 'simple exertions of eye and ear' are mingled with 'trains of active thought',[14] so that the 'whole being' of the poet is absorbed in 'the energy of sense':[15]

> Other poets *seek* for images to illustrate their conceptions; these men had no need to seek; they lived in a world of images; for the most important and extensive portion of their life consisted in those emotions, which are immediately conversant with the sensation.[16]

Hallam aligns Tennyson with 'the class we have already described as Poets of Sensation',[17] describing Tennyson's 'vivid, picturesque delineation of objects, and the peculiar skill with which he holds all of them *fused*, to borrow a metaphor from science, in a medium of strong emotion'.[18] But Hallam also foresaw how such poetry resulted in 'the melancholy, which so evidently characterises the spirit of modern poetry; hence that return of the mind upon itself, and the habit of seeking relief in idiosyncrasies rather than community of interest'.[19] The danger to the poet of 'perceiving the world through senses that are more sensitive than their own' is 'that the poems might end up abandoning ideas and feelings which once circulated as common currency between poets and their readers: a poet who detaches himself from his society risks finding himself with an audience of one'.[20]

Several critics have pointed out the inconsistencies in Hallam's separation of the poetry of reflection from the poetry of sensation, however. Isobel Armstrong, for instance, describes how, despite Hallam's rejection of reflection in the essay:

> consciousness does avail itself of reflections by presenting the train of associative sensation as a retrospective act, capable of reflexive analysis by as it were historicising the consciousness and working upon it with the analyst's understanding which comes from the acknowledgement of the latter-day poet that all experience is comprehended in a series of backwards questions.[21]

Seamus Perry notices, too, how Hallam's separation of sensation from reflection 'did not *exclude* thought from his verse, to be sure, but it did mean that the "elevated habits of thought [are] *implied*" – which was "more impressive, to our minds" . . . "than if the author had drawn up a set of opinions in verse"'.[22]

Others have described how Hallam's definition of the poetry of sensation is itself derived from Wordsworth's poetics. James Chandler, for instance, describes how Hallam's claim that in 'maintaining that the roots of all art and poetry lie in "daily life and experience," [Hallam] argues that it is within every reader's power to understand the artist's expressions and sympathize with the poet's passionate condition';[23] with those senses, in other words, that are 'more sensitive' than his or her own, and which place the poet with the possible audience of one. Chandler goes on to locate this power of sympathy directly within Wordsworth's 1815 'Essay, Supplementary to the Preface', 'the text in which Wordsworth tries hardest to formulate the doctrine that poetry does not depend on advances in opinion'.[24]

Steven C. Dillon goes further, claiming that Hallam's terms are a misreading of Wordsworth's poetics, suggesting that

> In order to set up Wordsworth as a poet of reflection, Hallam must reductively cut through the 'also' in Wordsworth's famous formulation: 'For all good poetry is the spontaneous overflow of powerful feelings: and though this be true, Poems to which any value can be attached were never produced on any variety of subjects but by a man who, being possessed of more than usual organic sensibility, had also thought long and deeply'.[25]

Dillon nevertheless confirms how Hallam's essay acts as a crucible for the paradigm shift from transcendence to immanence that takes place during the nineteenth century, as 'the vertical axis of imagination and epiphanic nature ("spots of time") moves towards a horizontal axis of empirical perception and continuous history'.[26]

Hallam's definition of poetry finds an analogue in John Stuart Mill's elevation of poetic feeling over thought. In Wordsworth, Mill claims in an essay of 1833,

> the poetry is almost always the mere setting of a thought. The thought may be more valuable than the setting, or it may be less valuable; but there can be no question as to which was first in his mind.[27]

There is, he goes on, 'an air of calm deliberateness about all [Wordsworth] writes, which is not characteristic of the poetic temperament'.[28] Mill's review that same year of Tennyson's *Poems, Chiefly Lyrical* and the 1832 *Poems*, however, reveals him as modifying his concept of the poetry of sensibility, arguing instead that 'poets must apply the faculty of cultivated reason to their nervous susceptibility and to their sensitivity to the laws of association'.[29] Tennyson's 'The Palace of Art', with its criticism of aesthetic isolation, begins, for Mill, to apply the faculty of 'cultivated reason', a practice he warns Tennyson he must continue to follow.[30]

'The Lotos Eaters' (1832; revised 1842) and 'The Lady of Shalott', in conjunction with 'The Palace of Art' itself, thus 'presage the destruction or decadence of the poetry of sensation and search both for another politics and a new aesthetic';[31] 'The Lotos Eaters' is 'at once the culminating expression of the poetry of sensation and its greatest critique', as Armstrong makes clear.[32] Towards the 1840s Tennyson's work pulls in two directions:

> One [takes] him towards the common-sense Wordsworthianism which assumed that simplicity of diction, permanent and universal moral truths which 'transcend' the immediately political and exemplary tales, are a way of gaining access to the sympathies of a wide audience.[33]

The other pull, meanwhile, is 'towards lyric sensuousness such as is to be found in the work of Monckton Milnes'.[34]

But the tension that Armstrong and others locate in Tennyson's use of the language of sensation is already manifest in 'The Lady of Shalott'. 'The Lady of Shalott' not only presages the search for a new poetic, but embodies that search, prefiguring the movement Tennyson is to make later in the 1840s in the English 'Idyls', for example, towards a simplicity of diction and the gaining of the sympathies of a wide audience. The poem absorbs a Wordsworthian reflective and 'unpoetical language' from which Hallam somewhat artificially separates it in his 1831 essay. Wordsworth's presence is clearly felt in the 1832 version of 'The Lady of Shalott', feeding Tennyson's discussion of some of the poem's major themes; the chapter augments the previous critical work done on the poem in this way. The level of borrowing from Wordsworth increases in the 1842 version of the poem, however, suggesting that Tennyson draws even more deeply from Wordsworth in the later poem, both to assuage the critics and to search for a new poetic; gaining the sympathies of a wide audience includes that of the critics, in fact. Tennyson was notoriously and painfully insecure about his poetic gifts, and the borrowings from Wordsworth play directly into this dynamic, scaffolding the poem with the earlier poet's language and allowing Tennyson to steady his poetic voice and reputation. But the borrowings in the poem do more than stream into Tennyson's critical insecurities, both complicating and constraining the poem's discussion of art, life and gender, enabling 'The Lady of Shalott' to sail further 'down the stream of time'.

The benign relationship suggested here itself echoes the supportive allusive model that Christopher Ricks outlines, working in a productive coalition or community of poets.[35] The borrowings work at the level of language and cadence rather than deep psychic fear and anxiety, a transmission that Harold Bloom regards in his account of the parricidal urges that he maintains exist between strong, male poets as '"something that happens"' and therefore of little consequence;[36] the poem is not born from anxiety or impulse, although the borrowings and echoes do reveal the anxieties attendant upon the creative process and can therefore be said to be working at a psychic level. Wordsworth's presence creates multiple effects in the poem, however, not all of which can be fully captured by Bloom's restrictive model of influence or Ricks' supportive model; some of the echoes from Wordsworth inform, some support, some seemingly establish a priority and overwhelm, some allow Tennyson to revise or, in Bloom's terms, defensively to weaken Wordsworth, some liberate, some inhibit, some direct the poem, others redirect it. Some indeed are generated by the echo of single words.[37]

'With a glassy countenance'

Like 'Mariana', Tennyson's 'The Lady of Shalott' seemingly exemplifies the picturesque poetry of sensation that Hallam describes, with objects delineated and held in a fusion of strong emotion. Here is the Lady of Shalott herself as she makes her way into Camelot:

> Lying, robed in snowy white
> That loosely flew to left and right –
> The leaves upon her falling light –
> Through the noises of the night
>   She floated down to Camelot:
> And as the boat-head wound along
> The willowy hills and fields among,
> They heard her singing her last song,
>   The Lady of Shalott.
>
> (ll. 136–44)

The Lady, robed in snowy white, is herself a sharply delineated object, and her plaintive singing fuses the scene in strong emotion. But the text is also inflected with Wordsworth's 'unpoetical', referential language, that language with which Hallam compares the language of sensation in his 1831 essay. These inflections complement the well-known allusive citations to Wordsworth's 'The Solitary Reaper' (1807), Keats' 'Ode to a Nightingale' (1819) and Shelley's 'To a Skylark' (1820) that the poem contains: Herbert F. Tucker, Jr, after Lionel Stevenson, notes the Shelleyan allusion of the Lady to an invisible singer, 'the high-born maiden / In a palace tower', and beyond that to Wordsworth's 'To the Cuckoo' (1807) and 'The Solitary Reaper', to which 'To a Skylark' was a response.[38] And Matthew Rowlinson confirms how,

> As a figure who sings without being seen, the Lady of Shalott at the beginning of the poem owes something to Keats's nightingale. The language Tennyson uses to describe his unseen Lady at the end of the poem's first section echoes the romantic diction of the pivotal seventh stanza of Keats's ode, from which he remembers words like *casement* and *fairy*, while the weary reaper who hears the Lady's song derives both from the figure of Ruth amid the alien corn and from Wordsworth's solitary reaper, who is herself the precursor of Ruth as she appears in Keats's poem.[39]

But there is another Wordsworth poem remembered as text in the poem, which comes into play after the breaking of the Lady's mirror:

In the stormy east-wind straining,
The pale yellow woods were waning,
The broad stream in his banks complaining,
Heavily the low sky raining
    Over towered Camelot;
Down she came and found a boat
Beneath a willow left afloat,
And round about the prow she wrote
    The Lady of Shalott.

And down the river's dim expanse
Like some bold seër in a trance,
Seeing all his own mischance –
With a glassy countenance
    Did she look to Camelot.
And at the closing of the day
She loosed the chain, and down she lay;
The broad stream bore her far away,
    The Lady of Shalott.

                                      (IV. ll. 118–35)

The use of the visual impression of landscape here to convey mood – the 'stormy east-wind straining', the 'low sky raining' – echoes Wordsworth's description of Sir George Beaumont's actual painting of the maritime sublime in the third section of Wordsworth's 1807 'Elegiac Stanzas: Suggested by a Picture of Peele Castle, in a Storm, Painted by Sir George Beaumont' (hereafter 'Elegiac Stanzas'), a poem, like 'The Lady of Shalott', centrally concerned with art, writing and image-making. 'The Lady of Shalott' absorbs the 'rueful sky',[40] 'fierce wind' (l. 52) of the 'Elegiac Stanzas' and turns them into its own 'pageantry of fear' (l. 48). The text's absorption of 'glassy' possibly also has a provenance in the 'Elegiac Stanzas', confirming Wordsworth's tendency to self-quote perhaps, as the adjective first appears in *An Evening Walk* (1793), but also confirming his predilection for ekphrastic poetry; Wordsworth often wrote in the ekphrastic mode during his poetic career, writing a number of ekphrastic poems, beginning with 'Elegiac Stanzas' and ending with 'To Luca Giordano', written in 1846.[41] 'Glassy' occurs in *An Evening Walk* in an early part of the poem, foreshadowing the speaker's subsequent descent into imaginative darkness: 'Into a gradual calm the zephyrs sink, / A blue rim borders all the lake's still brink',[42] and goes on to describe how 'The sails are dropp'd, the poplar's foliage sleeps, / And insects clothe, like dust, the glassy deeps' (I. ll. 129–30). 'Glassy' also occurs in the first section of Wordsworth's 'Elegiac Stanzas' where the speaker describes his memory-image of Peele Castle: 'I was thy Neighbour once, thou rugged Pile! / Four summer weeks I dwelt in sight of thee: / I saw thee every day; and all the while / Thy Form was sleeping on a glassy sea' (ll. 1–4). He goes on to claim that 'Whene'er I look'd, thy Image still was there; / It trembled, but it never pass'd away' (ll. 7–8). 'Image' here refers not just to the mirror image of Peele Castle in the water, but to the 'poet's internalizing of the sight into an "Image" reproducible in poetry',[43] a poetic power the speaker acknowledges he has lost and which becomes a mere 'fond delusion of my heart' (l. 29). 'Still' functions as both adverb and adjective in the text, evoking both the sense of the image the speaker creates remaining in place and in time, of never 'passing away' or 'dying', and a sense of stillness or calm. But, of course, the image does pass away for the speaker, becoming a mere memory-image, subsequently disturbing his sense of calm. A similar effect is achieved in *An Evening Walk*; here, 'still' also is linked to an image being held in place in the mind of the speaker, this time supported by the sense of dropped sails, sleeping foliage and the dusting of insects. But the image is also simultaneously displaced by the sense of sleep, and by the proximity with death, of sinking and of dust, which act to foreshadow the decline of the imagination that occurs later in the poem. 'Glassy''s affiliation with 'deep' in *An Evening Walk*, however, feeds into Tennyson's own description of the 'mighty Deep' ('Elegiac Stanzas', l. 11), allowing it to share in the illusory calm of Wordsworth's lake. 'Elegiac Stanzas' goes on to explore how the poet would have painted the castle if his were still the painter's hand and he were still in 'a state of "fond delusion"',[44] able to add 'the gleam, / The light that never was, on sea or land' (ll. 14–15). The writing 'allows us to inhabit this conditional state [of adding the gleam], even as it implies the poet's ultimate exile from it'.[45] Wordsworth's 'verbal painting' foregrounds the discontinuity between his imagined painting of a beautiful or picturesque landscape and Beaumont's image of the sublime: 'In superimposing his work on his friend's, Wordsworth discerns the terrifying discontinuity undermining the possibility of truth and its basis in something immutable.'[46] Rather than simply mediating the language of visual impression and sensation here, the text then also mediates Wordsworth's reflective, 'thoughtful' language and its engagement with questions surrounding the reproducible image. Hallam avers that the poet of sensation had no need to seek for images, that they lived in a world of images, and that the most important and extensive portion of their life consisted in those emotions which are immediately conversant with the sensation. Yet Tennyson does have the need to seek for images, images that are drawn not from the world, but from literary memory, and which are not simply conversant with sensation but rather with deep thought.

The absorption of Wordsworth's language in the text, and its own concern with the mediation of reproducible images in art and poetry, echoes 'The Lady of Shalott''s own concern with the mediation of the visual image, as the Lady weaves representations of the world she sees in her mirror:

> And moving through a mirror clear
> That hangs before her all the year,
> Shadows of the world appear.
> There she sees the highway near
>   Winding down to Camelot:
> There the river eddy whirls,
> And there the surly village-churls,
> And the red cloaks of market girls,
>   Pass onward from Shalott.
>
>   (II. ll. 46–54)

In the poem there is 'a structural analogy between the poem's [own] mimetic work and that of the Lady's weaving':[47] 'What the Lady weaves . . . is what she sees in the mirror' – which means that what she weaves 'refer[s] not only to the world as it exists outside the tower but also to its reflection inside, and to the representation of that reflection in the Lady's web'.[48] The 'characteristic topic of lyric in the nineteenth century is mediation; in the case of descriptive lyric it is the mediation of the visual image',[49] a pattern set by Wordsworth's 'Tintern Abbey' in 1798. Rowlinson confirms that, 'as the nineteenth century progressed, lyric came with increasing self-consciousness to reflect on its own mediated character';[50] in 'The Lady of Shalott', the 'representation of the mediation of visual images is one form of this reflection'.[51]

However, the topic of 'The Lady of Shalott''s 'narrative is indeed mediation's impossibility':[52] 'The Lady's corpse at the [close of the poem] does not in any sense preserve or make legible her song or her mode of life; these are on the contrary represented as irrecoverable.'[53]

Wordsworth's acknowledgement in the 'Elegiac Stanzas' of the disjunction between both poetic and visual art and their power to mediate the visual image and to convey truth and immutability is thus echoed in the disjunction which 'The Lady of Shalott' itself acknowledges in the mirror that cracks, the web that floats wide, and the Lady's own floating death. But Wordsworth does not conclude that mediation is impossible; the poet is still able to inhabit a conditional, illusory state in 'Elegiac Stanzas'. In mediating Wordsworth's 'glassy' image, Tennyson is therefore performing a retrospective act, echoing a Wordsworthian 'image' that is successfully mediated; Tennyson is drawing on the main topic of descriptive lyric – the mediation of the image – yet will nonetheless go on to conclude, through the Lady's silent death, that mediation is impossible. In so doing, the later poet draws from the very descriptive, referential poetry from which Hallam separates the poetry of sensation in his essay, drawing not only on its main topic but on its language, too, with its simple phrasing and diction.

Interestingly, in being described as 'glassy' the Lady in Tennyson's poem takes on the function of the mirror, as Armstrong points out.[54] The Lady herself mediates the two accounts of perception embedded in Hallam's essay: one based on associationist psychological theory,[55] with a dualistic opposition between subject and object;[56] the other a Kantian world which 'always includes the category of the self in its representations'.[57] In the former, the 'mirror is a *tabula rasa*. It reflects external images but it has no control over the Lady's perceptual faculties';[58] in the other, 'the images in the mirror become the result of the Lady's self-projection and are her own "shadows"'.[59] Lancelot as he 'flashed' into the Lady's 'crystal mirror' (III. l. 106), for instance, brings with him an associationist epistemology through an act of violent, explosive sexuality, precipitating the shattering of the Lady's mirror.[60] The absorption of Wordsworth's 'glassy' in the text, by contrast, strengthens the idealist position in the poem, reflecting off its own shiny surface. Moreover, its presence signals a Wordsworthian form of perception: in being 'glassy' and taking on the function of the mirror, the Lady comes to function as a metonym for Wordsworth's idealist epistemology, where subject and object fuse in the act of perception and 'exist as one through the act of self-reflection'.[61]

The Wordsworthian idealist position in the poem, ironically, is strengthened by Lancelot, the creator and perpetrator of associationist violence. Dillon qualifies 'the preeminence of beauty' in Hallam's essay by emphasising 'the inherent violence that accrues with an aesthetic of sensation'.[62] 'The Ballad of Oriana' (1830), Dillon maintains, 'virtually premises itself on a delight in violence, directed both towards oneself and against others':[63]

> The descriptions of battle and death are far from gruesome, but the effect nonetheless relies on a perverse pleasure taken in the death of the many-voweled heroine. Just so, *Idylls of the King* consistently moves toward violence in its narrative of the death of beauty.[64]

Not only does Lancelot bring with him a violent associationist epistemology as he 'flashes' into and shatters the mirror, but he also brings with him a very particular Wordsworthian epistemology, which carries within it the conflation of subject and object in the act of perception, that 'flash upon that inward eye' (II. l. 21) as Wordsworth has it in 'I WANDERED lonely as a Cloud' (1807). Riding on the 'burnished hooves' of his war horse (III. l. 101) into Shalott, Lancelot himself evokes Wordsworth's *An Evening Walk*. Self-reflexively, in Wordsworth's early poem, the still lake into which the speaker looks is described as glowing like a 'burnish'd mirror' (I. l. 126). Angela Leighton describes how a similar Tennysonian flash in *The Lover's Tale* (1879) is 'oddly anatomical'.[65] As she points out, Tennyson writes, for instance, in *The Lover's Tale*:

> 'The very face and form of Lionel / Flashed through my eyes into my innermost brain' (I. 365. 93–4) . . . [Yet] Lionel's 'form' seems to have to push 'through' the corporeal eye to reach the 'brain', so that the flash of recognition is audibly slowed up by the obstruction of a body.[66]

Leighton's reading fits with her analysis here of Tennyson as perhaps the 'most powerful, undeclared voice of English aestheticism'.[67] Writing of Tennyson's 'flashpoints', Leighton suggests that 'displaced touch' becomes 'a defining characteristic [as] again and again the moment of revelation, of spiritual or imaginative intuition, is slightly held up by the sense of a body'.[68] Dillon too draws a parallel between Hallam's sensation and current evaluation of categories of experience:

> An argument on behalf of the Body, for example, may not look too much different from Hallam's; this argument would take place today in the wake of enormous philosophical sophistication (after Heidegger, et al.), but in order to make its case, it may seem obliged to simplify radically. But the simplification will be in appearance only.[69]

The Wordsworthian echoes that resonate through 'The Lady of Shalott', however, question Tennyson's commitment both to the poetry of sensation and to the body. The sense of light in these images is intrinsic to the Wordsworthian imaginative process – the speaker of 'Elegiac Stanzas' watches himself adding the light that never was, for instance. There is an undoubted focus in 'The Lady of Shalott' on the body, in keeping with its mediation of an associationist epistemology and the language of sensation. Lancelot's sheer erotic physicality features heavily in the poem: 'And from his blazoned baldric slung / A mighty silver bugle hung, / And as he rode his armour rung' (III. ll. 87–9); 'All in the blue unclouded weather / Thick-jewelled shone the saddle-leather, / The helmet and the helmet-feather / Burned like one burning flame together, / As he rode down to Camelot' (III. ll. 91–5); and 'From underneath his helmet flowed / His coal-black curls as on he rode' (III. ll. 102–3). The speaker describes how 'A red-cross knight for ever kneeled / To a lady in his shield' (III. ll. 78–9), an image that suggests a Spenserian influence, according to Ricks.[70] The undoubted sense of a body here, however, armoured, jewelled, with flaming helmet and feather at one, his knightly status reflected in the supplicant knight in his shield, is combined with an equally prominent sense of the light of the Wordsworthian imagination, complementing the reflective light of the burnished hooves of Lancelot's war horse: the sun 'came dazzling through the leaves / And flamed upon the brazen greaves' (III. ll. 75–6); Lancelot's shield 'sparkled' (III. l. 80) on the yellow field beside remote Shalott; the 'gemmy bridle glittered free, / Like to some branch of stars we see / Hung in the golden Galaxy' (III. ll. 82–4); his broad clear brow in 'sunlight glowed' (III. l. 100). Words like 'glittering' and 'glowing' have a ubiquity in Romantic literature – one thinks of the ancient mariner's sinister 'glittering eye' in Samuel Taylor Coleridge's 'The Ancient Mariner', for instance[71] – but Wordsworth himself frequently draws on these phrases in his own poetry as expressions of the imaginative process: 'glittering' features in *An Evening Walk*, where 'Never shall ruthless minister of Death / 'Mid thy soft glooms the glittering steel unsheath' (I. ll. 77–8); similarly, in *An Evening Walk* 'brightly blue, the burnish'd mirror glows' (I. l. 126). In drawing on Wordsworth's language in this way, Tennyson's poem forces back into prominence Wordsworth's focus on mind, and of the mind's productive and essential idealist relationship with object. The prominent, and destructive, sense of body in the poem is pervaded by an equally strong sense of the light of the Wordsworthian imagination. If the movement of the century is from transcendence to immanence, then that movement appears to be checked here, as the poem seeks out the light of Wordsworthian imaginative transcendence as an antidote to the violence of the language of sensation: Wordsworth's burnished mirror replaces the mirror that Lancelot so violently shatters.

The move towards the light of the Wordsworthian imagination is underpinned by the allusion to Wordsworth in Tennyson's phrase, 'All in the blue unclouded weather' (III. l. 91), confirming Tennyson's ear for rhythm and sound, as well as rhyme.[72] In Wordsworth's 'The Green Linnet' (1807) the speaker describes the visit of the 'happiest guest' (I. l. 9) to his 'sequestered nook' (I. l. 5) in 'spring's unclouded weather' (I. l. 4):

> BENEATH these fruit-tree boughs that shed
> Their snow-white blossoms on my head,
> With brightest sunshine round me spread
>   Of spring's unclouded weather,
> In this sequestered nook how sweet
> To sit upon my Orchard-seat!
> And Birds and Flowers once more to greet,
>   My last year's Friends together.
>
> (I. ll. 1–8)

Wordsworth's iambics settle into the blue unclouded weather of Tennyson's tetrameter line. There is also a clear allusion to the speaker's dazzled sight as he views the green linnet in Tennyson's sun that 'came dazzling through the leaves' (III. l. 75), when Lancelot first comes into view. But in Wordsworth's poem the speaker's description of the 'spring's unclouded weather' is coloured by his imagination, as is his view of the dazzling sun and green linnet; in each, his mind fuses with its object in an act of reflection. Tennyson's 'blue unclouded weather', on the contrary, seemingly confirms his designation as a poet of sensation: Tennyson gives his unclouded weather a specificity, loading it with the kind of rich visual detail that would later appeal to the Pre-Raphaelite movement; he turns the air 'blue', as it were. 'Susceptible of the slightest impulse from external nature',[73] Tennyson here seemingly trembles 'into emotion at colours, and sounds, and movements, unperceived or unregarded by duller temperaments',[74] as his whole being is absorbed 'into the energy of sense'.[75] Yet in drawing on Wordsworth's phrasing, Tennyson acknowledges both an alternative epistemological model and the part that imagination or mind plays in perception. Tennyson's poem performs a further nod to Wordsworth through its insistent end-rhymes, enacting through rhyme – weather and together – its affinity with Wordsworth's poetry. That 'weather' and 'together' themselves echo Wordsworth's own rhyme pattern in lines 4 and 8 of

'The Green Linnet' serves only to emphasise the productive relationship that exists between the two poets in the poem. If Tennyson establishes Wordsworth's priority in the text through the re-establishment of the light of the Wordsworthian imagination and the Lady's 'glassy' functioning, here Tennyson's poetics blend with Wordsworth's in a creative alliance or fusion. Peter McDonald notes a 'self-awareness' in Tennyson's use of rhyme derived from the erosion of the boundary between repetition and rhyme established by Wordsworth.[76] That Tennyson is self-aware in his use of a Wordsworthian rhyme pattern here is open to debate, but it is certainly true that the later poet is engaging with Wordsworth's poetic practice on a deeply intimate level.

There is another text with which the section above blends, however, and that is Keats' 'Ode to a Nightingale'. Tennyson's poem describes how as Lancelot 'rode down to Camelot[,] / As often through the purple night, / Below the starry clusters bright, / Some bearded meteor, trailing light, / Moves over still Shalott' (III. ll. 95–9). The 'starry clusters bright' resonate with echoes of Keats' poem, where the speaker describes the marvellous world of the imagination, where:

> tender is the night,
> And haply the Queen-Moon is on her throne,
>   Cluster'd around by all her starry Fays;
>   But here there is no light,
> Save what from heaven is with the breezes blown
>   Through verdurous glooms and winding mossy ways.[77]

Like 'The Lady of Shalott', Keats' poem engages with the question of whether art allows an escape from reality and human experience, only to conclude, unlike Tennyson's poem, that the 'visionary' world of art creates perhaps its own form of reality. In both 'The Green Linnet' and 'Ode to a Nightingale' 'the song or flight of the bird becomes an emblem of the poet's own voice, of his vocation, in the original sense of a "calling or summons", as a poet'.[78] The play of these poems in 'The Lady of Shalott' underpins Tennyson's discussion of his own vocation, his own voice in the poem. As we shall see in Chapter 4, Tennyson again draws on 'The Green Linnet' in *Maud* (1855), thereby engaging with the subject of his own poetic vocation. But the presence of Keats' 'Ode' in the 'blue unclouded weather' section of 'The Lady of Shalott' emphasises Tennyson's closeness to Keats' sensuous language; conversely, the presence of Wordsworth's 'unpoetic' language simultaneously emphasises Tennyson's lack of commitment to it.

Despite Tennyson's productive alliance with Wordsworth in 'The Lady of Shalott', however, the mirror in the poem, and therefore the

Lady and her 'idealist' form of representation, crack 'from side to side' (III. l. 115), acting as a synecdoche of the disjunction between mind and object, word and image that Wordsworth's poem itself acknowledges in the speaker's apostrophe to the image-making poet he once was. The associationist epistemology is also 'cracked' here, of course, and the Lady with it – she breaks into discrete fragments, as 'Hallam's fragments of being reappear as isolated sensation in the external world. "She saw the water-lily bloom, / She saw the helmet and the plume"'.[79] But the mirror's fracture is miraculously healed in the poem,[80] however, suggesting specifically that Wordsworth's disjunction between mind and nature is itself potentially assuaged. As glassy mirror, the Lady's countenance remains whole, thereby implying that the fractured mirror itself paradoxically remains whole, or is re-pieced together. The act of healing that takes place thus enables the mirror's acts of idealist representation also to be sustained in the poem: the Lady is able to 'look' to Camelot (IV. l. 131), for instance; she is 'Like some bold seër in a trance, / Seeing all his own mischance –' (IV. ll. 128–9). The associationist fracture of the Lady offers no such healing. Her passive body is carried along, out of Shalott, as 'the broad stream bore her far away' (IV. l. 134): 'Lying, robed in snowy white / That loosely flew to left and right – / The leaves upon her falling light – / Through the noises of the night / She floated down to Camelot' (IV. ll. 136–40). Robes fly loosely to left and right; leaves fall light; and the night is full of noises, yet the Lady can only float, encased in her ghostly mantle, down to Camelot. By contrast, the idealism still at work in the poem restores the sense of agency needed in the act of 'looking'. This sense of looking – of projecting the self in its representations – rehabilitates or reconstructs the Wordsworthian epistemological model in the poem. Despite her fracture into discrete parts, the Lady retains a coherent identity, still able to 'look'; she is not simply a passive body of sensation, floating inertly to her death. Margaret A. Lourie positions the Lady's boat journey in relation to Shelley: 'the Lady looks outside herself (back to Shelley perhaps)?'[81] But here the Lady just as equally 'looks' both forward and back to Wordsworth. There is a sense that the Wordsworthian act of healing specifically counters the violence inherent in the associationist language of sensation – Lancelot's violent shattering of the mirror, for instance, symbolised by his shield and bugle, which both denote the past and future acts of violence of the 'bold Sir Lancelot' (III. l. 77); the Lady's violent fracture into discrete parts. In 'looking' in this way, the Lady privileges Wordsworth's epistemological model over and above the associationist model at work in the poem, positioning active thought in contradistinction to passive feeling. The allusion to Wordsworth's 'Intimations' ode (1807) contained within the Lady as 'bold seër' – 'Mighty Prophet! Seer blest! / On whom those truths do rest, / Which we are toiling all our lives to find, / In darkness lost, the darkness of the grave' (IV. ll. 114–17) – might be seen to underpin the movement towards Wordsworth taking place in the poem. The Wordsworthian echoes and allusions here also work to draw attention to the visionary or revelatory quality inherent in the Lady's experience of having 'cracked', completing the Wordsworthian 'priority' being established in the poem.

The Lady's rejuvenated ability to 'look' also enables her to embrace the social, something denied to her through the language of sensation, although as Joseph Chadwick maintains, the Lady's perceptions are already socially mediated:[82] Beatrice Sanford Russell, quoting Sharon Cameron, explains how '"the reduction to sensation without thoughts that appropriate it (or a seeing through such thoughts) unsocializes perception," because it severs the connection between experiential phenomena and the more personal conceptual organization of these phenomena'.[83] The language of reflection, on the contrary, provides a way in which the missing link between the phenomena experienced and the personal organisation of these phenomena can be restored. In this way, the Lady's 'look' emblematises how the phenomena experienced – looking down to Camelot – and the personal organisation of these phenomena have been reconnected, corroborating the blurring of the social and artistic self that is already taking place in the poem; Chadwick notes, for instance, how the social world creates the problems of isolation discussed in the poem.[84] In her act of looking, the Lady thereby offers Tennyson an alternative means by which to escape the introspection conferred by the language of sensation, with its 'return of the mind upon itself, and the habit of seeking relief in idiosyncrasies rather than community of interest'.

The poem ends by paying homage to Wordsworth through Lancelot's comment on the Lady's 'lovely face' (IV. l. 169). In describing the Lady's face as 'lovely', the poem returns once more to *An Evening Walk*. In Wordsworth's poem, in a section of the poem where the imagination begins its recovery after its descent into darkness, the moon is described as having a 'lovely face':

See, oe'r the eastern hill, where darkness broods
O'er all its vanished dells, and lawns, and woods;
Where but a mass of shade the sight can trace,
She lifts in silence up her lovely face;

Above the gloomy valley flings her light,
Far to the western slopes with hamlets white;
And gives, where woods the chequered upland strew,
To the green corn of summer, autumn's hue.

(I. ll. 348–55)

The moon's sense of actively flinging light suggests the rebuilding of
the imagination after its decline into brooding darkness in the poem,
and, by association, the resurgence of Wordsworth's epistemology in
Tennyson's poem. The play of light and shade here complements the
play of light and shade in Tennyson's poem (in the mirror and the
flash of Lancelot, combined with the shadows the Lady self-creates);
the Wordsworthian imaginative process contains darkness as well as
light – the Lady has created her own shadows of sensation as well as
being submissively in receipt of them. Autumn also echoes the move
that has already taken place from summer to autumn in the poem
(and therefore the blurring of the real and the aesthetic worlds, as
noted above).[85] Lancelot's somewhat bathetic, trivial summary of the
Lady of Shalott – '"She has a lovely face"' – has been met with criticism, even incredulity,[86] although its inadequacy is seen as evidence
of the poem's delight in 'half-revealing' and 'half-concealing':[87]

> none of the other things [Tennyson] might have said, such as 'Can
> I watch the autopsy?' or 'Do you think I could have the boat after we
> bury her?' are likely to strike us as any better; the poem confesses the
> inadequacy of our drive to make sense of the world even as it is laying
> tempting clues for us to follow.[88]

But the summary's provenance in Wordsworth goes some way to
explaining Tennyson's 'unpoetic' phrasing; in sharing the 'lovely face'
of Wordsworth's moon, the Lady gains in visionary power and influence, augmenting the Wordsworthian epistemological model in the
poem: she too is imbued with transcendental significance. Further,
the Lady of Shalott pays the price with her life for entering the public
world and of entering language, her name written on her barge as she
floats to Camelot. The poem thus narrates 'the substitution of a visible (indeed legible . . .) sign for a voice'.[89] If the Lady is denied a voice,
then she nevertheless retains a lovely face, however, which offers her
a chance of immortality gained through the power of the imagination. In adopting Wordsworth's phrase and turning it into speech,
Lancelot participates in the Wordsworthian epistemology at work in
the poem, colouring his perception of the Lady with his imagination;

he does not rely on pure emotion to mediate sense here. Rather, his view of the Lady's lovely face is fuelled by his imagination. Both the lady and Lancelot have become active 'seërs'. Further, that the 'lovely face' comes at the close of the poem, when the Lady's death signals mediation's impossibility, indicates how the poem retains the possibility of the mediation of the image while simultaneously denying it, even though this is inevitably a retrospective act. The 1832 version of the text omits to position Lancelot among the onlookers at the end of the poem, closing with the words of the Lady of Shalott herself: "*The web was woven curiously / The charm is broken utterly, / Draw near and fear not – this is I, / The Lady of Shalott*".[90] In including Lancelot's comment on the Lady's lovely face, the 1842 text therefore affords Wordsworth a priority that the earlier version of the poem does not support, allowing Tennyson in turn to give 'voice' to Lancelot and to give a 'face' to the Lady of Shalott.

The start of the poem also borrows Wordsworth's language and phrasing. The speaker describes how:

Willows whiten, aspens quiver,
Little breezes dusk and shiver
Through the wave that runs for ever
By the island in the river
  Flowing down to Camelot.
Four gray walls, and four gray towers,
Overlook a space of flowers,
And the silent isle imbowers
  The Lady of Shalott.

          (I. ll. 10–18)

Space features at the close of the poem: Lancelot 'muses a little space' (IV. l. 168). Ricks quotes E. E. Duncan-Jones on 'a little space', who suggests that the phrase comes from Scott, *Marmion* I xxi, 'The Captain mused a little space'.[91] The 'space of flowers' at the start of the poem, however, is reminiscent of one of the Pastor's domestic vignettes in Book VI of Wordsworth's *The Excursion* (1814). Here, the Daughter of the house tends a garden, enclosed within which is her own garden 'space':

– Brought from the woods the honeysuckle twines
Around the porch, and seems, in that trim place,
A Plant no longer wild; the cultured rose
There blossoms, strong in health, and will be soon
Roof-high; the wild pink crowns the garden-wall,

And with the flowers are intermingled stones
Sparry and bright, rough scatterings of the hills.
These ornaments, that fade not with the year,
A hardy Girl continues to provide;
Who mounting fearlessly the rocky heights,
Her Father's prompt Attendant, does for him
All that a Boy could do; but with delight
More keen and prouder daring; yet hath she,
Within the garden, like the rest, a bed
For her own flowers and favourite herbs – a space,
By sacred charter, holden for her use.

(V. vi. ll. 1141–56)

The Daughter's bed of flowers and favourite herbs is a private space, appointed by sacred charter for her own use; the sense of privacy is emphasised by a 'rill' that 'Flows on in solitude' (V. vi. l. 1162) through the garden. But in the poem, the Daughter does not partake of this experience; rather, it is the Pastor who describes his experience of her garden, freely enjoying the fruits of her labour, often without permission: '– These, and whatever else the garden bears / Of fruit or flower, permission asked or not, / I freely gather' (V. vi. ll. 1157–9). The Daughter's garden space thus functions as a confined space, patriarchally controlled, a symbol of her proscribed life (as well as her abused labour). The space of flowers in 'The Lady of Shalott' has a similar function, acting as a symbol of the Lady's confinement and removal from life. Embowered in her four grey walls, the Lady can but overlook the space of flowers; she is prohibited from entering a space restricted to others' use. Tennyson's end-rhymes here mimic the Lady's confinement, with towers and imbowers acting to enclose the space of 'flowers'. Space in Tennyson has been described as a metaphor for experience – Ulysses' margin that fades, for instance[92] – but here space acts as a metaphor for forbidden experience; the four grey walls extend the metaphor by acting as a boundary between life and the removal from life in the world of art. Yet, the Lady is simultaneously separated from the space of flowers and absorbed within it, confirming how inner and outer worlds, life and art, are combined rather than dichotomised in the poem: in being embowered in Shalott, the Lady is enclosed or sheltered within a bower of flowers, meaning that she shares the space of flowers rather than simply overlooks it. Shelley's 'To a Skylark', for example, from which Tennyson draws for his high-born maiden in a tower according to Tucker, is 'Like a rose embowered / In its own green leaves'.[93] The Lady is therefore as much embowered in her space of flowers as her four grey towers, as Shelley's elusive and enigmatic songbird blends its notes with Wordsworth's own maiden. Tennyson thus breaks down the patriarchal and artistic distinctions that Wordsworth's poem perpetuates, allowing the Lady momentarily to escape the restrictions to which his own poem nevertheless insists she is already doomed. In drawing his material from Wordsworth's poem, Tennyson, however, both participates in the 'social, religious, and didactic' tone of the earlier poem and subtly undercuts it,[94] prefiguring the analysis of 'the cultural myth of patriarchy' he makes in poems like *Idylls of the King*.[95]

Tennyson continues to draw from *The Excursion* in his account of the Lady's weaving. Wordsworth's speaker in the poem goes on to describe how, as night falls, he cannot refrain from gazing at the widower and his daughters at work in their homely abode:

> This Dwelling charms me; often, I stop short;
> (Who could refrain?) and feed by stealth my sight
> With prospect of the Company within,
> Laid open through the blazing window: – there
> I see the eldest Daughter at her wheel
> Spinning amain, as if to overtake
> The never-halting time; or, in her turn,
> Teaching some Novice of the Sisterhood
> That skill in this, or other household work;
> Which, from her Father's honoured hand, herself
> While she was yet a little-one, had learned.
> – Mild man! he is not gay, but they are gay;
> And the whole house seems filled with gaiety.
>
> (V. vi. ll. 1167–79)

The scene on which the Pastor gazes is one of domestic harmony and bliss, with the eldest Daughter of the house passing on her household skills to the 'Sisterhood', sitting at her wheel and spinning amain. Tennyson borrows from Wordsworth in his account of the Lady of Shalott at her weaving: just as the Lady by 'night and day' weaves a magic web with 'colours gay', so the eldest daughter at her wheel spins at night as if to overtake never-halting time; the daughters of the house are gay with happiness, while the Lady's magic web is woven 'with colours gay' (II. l. 38); Wordsworth's rill runs on in solitude, Tennyson's Shalott is an 'island in the river' (I. l. 13). Yet Wordsworth's speaker views the widower's daughters through the blazing window; the Lady weaving behind her castle walls, by contrast, is heard but never seen until her body enters the public arena and is subject to the public, largely masculine, gaze – it is 'Knight and burgher, lord and dame' (IV. l. 160) that come to view the Lady's body; Wordsworth's speaker describes a scene of domestic household work, Tennyson an aristocratic woman working in isolation at her weave. The 1832 version of the poem contains neither the lady who weaves by night and day nor the colours gay,[96] again suggesting that Tennyson returns to Wordsworth for his sourcing in the 1842 version of the poem, building around the space of flowers from the 1832 version, echoing and reworking the earlier poem's tropes of private versus public space, the patriarchal gaze and the nature of women's work. *The Excursion* was an unpopular poem when first published (Byron called it a '"drowsy, frowsy poem"'),[97] although it gained in popularity as the century wore on. William Allingham quotes Tennyson himself as bemoaning its '"long dreary plains of prose"'.[98] Nevertheless, by the time of the publication of the 1842 version of 'The Lady of Shalott', Wordsworth had consolidated his reputation as the pre-eminent poet of his age, largely on the basis of the 'dreary' *Excursion*. In borrowing so liberally from the dreary plains of prose of Wordsworth's 1814 poem, then, Tennyson is able to secure the critical reputation, and perhaps reception, of his revised work by harnessing the cultural authority of his precursor. He does so, of course, by once more borrowing Wordsworth's unpoetical, 'dreary' language.

Gazing features prominently in Wordsworth's 'The Two April Mornings', one of the 'Matthew' poems of 1800, written when Wordsworth was visiting Goslar in Germany. While spending 'A day among the hills' (IV. l. 12), Matthew is reminded of a similar day thirty years before when he stumbled, when fishing, across the grave of his daughter: '"Yon cloud with that long purple cleft / Brings fresh into my mind / A day like this which I have left / Full thirty years behind"' (IV. ll. 21–4). He goes on to recount how, turning from the grave, he met '"A blooming Girl, whose hair was wet / With points of morning dew"' (IV. ll. 43–4), who stirs the memories and emotions of his daughter's loss. He looks at this girl, but does not wish her his: '"There came from me a sigh of pain / Which I could ill confine; / I looked at her and looked again: / – And did not wish her mine"' (IV. ll. 53–6). Something of Matthew's 'looking' or insistent gaze runs through the Lady who looks 'to Camelot' (IV. l. 131), as well as through the knight and burgher who 'read' the Lady's name on the prow of her boat as she enters the public domain. It runs too through Tennyson's description of the road that runs by many-towered Camelot – 'And up and down the people go, / Gazing where the lilies blow / Round an island there below, / The island of Shalott' (I. ll. 6–9). Tennyson's 'people' indulge in the same kind of scrutiny of 'where the lilies blow' as Matthew does of the girl whose hair is wet with points of dew, although Matthew's looking is hedged by memory and an awareness of the differences to looking that time creates. Both scenes carry a sense of indeterminacy, however: Matthew looks at the girl and looks again, trying to match his memory with the blooming girl who stands before him; the people in Tennyson's poem gaze 'where' the lilies blow rather than at the lilies themselves, raising the possibility through the adverbial 'where' that the lilies exist in memory as much as in the present. The 1832 version of the poem lacks the people-gazing scene, suggesting that Tennyson returns to Wordsworth in support of his rewriting in 1842.[99]

'The Two April Mornings' ends with the speaker recording Matthew's death: 'Matthew is in his grave, yet now, / Methinks, I see him stand, / As at that moment, with a bough / Of wilding in his hand' (IV. ll. 57–60). Memory again mixes with looking here, as the speaker remembers seeing Matthew stand with a bough of wilding in his hand, although it is not clear when 'that moment' is. Wordsworth's language is absorbed into Tennyson's poem in the description of the Lady at her casement: 'But who hath seen her wave her hand? / Or at the casement seen her stand? / Or is she known in all the land, / The Lady of Shalott?' (I. ll. 24–7). Unlike Wordsworth, Tennyson records a moment of not seeing or remembering: Who has seen her wave her hand, or at the casement stand? Wordsworth's speaker sees Matthew in an image forged from memory, where the Lady is neither seen nor remembered. The interplay between the two poems runs through the reworking of the 'hand' and 'stand' rhymes. In Wordsworth, seeing and the object of that seeing, image and memory, combine, which is given prominence through the abab end-rhymes: the speaker sees Matthew 'stand' with a bough of wilding in his 'hand'. In Tennyson, however, the rhyme acts to emphasise how the subject and its object have been dislocated – there is no one who has seen the Lady 'wave' her hand or seen her 'stand', and no one to remember having seen. Again, the lines are added to the 1842 version of the poem, suggesting that Tennyson turns to Wordsworth in the 1842 poem.[100] The casement – Keats' casement, as Rowlinson points out – fails to act as a conduit to the imagination or the treasures that memory can unlock.

Douglas-Fairhurst describes how 'The Lady of Shalott' offers itself as 'a fable of writing',[101] partly through the way in which its lines of verse 'reach out into the margin that separates art from the world of their readers, before nervously recoiling back on themselves',[102] mimicking the way in which Tennyson's work 'is shaped by rival centrifugal and centripetal forces, the desire to expand into public life and the desire to retreat into something more "self-involved"'.[103] In its exploration of art and life, 'The Lady of Shalott' thus mirrors Tennyson's own concerns between the demands of a poetry concerned purely with private experience and a poetry that moves away from the self and engages with life, politics and generalised humanity: 'From 1798 onward, Wordsworth's principal endeavour was to become the poet of *The Recluse*, or to move beyond an imagination relevant only to a personal case history to demonstrate the imagination's workings in human life more generally.'[104] The presence of Wordsworth's language enables Tennyson to explore this divide: the presence of Wordsworth's *The Excursion*, for instance, allows Tennyson to move into a poetry that is concerned more with generalised humanity, and less concerned with the self, while the reflective language in the poem enables Tennyson to probe his own private concerns, including his commitment to the poetry of sensation and the epistemology that underpins it as well as what is required from him in terms of being a public poet.

'A gleaming shape she floated by'

In floating past Camelot at the close of the poem the Lady, through death, becomes an artwork, but also an 'image': 'a gleaming shape she floated by, / Dead-pale between the houses high, / Silent into Camelot' (IV. ll. 156–8). 'Gleaming' functions as a resonant word in Wordsworth and in the 'Elegiac Stanzas' in particular, where it acts as a reminder of the speaker's lost image-making powers. The poet adds the gleam, the light that never was, however, allowing him to inhabit a conditional state; and so, in becoming an image, a gleaming shape, the Lady becomes a Wordsworthian 'image', strengthening the Wordsworthian epistemology at work in the poem and Tennyson's reliance on reflective images rather than those grounded in sense. Gleaming is also a synonym for glassy, strengthening the Wordsworthian function in the poem, with the words gleaming and glassy themselves thus creating a mirror image. The phrase is inserted into the 1842 version of the poem, suggesting that Tennyson's echoing or borrowing of Wordsworth's language increases in intensity in the ten years from the poem's first publication. The 1832 version reads a 'pale, pale corpse'.[105] But there is another Wordsworth poem here on which Tennyson draws for his 'gleaming shape': 'SHE was a Phantom of delight', Wordsworth's 1807 paean to his wife:

> SHE was a Phantom of delight
> When first she gleamed upon my sight;
> A lovely Apparition, sent
> To be a moment's ornament;
> Her eyes as stars of Twilight fair;
> Like Twilight's, too, her dusky hair;
> But all things else about her drawn
> From May-time and the cheerful Dawn;
> A dancing Shape, and Image gay,
> To haunt, to startle, and way-lay.
>
> (II. ll. 1–10)

Here, the speaker describes how she was a phantom of delight that first 'gleamed' upon his sight; she is a 'dancing Shape', an epiphanic revelation, an 'Image gay'. In Tennyson, Wordsworth's dancing Shape is transformed into the 'gleaming shape' of the Lady as she floats down to Camelot, dead-pale between the houses high. But the Lady retains something of the Phantom's epiphanic quality, becoming an Apparition, ghostly, but also a revelation. In Wordsworth the speaker describes how the dancing shape has the power to 'haunt, to startle, and way-lay', and something of this power is carried into Tennyson's poem: the speaker at the close of 'The Lady of Shalott' records how the vision of the Lady on her barge inspires shock and fear in the assembled crowd of knights and burghers: 'Who is this? and what is here? / And in the lighted palace near / Died the sound of royal cheer; / And they crossed themselves for fear, / All the knights at Camelot' (iv. ll. 163–7). She becomes, in her own way, 'a moment's ornament'.

Tennyson turns to the same poem in his description of the Lady's 'glassy countenance': in Wordsworth, the 'Phantom of delight' is described as having a 'countenance in which did meet / Sweet records, promises as sweet' (II. ll. 15–16). She has 'household motions light and free, / And steps of virgin-liberty' (II. ll. 13–14). But Wordsworth goes on to describe how this woman is 'A Creature not too bright or good / For human nature's daily food; / For transient sorrows, simple wiles, / Praise, blame, love, kisses, tears, and smiles' (II. ll. 17–20). In harvesting his image of the Lady's glassy countenance from Wordsworth's poem, then, Tennyson taps into a 'femininity constituted through domestic, privatized subjectivity',[106] a subjectivity that is itself a point of discussion in his own poem; in confining the Lady of Shalott to her weaving Tennyson's poem itself engages with both the artist's and women's place within society. Wordsworth's speaker goes on to acknowledge, with the benefit of an 'eye serene' (II. l. 21), the woman as 'A Being breathing thoughtful breath / A Traveller betwixt life and death; / The reason firm, the temperate will, / Endurance, foresight, strength, and skill / A perfect Woman, nobly planned, / To warn, to comfort, and command' (II. ll. 23–8). The Lady, too, shares the Phantom's liminal state, travelling between life and death on her journey from Shalott to Camelot. Unlike the Phantom, however, the Lady does not reach the point at which she is in 'command'. Wordsworth's speaker moves from unaccountable delight in his lovely Apparition to an acknowledgement, in the third stanza, of her earthly qualities, although she remains 'yet a Spirit still, and bright / With something of an angel light' (II. ll. 29–30). Tennyson's poem reverses this trajectory, with the Lady moving from the earthly, weaving at her web, to the visionary, appearing as a gleaming shape.

Joseph Chadwick maintains that the Lady herself becomes an 'antidiscursive poet of sensation' in the poem,[107] but in being both 'glassy' and 'gleaming' she is equally a Wordsworthian poet of reflection, who creates her own self-projected shadows in the mirror. Chadwick envisions the destruction of the poem of sensation, but attributes this to its loss of autonomy, a loss closely linked to the Lady of Shalott's femininity:

> As a feminine emblem of the artist and the artwork, the Lady undermines artistic autonomy by revealing it to be another form of the same kind of confining privacy which removes certain women from the public social world. As an artist and eventually an artwork representing the situation of a certain form of femininity, the Lady undermines the privatized subjectivity of that femininity by revealing it to be vulnerable to the same annihilating objectification Hallam sees the public meting out to the poet of sensation and his works.[108]

But if the poet of sensation is destroyed through an objectified loss of autonomy, then the poetry of reflection survives, as it escapes the annihilating objectification to which the poet and poetry of sensation are subject. In borrowing the Lady's gleaming shape, glassy countenance and lovely face from Wordsworth, 'The Lady of Shalott' may participate in Wordsworth's own objectification of femininity, but the poetry of reflection itself transcends the annihilating objectification to which the poetry of sensation and the feminine artist are subject. Carol T. Christ notes how, 'fearful of the feminization of culture, the poet of the period strove to make the female subject bear his name'.[109] Dorothy Mermin also notes the limitations of the feminine artist:

> She could not just reverse the roles in her poetry and create a comparable male self-projection, since the male in this set of opposites is defined as experienced, complexly self-conscious, and part of the public world and therefore could not serve as a figure for the poet.[110]

Tennyson keys into the feminisation of culture by making the Lady of Shalott bear his name. However, in becoming a poet of reflection, the Lady also subverts the naming to which she is subjected; she is able to reverse roles and 'create a comparable male self-projection', becoming, as Wordsworth frames it in the 'Preface to the Second Edition' of *Lyrical Ballads* (1802), 'a man speaking to men'.[111] In drawing on Wordsworth's language, then, Tennyson reverses the role of the female artist in Victorian poetry, allowing the Lady of Shalott a place in the public sphere that is denied her both through the language of sensation and Victorian culture at large. Tennyson inherits the Romantic idea of the grandeur of art, an aesthetic empowered 'with wonderful autonomy and grandeur',[112] an aesthetic which, as 'The Lady of Shalott' attests, Tennyson was to find both irresistible and unsustainable.[113] In privileging Wordsworth's model in the poem, Tennyson thus returns to a Romantic aesthetic that celebrates the artist's autonomous status and removal from public life and the public good. The Lady as 'gleaming shape' does not signal the death of the artwork as it enters public life, but rather the rejuvenation of the autonomous Romantic poet, but this in itself is not enough to secure the Lady a role beyond her 'Four gray walls'.

Garden 'Idyls'

The 1842 rewriting of 'The Lady of Shalott' sees Tennyson draw more deeply on Wordsworth, with Wordsworth's presence helping to steady the later version of the poem and to feed its discussion of issues relating to gender, art and life. Wordsworth's presence complicates and at times clarifies these issues too. Tennyson's borrowings from Wordsworth also help to steady Tennyson's deep-rooted compositional anxiety, as well as allowing him to engage with a more generalised concern with humanity and to secure his public voice. In turn, by drawing on *The Excursion* and a range of Wordsworthian

poems, Tennyson helps to balance and expand Wordsworth's reputation, offering a more complex view of the earlier poet than the ste-
reotypically confident and prophetic Wordsworth that the Victorians
were busy constructing. Yet, the borrowings from Wordsworth signal
Tennyson's unease at being corralled by Hallam's review and his designation as a poet of sensation, repeatedly testing and questioning his
own poetic identity. Wordsworth is at times prioritised in the poem;
at other times, Tennyson asserts his own priority in what could seem
like acts of Bloomian revisionism and self-assertion. The patterns
of borrowing or echo at work in the poem – of informing, feeding,
directing, redirecting, revising, complicating, problematising – cannot
be contained by one overarching, prescriptive model of influence; nor
can they be subsumed under the umbrella of a benign cooperative of
poets. That the Lady of Shalott as a poet of reflection enters the world
as an autonomous Romantic artist means that Wordsworth does not
fully address Tennyson's artistic and poetic concerns. Nonetheless, it
is the complex, echoing presence of Wordsworth that holds both poet
and poem together.

Other Tennyson poems from 1842 display an affiliation with
Wordsworth, either thematically or linguistically, or both. These
include 'Break, break, break', written on the death of Hallam,[114]
which engages with the themes of return and expressibility, and does
so in part using Wordsworth's language: the 'thoughts that arise'
(l. 4) in Tennyson's speaker but cannot be uttered owe a debt to
Wordsworth's 'Lines written in early Spring' (1798), in which the
reclining speaker describes 'that sweet mood when pleasant thoughts /
Bring sad thoughts to the mind' (IV. ll. 3–4). Wordsworth's 'thoughts'
arise from a sweet mood, while the focus of the speaker in Tennyson's
poem is the unutterability of the thoughts that do arise in him, which
are counterpointed with the crashing volubility of the sea through
the end-rhymes 'Sea' and 'me'. Unlike the sea, the speaker's thoughts
have no stones on which to break their silence. 'The Two Voices',
another poem connected with the death of Hallam,[115] may owe its
title to Wordsworth's sonnet, 'Two Voices Are There' (1807), which
Tennyson read in spring 1835.[116] The allusion to 'The Ancient Mariner' in the speaker's 'blessing' of the family on its way to church
'fixes Tennyson's claim, that his is, like Coleridge's, a conversion
poem'.[117] But 'The Two Voices' also draws liberally on Wordsworth's
language: in an echo of the girl '"whose hair was wet / With points
of morning dew"' (IV. ll. 43–4) from 'The Two April Mornings', the
dragonfly of the opening of Tennyson's poem flies through '"crofts
and pastures wet with dew"' (l. 14). If Tennyson's poem owes its

title to Wordsworth's 'Two Voices Are There', then it owes some of its language, as well as its title in part, to 'The Two April Mornings'. In a reminder of 'Tintern Abbey''s 'living air' (II. l. 99), the dragonfly in Tennyson's poem appears as '"A living flash of light"' (l. 15). In its echoes of Wordsworth 'The Two Voices' therefore harbours a pantheistic alternative to its main Christian narrative, which is made conclusive towards the end of the poem through 'Nature's living motion' (l. 449), which 'lent / The pulse of hope to discontent' (ll. 449–50). The 'living air' (II. l. 98) of 'Tintern Abbey' becomes a motion, combining with the pulses or 'sensations sweet, / Felt in the blood' (II. ll. 28–9) of that same poem to offer Tennyson's speaker a route out of misery and despair. From this perspective, the dragonfly of Tennyson's poem, as it flies through crofts and pastures wet with dew, goes through its own kind of pantheistic baptism or rebirth, complementing the Christian 'conversion' of the speaker himself.

But there is another group of poems from 1842 that specifically engage with Wordsworth's unpoetical language and unpoetical universe, poems that were later termed the English or Domestic 'Idyls'; these include 'Dora', 'Audley Court', 'Walking to the Mail' and 'The Gardener's Daughter Or, The Pictures' (hereafter 'The Gardener's Daughter'). The poems return thematically and linguistically to Wordsworth – they borrow Wordsworth's ordinary language and ordinary themes and ordinary people too, making explicit the pattern at work in 'The Lady of Shalott'. Tennyson attempts a Wordsworthian simplicity in 'Dora', such as that of Wordsworth's blank verse narrative, 'Michael: A Pastoral Poem' (hereafter 'Michael'), which Edward Fitzgerald read to Tennyson in 1835 on a trip to the Speddings' house, Mirehouse, by Bassenthwaite Lake in the Lake District.[118] Fitzgerald quotes Tennyson, in fact, as saying that he 'remembered the time when he could see nothing in "Michael" which he now read us in admiration'.[119] Wordsworth for his part is rather apocryphally accredited with saying of 'Dora': '"Mr Tennyson, I have been endeavouring all my life to write a pastoral like your 'Dora' and have not succeeded."'[120] Like Wordsworth's 'Michael', 'Dora' is one of 'those domestic tales' ('Michael', I. l. 22), a 'history / Homely and rude' ('Michael', I. ll. 34–5). Both 'Michael' and 'Dora' share common tropes, a common language and a common metre. Both poems feature lost and recalcitrant sons. Michael's son Luke and the farmer's son William in 'Dora', as well as brothers' sons in both poems, form the fulcrum on which the narratives of the two poems revolve in their tales of 'simple' ('Michael', I. l. 207) households. The poems also share in the same 'simple' phrasing: Wordsworth's Michael is referred to as 'The old Man' (I. l. 316; I. l. 452), Tennyson's farmer as 'the old man';[121] Michael's son Luke carries within his cheek two steady roses that were 'five years old' (I. l. 179), Tennyson's farmer observes that there has not been for these 'five years' (l. 63) a full harvest. Both poems in this way remember 'Tintern Abbey''s 'five years' that have past (II. l. 1). Similarly, the later poem echoes and reworks scenes from the earlier Wordsworth poem: Michael hears Luke as a babe by the fireside 'First uttering, without words, a natural tune; / While thou, a feeding babe, didst in thy joy / Sing at thy Mother's breast' (II. ll. 347–9). In 'Dora', William's son, the farmer's grandson, sits in the hollow of the farmer's arm, stretching out and babbling for 'the golden seal, that hung / From Allan's watch, and sparkled by the fire' (ll. 132–3).

The idyll has its roots in Theocritus and is 'essentially an urban poetic form, one that emerges in nostalgia for a pastoral way of life',[122] although Tennyson's use of the term is notably vague, reflected in his idiosyncratic spelling of 'idyl'.[123] Nostalgia for a pastoral way of life in 'The Gardener's Daughter' nonetheless reveals Tennyson as not only indebted to Theocritus, especially in the Seventh Idyll,[124] but also to the Pastor's domestic vignette from Book VI of Wordsworth's *The Excursion*. Rose, the Gardener's daughter, her name itself a reminder of the 'cultured rose' of Book VI of Wordsworth's poem, occupies a private garden, 'Not wholly in the busy world, nor quite / Beyond it' (ll. 33–4). Verbal echoes in Tennyson's poem emphasise the garden's connections with that of its predecessor in *The Excursion*: the speaker of Book VI describes the garden as 'this trim place' (V. vi. l. 1142); in 'The Gardener's Daughter', the deictic 'this' turns to 'that' as the speaker describes how the Gardener's daughter 'In that still place . . . hoarded in herself, / Grew, seldom seen' (ll. 48–9), as trimness transmutes into stillness. Each of the gardens is a private space, removed from public view, much like the daughters in the poems. And yet in both poems, this private space is disturbed by a male imposter or onlooker; in Book VI of *The Excursion*, the Pastor freely partakes of whatever the garden bears, whether fruit or flower, while in Tennyson's poem the speaker 'looked upon' (l. 61) or 'beheld' (l. 121) the Gardener's daughter in her sequestered place, freely partaking of her image, just as the Pastor partakes of the garden's offerings. Tennyson's poem concludes with the Gardener's daughter offering to the speaker 'the greatest gift' (l. 224), 'A woman's heart' (l. 225), although Tennyson does not confirm that the marriage has taken place, only that Rose has become 'the most blessèd memory of mine age' (l. 273). Wordsworth's Pastor observes in the Daughter spinning at her wheel the survival of her mother's spirit on earth; in potentially becoming a wife, Rose becomes an extension of the spirit of domestic bliss, fulfilling the destiny of Wordsworth's hardy Girl. Tennyson, according to Armstrong, suffers a failure of nerve or a loss of confidence in the English 'Idyls':[125] the poems retreat from the poetry of sensation and the daring experimentalism of 'The Lady of Shalott' into a domesticated and conventional Wordsworthianism. Yet 'The Lady of Shalott' and 'The Gardener's Daughter' form part of a whole, both drawing from and reworking Wordsworth's pastoral vignette from *The Excursion*. The movement back to Wordsworth is therefore less of a retreat or a failure of nerve than a facilitation, allowing Tennyson once again to question the poetry of sensation and his own role within it, as well as allowing an exploration of the theme of gendered space.

Tennyson draws on Wordsworth's 'ordinary' language in the so-called Lincolnshire dialect poems, 'Northern Farmer, Old Style' (1864), 'Northern Farmer, New Style' (1869) and 'The Northern Cobbler' (1880). Tennyson also turns to Wordsworth's scenes of ordinary life in the 1880 *Ballads and Other Poems* such as 'Rizpah', 'In the Children's Hospital' and 'The Village Wife', leading to suggestions that he turns away from his own ballad experiments of the 1830s and 1840s to adapt the Wordsworthian ballad, with its emphasis on incidents and situations from common life;[126] the title of Tennyson's collection is itself a reminder of Wordsworth's *Lyrical Ballads* (1800).[127] Yet, rather than a turning away from his own early ballads like 'The Lady of Shalott', the later ballads act as a continuation of them; the Wordsworthian 'prosaic' language at work in 'The Lady of Shalott' and the scenes of ordinary life that it embraces, from the Daughter of the house at her wheel to Matthew of 'The Two April Mornings', prefigure the move towards Wordsworth that Tennyson is to make in these later works.

The year 1842 saw the publication of Tennyson's monologue, 'Ulysses', first written in 1833 soon after the death of Arthur Hallam, but rewritten for later publication. Tennyson considered the 1833 'Ulysses' to be an 'Idyl', when he printed it in the 1842 trail pamphlet, *Morte-D'Arthur; Dora; and Other Idyls*.[128] The poem is predicated on distancing the solipsism of the lyrical speaker,[129] and is therefore in theory distanced from Wordsworth's lyrical voice. Yet, as in 'The Lady of Shalott', the poem absorbs Wordsworth's language, with Tennyson echoing, reworking, revising, drawing from his predecessor; but whereas in 'The Lady of Shalott' Tennyson returns to Wordsworth ostensibly to stabilise the poem, in 'Ulysses' Tennyson attempts to break free from Wordsworth in order to stabilise a 'new' poetic form – the monologue. Yet, as the next chapter will show, the echoes and borrowings at work within the poem create complex effects, with Tennyson's revision of Wordsworth mirrored by his dependency on him.

Notes

1. Tennyson, *The Poems of Tennyson*, I, IV. l. 169 (p. 395). All further references in the chapter to Tennyson's poems are to this edition and appear parenthetically in the text unless otherwise stated.
2. Tennyson, *The Poems of Tennyson*, I, p. 387.
3. Tennyson, *The Poems of Tennyson*, I, p. 387.
4. Tennyson, *The Poems of Tennyson*, I, p. 387.
5. Tennyson, *The Poems of Tennyson*, I, p. 387.
6. Croker, *Quarterly Review*.
7. Douglas-Fairhurst, 'Tennyson', p. 608.
8. Douglas-Fairhurst, 'Tennyson', p. 608.
9. Douglas-Fairhurst, 'Tennyson', p. 608.
10. Douglas-Fairhurst, 'Tennyson', p. 608.
11. Douglas-Fairhurst, 'Tennyson', p. 608.
12. Hallam, 'On Some of the Characteristics of Modern Poetry', p. 93.
13. Hallam, 'On Some of the Characteristics of Modern Poetry', p. 91.
14. Hallam, 'On Some of the Characteristics of Modern Poetry', p. 94.
15. Hallam, 'On Some of the Characteristics of Modern Poetry', p. 94.
16. Hallam, 'On Some of the Characteristics of Modern Poetry', p. 94.
17. Hallam, 'On Some of the Characteristics of Modern Poetry', p. 107.
18. Hallam, 'On Some of the Characteristics of Modern Poetry', p. 109.
19. Hallam, 'On Some of the Characteristics of Modern Poetry', p. 105.
20. Douglas-Fairhurst, 'Tennyson', p. 608.
21. Armstrong, *Victorian Poetry*, p. 67.
22. Perry, *Alfred Tennyson*, pp. 8–9, quoting from Hallam's review, in Jump, *Tennyson: The Critical Heritage*, p. 42.
23. Chandler, 'Hallam, Tennyson, and the Poetry of Sensation', p. 533.
24. Chandler, 'Hallam, Tennyson, and the Poetry of Sensation', p. 533.
25. Dillon, 'Canonical and Sensational', p. 98.
26. Dillon, 'Canonical and Sensational', p. 95. Dillon draws here from Bruns, 'The Formal Nature of Victorian Thinking', pp. 404–18.
27. Mill, 'Thoughts on Poetry and its Varieties', p. 358.
28. Mill, 'Thoughts on Poetry and its Varieties', pp. 358–9.
29. Christ, 'Introduction: Victorian Poetics', p. 5.
30. Christ, 'Introduction: Victorian Poetics', p. 5.
31. Armstrong, *Victorian Poetry*, p. 77.
32. Armstrong, *Victorian Poetry*, p. 87.
33. Armstrong, *Victorian Poetry*, pp. 96–7.
34. Armstrong, *Victorian Poetry*, p. 97.

35. Ricks, *Allusion to the Poets*, pp. 179–216.
36. Bloom, *The Anxiety of Influence*, p. 71.
37. Hollander describes how 'A single word or phrase . . . amplified or not by a phonetic scheme, may easily carry rumors of its resounding cave', and this effect makes itself manifest in 'The Lady of Shalott' through Tennyson's echoing of single Wordsworthian words. See Hollander, *The Figure of Echo*, p. 95.
38. Tucker, *Tennyson and the Doom of Romanticism*, pp. 103–4; Stevenson, 'The "High-Born" Maiden Symbol', pp. 126–36. As noted by Plasa, '"Cracked from Side to Side"', p. 253, n. 18.
39. Rowlinson, *Tennyson's Fixations*, p. 89.
40. Wordsworth, 'Elegiac Stanzas: Suggested by a Picture of Peele Castle, in a Storm, Painted by Sir George Beaumont', in *Poems, in Two Volumes*, II, l. 48 (p. 144). Subsequent references to this poem are to this edition and appear parenthetically in the text.
41. Simonsen, *Wordsworth and Word-Preserving Arts*, p. 5.
42. Wordsworth, *The Poetical Works of William Wordsworth in Five Volumes*, I, ll. 117–18 (p. 58). All other references in the chapter to Wordsworth's poems are to these volumes and appear parenthetically in the text unless otherwise stated. References are given by volume and line number.
43. O'Neill, *Romanticism and the Self-Conscious Poem*, p. 54.
44. O'Neill, *Romanticism and the Self-Conscious Poem*, p. 54.
45. O'Neill, *Romanticism and the Self-Conscious Poem*, p. 54.
46. Starzyk, '"If Mine Had Been the Painter's Hand"', p. 46.
47. Rowlinson, 'Lyric', p. 65.
48. Rowlinson, 'Lyric', p. 65.
49. Rowlinson, 'Lyric', p. 67.
50. Rowlinson, 'Lyric', p. 67.
51. Rowlinson, 'Lyric', p. 68.
52. Rowlinson, 'Lyric', p. 64.
53. Rowlinson, 'Lyric', p. 64.
54. Armstrong, *Victorian Poetry*, p. 86.
55. Armstrong, *Victorian Poetry*, p. 62.
56. Armstrong, *Victorian Poetry*, p. 62.
57. Armstrong, 'Tennyson's "The Lady of Shalott"', p. 64.
58. Armstrong, 'Tennyson's "The Lady of Shalott"', p. 63.
59. Armstrong, 'Tennyson's "The Lady of Shalott"', p. 63.
60. Armstrong, 'Tennyson's "The Lady of Shalott"', p. 69.
61. Armstrong, 'Tennyson's "The Lady of Shalott"', p. 68.
62. Dillon, 'Canonical and Sensational', p. 96.
63. Dillon, 'Canonical and Sensational', p. 96.
64. Dillon, 'Canonical and Sensational', p. 96.
65. Leighton, *On Form*, p. 60.
66. Leighton, *On Form*, p. 60.

67. Leighton, *On Form*, p. 57.
68. Leighton, *On Form*, p. 61. The example Leighton gives here is of Tennyson's *In Memoriam*, Section XCV.
69. Dillon, 'Canonical and Sensational', p. 105.
70. Tennyson, *The Poems of Tennyson*, l, p. 392, l. 78.
71. Coleridge, *The Complete Poetical Works*, l, l. 3 (p. 187).
72. McDonald notes Tennyson's 'ear' for rhythm, sound and phrasing. See McDonald, *Sound Intentions*, p. 23.
73. Hallam, 'On Some of the Characteristics of Modern Poetry', p. 93.
74. Hallam, 'On Some of the Characteristics of Modern Poetry', p. 94.
75. Hallam, 'On Some of the Characteristics of Modern Poetry', p. 94.
76. McDonald, *Sound Intentions*, p. 26.
77. Keats, *Selected Poems and Letters of Keats*, ll. 35–40 (p. 125).
78. Sprinker, '"A Counterpoint of Dissonance"', p. 6.
79. Armstrong, 'Tennyson's "The Lady of Shalott"', p. 93.
80. Plasa, '"Cracked from Side to Side"', p. 251; the rehabilitation of the mirror is also noted by Jordan, *Alfred Tennyson*, p. 58.
81. Lourie, 'Below the Thunders of the Upper Deep', p. 20.
82. Chadwick, 'A Blessing and a Curse', p. 89.
83. Sanford Russell, 'How to Exist Where You Are', pp. 391–2, quoting Cameron, *Impersonality: Seven Essays*, pp. 5–6.
84. Chadwick, 'A Blessing and a Curse', pp. 83–9.
85. Chadwick, 'A Blessing and a Curse', pp. 83–9; see also Plasa, '"Cracked from Side to Side"', pp. 247–63.
86. Douglas-Fairhurst, 'Tennyson', p. 608.
87. Douglas-Fairhurst, 'Tennyson', p. 608.
88. Douglas-Fairhurst, 'Tennyson', p. 608.
89. Rowlinson, 'Lyric', p. 64.
90. Tennyson, *The Poems of Tennyson*, I, p. 395, ll. 163–71.
91. Tennyson, *The Poems of Tennyson*, I, p. 395, l. 168.
92. Decker, 'Tennyson's Limitations', p. 65.
93. Shelley, *The Complete Works of Percy Bysshe Shelley*, ll. 51–2 (p. 603).
94. Gravil, 'Introduction', p. 2.
95. See Shires, 'Patriarchy, Dead Men and Tennyson's *Idylls of the King*', p. 408.
96. See Tennyson, *The Poems of Tennyson*, I, p. 390, n. 37–40. Armstrong suggests that the poem draws on the myth of the weaving lady in Arachne and Penelope, which it fuses with the myths of reflection carried by Narcissus and Echo. See Armstrong, *Victorian Poetry*, p. 83.
97. Gravil, 'Introduction', p. 2.
98. See Page, *Tennyson: Interviews and Recollections*, p. 135, quoted in Perry, 'Two Voices', p. 14.
99. See Tennyson, *The Poems of Tennyson*, I, ll. 6–9 (p. 388). Lines 6–9 of the 1832 version read: 'The yellowleavèd waterlily / The greensheathèd daffodilly, / Tremble in the water chilly, / Round about Shalott'.

100. Tennyson, *The Poems of Tennyson*, I, ll. 24–6 (p. 389). Lines 24–6 of the 1832 poem read: 'A pearlgarland winds her head; / She leaneth on a velvet bed, / Full royally apparellèd'.
101. Douglas-Fairhurst, 'Tennyson', p. 608.
102. Douglas-Fairhurst, 'Tennyson', p. 609.
103. Douglas-Fairhurst, 'Tennyson', p. 609.
104. Larkin, *Wordsworth and Coleridge*, p. 33.
105. See Tennyson, *The Poems of Tennyson*, I, p. 394, l. 156.
106. Chadwick, 'A Blessing and a Curse', p. 95.
107. Chadwick, 'A Blessing and a Curse', p. 94.
108. Chadwick, 'A Blessing and a Curse', p. 95.
109. Christ, 'The Feminine Subject in Victorian Poetry', p. 400.
110. Mermin, 'The Damsel, the Knight, and the Victorian Woman Poet', p. 68.
111. Wordsworth, 'Preface to the Second Edition', p. 370.
112. Perry, *Alfred Tennyson*, p. 17.
113. Perry, *Alfred Tennyson*, p. 17.
114. Tennyson, *The Poems of Tennyson*, II, p. 24.
115. Tennyson, *The Poems of Tennyson*, I, p. 570. Ricks here raises the possibility, however, that Tennyson began the poem before the death of Hallam.
116. Tennyson, *The Poems of Tennyson*, I, p. 570, quoting from *Alfred Lord Tennyson: A Memoir*, p. 151.
117. Cronin, *Romantic Victorians*, p. 231.
118. Tennyson, *The Poems of Tennyson*, II, p. 68.
119. Tennyson, *Alfred Lord Tennyson: A Memoir*, I, p. 151.
120. Tennyson, *Alfred Lord Tennyson: A Memoir*, I, p. 265.
121. Tennyson, *The Poems of Tennyson*, II, l. 22 (p. 69). All other references to 'Dora' are to this edition and appear parenthetically in the text.
122. Peterson, 'Domestic and Idyllic', p. 50.
123. Perry, for instance, claims that Tennyson 'did not firmly mean anything' by the term. See Perry, *Alfred Tennyson*, p. 96.
124. Ricks, in Tennyson, *The Poems of Tennyson*, I, p. 552. Ricks also notes how the poem brings together Tennyson's friendship for Hallam and Hallam's love for Tennyson's sister Emily.
125. Armstrong, *Victorian Poetry*, p. 94.
126. Sylvia, 'Reading Tennyson's *Ballads and Other Poems*', pp. 28–9.
127. Sylvia, 'Reading Tennyson's *Ballads and Other Poems*', p. 28.
128. O'Donnell, 'Tennyson's "English Idyls"', p. 141.
129. Christ, *Victorian and Modern Poetics*, p. 26.

Chapter 2

'All experience is an arch':[1] Tennyson's 'Ulysses' and the Revision of Wordsworth

Tennyson wrote 'Ulysses' on 20 October 1833, soon after he heard the news of Arthur Henry Hallam's unexpected death,[2] and subsequently reworked the poem for publication in 1842. The poet notably declares, in a comment which post-dates the poem's publication, that

> There is more about myself in *Ulysses*, which was written under the sense of loss and that all had gone by, but that still life must be fought out to the end. It was more written with the feeling of his loss upon me than many poems in *In Memoriam*.[3]

Tennyson wrote 'Tithonus' in the same year, as a companion piece or 'pendent' to 'Ulysses',[4] as he tries to find a way of assuaging his grief, resulting in the two poems subsequently being viewed as a pair.[5] The poem takes the form of a dramatic monologue and is based on two sources – Homer's *Odyssey* xi 100–37 and Dante's *Inferno* xxxvi 90ff, with Dante regarded as the more important of the two[6] – and recounts Ulysses' last, fatal voyage. Christopher Decker points out, however, that the poem takes place 'at some indefinite point in time between the end of the events recounted in the *Odyssey* and the final voyage described, in another analepsis, by Ulysses in Canto 26 of the *Inferno*'.[7]

'Ulysses' attracted much critical attention at the time of its publication and has continued to do so since, although its speaker, and its primary message about the 'need of going forward', have not been viewed without irony in recent years: Christopher Ricks, in a much-quoted reading, reveals how Ulysses' sense of steely determination is undermined by his lack of use of the future tense.[8] The poem has also been viewed as articulating a 'Romantic religion, a structure of transcendence without a grounding dogma [which] . . . secularizes the patterns of earlier Christian psychology',[9] and as propounding a proto-imperialist agenda: 'Ulysses, like Tennyson and Columbus, takes with him the dominant language of the world and imposes its cultural requirements wherever he goes.'[10]

The poem alludes to several prior texts that help to make up its composition. Ricks, in his gloss to the poem, cites possible allusions to Shakespeare's *Hamlet* IV iv 33–9 in the 'sleep and feed' of line 5;[11] 'the still-vexed Bermoothes' of *The Tempest* I ii 229 in the 'vext sea' of line 11;[12] *Troilus and Cressida* in the 'rust unburnished' of line 23;[13] and Percy Bysshe Shelley's *Revolt of Islam* III xxxii 3–4 in the 'dim sea' of lines 10–11.[14] Herbert F. Tucker, Jr, also points to how 'Ulysses' shares its 'something more' (l. 27) with Wordsworth's 'Tintern Abbey',[15] as it does the 'eternal silence' of line 27 with the 'Intimations' ode's own 'eternal Silence' (IX. l. 160),[16] the latter of which is 'especially germane to Tennyson's purpose in "Ulysses," since there for once Wordsworth explicitly forswears the "simple creed" of unmediated participation in experience';[17] similarly, 'Tennyson's "feeling about the need of going forward" . . . answers very closely to Wordsworth's "We will grieve not, rather find / Strength in what remains behind"' from the 'Intimations' ode.[18] As Tucker concludes, 'the verbal echo urges the comparison upon us, and I suspect it does so with Tennyson's blessing'.[19]

Tucker mentions, too, how the rhythm and syntax of lines 55–6 of the poem, with their 'long day' that wanes, alludes to Shelley's *Adonais* (1821) and 'The soft sky [that] smiles, – the low wind [that] whispers near'.[20] Michael O'Neill, expanding on the Shelleyan allusions Tucker 'sensitively hears' in the text,[21] advocates that

> The Victorian poet both chastens Romantic longing and suggests that his own temperament's and era's would-be stoic awareness that 'that which we are, we are' (l. 67) lurked in the poetry of a precursor whose sight seemed forever set on what was 'yet to be' (*Prometheus Unbound*, III. iii. 56).[22]

Decker, meanwhile, foregrounds the Shakespearean allusions in the poem, seeing them as enabling Tennyson to express 'his desire to believe in spiritual survival by invoking and blessing the consubstantial presence of an absent precursor within the pale of a new poem'.[23]

But 'Ulysses' also sports a gallery of Wordsworthian echoes, echoes that have thus far been overlooked, ignored or simply not heard by previous critics. The poem is not regarded as overtly Wordsworthian, unlike its companion piece, 'Tithonus', which shares with Wordsworth's 'Tintern Abbey' (1798) that sense of the self re-encountering itself in time. 'Ulysses' contains many more 'borrowings' from Wordsworth's poetry than those listed above, nonetheless, including from 'Tintern Abbey' and the 'Intimations' ode. As in 'The Lady of Shalott' (1832; revised 1842), these borrowings include 'single' words.[24] Echoes from 'Tintern Abbey', *An Evening Walk* (1793) and the 'Intimations' ode (1807), as well a range of other Wordsworth poems, sound through the poem, providing an alternative commentary to the one the poem ostensibly supports. These echoes compromise the poem's meaning, or at least give it a meaning different from the one the poet might have intended, or readers have hitherto 'read' from it. 'The Lady of Shalott' liberally absorbs Wordsworth's language; but here there are different effects, different consequences: if Tennyson borrows from Wordsworth in 'The Lady of Shalott' in order to loosen the restrictive epistemology in which he has been placed through his designation as a poet of sensation, in 'Ulysses' his borrowings allow him to distance the Romantic lyric's focus on self and to consolidate a new poetic form. As Robert Langbaum has made clear, the dramatic monologue develops from the Romantic lyric but is predicated on a move away from lyrical interiority to performative or rhetorical speech, a process that, for Langbaum, involves 'a tension between sympathy and moral judgment';[25] Tennyson, alongside Robert Browning, is himself instrumental in developing the form.[26] In revising Wordsworth, Tennyson is thus establishing his poetic difference from Wordsworth, or at least setting his poetry in relation to the poetry that precedes it.

Revisionary processes inevitably evoke Harold Bloom's intra-poetic model of family romance,[27] and Tennyson's reworking of Wordsworth could be viewed as the later poet's attempt to weaken a dominant Wordsworth in order to strengthen his own poetic hand. Yet, in borrowing Wordsworth's language in the poem, Tennyson reveals himself to be as dependent on Wordsworth as he is independent from him; difference can function only alongside dependence, as the chapter will demonstrate.

The study of the Wordsworthian echoes at work in the poem draws on Sigmund Freud's theory of mourning and melancholia. The application of Freud's theory to the processes of borrowing at work in 'Ulysses' again seemingly evokes Bloom's revisionary model, yet Tennyson's 'consumption' of Wordsworth differentiates itself from Bloom in several ways, not least because it reveals Tennyson as seeking to reaffiliate himself with Wordsworth rather than defensively protecting himself from him in one or more of Bloom's revisionary ratios.

Interestingly, the poem is also revising Hallam's own allusions to Wordsworth in his 1829 poem, 'Timbuctoo'. Both Tennyson and Hallam competed for the 1829 University of Cambridge Chancellor's Gold Medal poem prize, based on the famed Saharan city of Timbuktu, with Tennyson's poem securing the coveted medal.[28] Each of these poems engages with the 'city of the imagination',[29] although Tennyson's poem concludes with an acknowledgement that the city will 'lose its power in the world'.[30] Hallam's 'Timbuctoo' alludes to Wordsworth's 'Tintern Abbey' and 'Intimations' ode in its exploration of imaginative transcendence, but, like 'Ulysses', echoes Wordsworth, too. Hearing a double echo, 'Ulysses' picks up Hallam's poem's Wordsworthian language and reworks it, exposing a little-explored line of connection that exists between the two poems.

Weaving a Rainbow

The 'Intimations' ode describes a process of imaginative loss and recovery, a loss precipitated in the poem by the speaker's alienation from nature through the growth of self-consciousness. The speaker of the poem notes how

> THERE was a time when meadow, grove, and stream,
> The earth, and every common sight,
>   To me did seem
>   Apparelled in celestial light,
> The glory and the freshness of a dream.
> It is not now as it hath been of yore; –
>   Turn wheresoe'er I may,
>   By night or day,
> The things which I have seen I now can see no more.
>
> (IV. i. ll. 1–9)

Recompense for the speaker's visionary loss comes through 'the soothing thoughts that spring / Out of human suffering' (IV. x. ll. 183–4), and 'In the faith that looks through death, / In years that bring the philosophic mind' (IV. x. ll. 185–6). But there is also imaginative recompense to be found in 'the meanest flower that blows' (IV. xi. l. 202), as the connection between nature and 'the human heart by which we live' (IV. xi. l. 200) is restored. The speaker's loss of imaginative power is assuaged through the very 'nature' from which it has felt itself estranged,[31] in the 'Thoughts that do often lie too deep for tears' (IV. xi. l. 203). It is the 'meanest', or humblest,[32] things in nature which bring comfort to the speaker at the close of the Ode, re-establishing the connection with 'The earth, and every common sight' (IV. i. l. 2) that is dislocated at the start of the poem: 'Fountains, Meadows, Hills, and Groves' (IV. xi. l. 187); 'the Brooks which down their channels fret' (IV. xi. l. 192). In Wordsworth, however, growth is nevertheless engendered through this 'narrative' of loss;[33] 'loss and grief serve as providential catalysts of his imagination'.[34]

The 'Intimations' ode resonates throughout 'Ulysses', bringing with it its account of imaginative loss and recovery, made evident through the echoes and borrowings that make up the poem's principal moment of imaginative transcendence, namely, Ulysses' claim that 'all experience is an arch wherethrough / Gleams that untravelled world, whose margin fades / For ever and for ever when I move' (ll. 19–21). J. Pettigrew, according to Ricks' gloss to the poem, cites the source of 'the unpeopled world' as Henry Francis Cary's Dante, *Inferno* xxvi 117 as the possible origin for these lines,[35] while M. Alexander claims *Hamlet* III i 79–80, 'The undiscovered country, from whose bourn / No traveller returns', as an alternative source.[36] Ricks also quotes E. H. Duncan on how the arch itself is 'not apparently indebted to Dante'.[37] Interestingly, the arch complies with a familiar Romantic trope, the window casement, which Robert Douglas-Fairhurst describes as a 'textual frame that opens on to a parallel world of the imagination'.[38] But there is also an allusion to 'arch' here, which is evocative of the 'Intimations' ode and other, related Wordsworth poems. Rather than an architectural metaphor (Richard Cronin reveals how Edward Lear reincarnates Tennyson's metaphor in solid Roman brick, for instance, in his watercolour, *The Campagna as seen through an Arch on the Appian Way*[39]), the arch corresponds to Wordsworth's use of the rainbow as a Romantic trope for the imagination. Significantly, the Latin origin of 'arch' is *arcus* or bow (*OED*). Both the Romantics and the Victorians use the metaphor of the rainbow as a means by which to draw attention to the imagination's role in creating moments of personal, or even theological, transcendence: John Keble in 'The Third Sunday after the Epiphany', which appears in *The Christian Year* of 1827, uses the motif of the rainbow to emphasise the objective truth of the sacrament, but also to show how the act of 'marking' a rainbow in the sky reveals how theology itself is inseparable from the act of individual perception;[40] Gerard Manley Hopkins, in an untitled poem of 1864, uses the rainbow to reveal how the mind finds inscapes of Christ in nature, of how 'The rainbow shines, but only in the thought / Of him that looks'.[41]

The rainbow itself has a long history as a religious trope, but its 'symbolic import' is rejected by the Romantic poets for whom its 'sense of wonder' evaporates:[42] Shelley sees the rainbow as an emblem of transience in 'When the Lamp is Shattered' and 'Hymn to Intellectual Beauty',[43] and mocks the notions of rainbow and covenant in 'a blasphemous parody of *Queen Mab*'.[44] A second-generation Romantic poet like John Keats laments the way in which the discoveries of Newton '"destroyed the poetry of the rainbow by reducing it to the prismatic colours"'.[45] However, 'few Victorian poets were likely to take such pleasure in directly mocking the religious tradition upon which this symbolism had been based'.[46] Rather, poets like Tennyson and Robert Browning 'simply employ the rainbow at times as a beautiful optical phenomenon',[47] or 'find some literary device to insulate it from questions of belief';[48] often, they 'make use of the rainbow precisely because it is problematic'.[49] For example, Tennyson's '"The Two Voices" exemplifies a poem that draws upon the rainbow as emblem of hope and grace without having to admit literal belief in it'.[50]

In the 'Intimations' ode, the rainbow is an object in nature which stimulates imaginative awareness in the speaker, yet is also a reminder of the fragility of the creative, imaginative act, which, like the rainbow itself, comes and goes. George P. Landow points to how Wordsworth 'takes the fact that the "Rainbow comes and goes" as a sign of our earthly state',[51] but the rainbow bears an imaginative load also, which counteracts, yet at the same time supports, any religious symbolism it may have, as in the 'Intimations' ode:

> The Rainbow comes and goes,
> And lovely is the Rose,
> The Moon doth with delight
> Look round her when the heavens are bare,
> Waters on a starry night
> Are beautiful and fair;
> The sunshine is a glorious birth;
> But yet I know, where'er I go,
> That there hath passed away a glory from the earth.
>
> (IV. ii. ll. 10–18)

The dead-beat, perfunctory rhythm of the opening lines here reflects the speaker's acknowledgement that imaginative glory is for the moment spent. In 'MY heart leaps up' (1807), Wordsworth writes of how 'MY heart leaps up when I behold / A Rainbow in the sky: / So was it when my life began; / So is it now I am a Man; / So be it when I shall grow old, / Or let me die!' (I. ll. 1–6). The rainbow becomes a trope for the speaker's imaginative power, a power with which the speaker was invested as child, and with which he hopes he will continue to be invested as an old man, as 'The Child is Father of the Man' (I. l. 7). Imaginative power is linked too to a heart that can leap with the 'spontaneous overflow of powerful feelings'.[52] Significantly, the last three lines of 'MY heart leaps up' – 'The Child is Father of the Man; / And I could wish my days to be / Bound each to each by natural piety' (I. ll. 7–9) – form an epigraph to the 'Intimations' ode, emphasising the linkage between the two texts.

The arch of the rainbow is a somewhat submerged presence in both the 'Intimations' ode and 'MY heart leaps up': Wordsworth writes of the 'Rainbow' in his own texts, but not their arch; Tennyson writes of the 'arch' in 'Ulysses', but not its bow. Wordsworth and Tennyson's poems thus become two halves of a whole, with the 'rainbow arch' an emblematic trope transmitted between them. 'Arch', and its submerged (rain) bow, both permeate 'Ulysses', signifying the fragility of the transcendental imagination, and qualifying Ulysses' search for imaginative immortality through his 'arch' of experience as a result of the intertextual arch of influence created between the two poems. Tennyson 'weaves' a rainbow – in an intertextual sense – from the poetic works that precede his.[53]

Crucially, the rainbow in Wordsworth's ''TIS said, that some have died for love' (1800) is associated with 'arch' as imaginative projection, as it is in 'Fair Prime of Life!' (1827), making the connection drawn above between arch and rainbow in 'Ulysses' explicit. In 'Fair Prime of Life!' the 'rainbow arch' (II. l. 4) is supplementary to 'Fancy's errands' (II. l. 5), and thereby directly connected to the creative imaginative, as 'Fancy', in the Wordsworthian sense, is an inferior faculty, working in support of the superior faculty, 'imagination':[54]

> FAIR Prime of life! were it enough to gild
> With ready sunbeams every straggling shower;
> And, if an unexpected cloud should lower,
> Swiftly thereon a rainbow arch to build
> For Fancy's errands, – then, from fields half-tilled

Gathering green weeds to mix with poppy flower,
Thee might thy Minions crown, and chant thy power,
Unpitied by the wise, all censure stilled.

(II. ll. 1–8)

In "'TIS said, that some have died for love', both 'arch' and 'rainbow' are related to death and imaginative loss, and to the loss of nature as an imaginative source. Wordsworth writes of a 'wretched Man' (l. 4), who, having slain his love, opines:

'Thou Eglantine, whose arch so proudly towers,
(Even like a rainbow spanning half the Vale)
Thou one fair shrub, oh! shed thy flowers,
And stir not in the gale.
For thus to see thee nodding in the air,
To see thy arch thus stretch and bend,
Thus rise and thus descend, –
Disturbs me till the sight is more than I can bear.'

(I. ll. 37–44)

The wretched man draws equivalence between the arch of the eglantine and the rainbow, projecting an image of the eglantine as standing proud as a rainbow spanning half the vale. But the projection is also one of loss, as the eglantine as rainbow is an imaginative projection of his lost love: the lost love was once as alive and vital as the eglantine. He wishes pre-emptively to destroy the eglantine, to negate it before its own death, so that he does not have to be reminded of his loss. But by wishing to destroy the eglantine, he is, by association, also wishing to destroy his imaginative projection.

The projections of loss, death and pre-emptive imaginative death are mediated through the poem's borrowing of 'arch' as rainbow in 'Ulysses', and serve to threaten Ulysses' imaginative project, which is already perturbed by potential imaginative loss, and the search for its recovery, through its intertextual linkage to the 'Intimations' ode and 'MY heart leaps up'. Significantly, in Wordsworth's text, it is the wretched man for whom the rainbow's arch signifies death and imaginative loss: the speaker steps away from such loss to celebrate the 'happiness' he has 'known to-day' (I. l. 52). Imaginative and literal loss are contained or compartmentalised, with the speaker's own imaginative power remaining seemingly intact.

Other allusions to the 'Intimations' ode also resonate through 'Ulysses', moving centrifugally around the sense of imaginative loss that has been introduced into the text through the allusion to the 'rainbow arch': 'for ever' (IV. x. l. 176) and the setting 'sun' (IV. xi. l. 196) find their way into the poem, sitting alongside the 'eternal silence' of line 27. The borrowing of 'for ever', where, in the 'Intimations' ode, the speaker states, 'What though the radiance which was once so bright / Be now for ever taken from my sight' (IV. x. ll. 175–6), colours Ulysses' imaginative projection through the arch of experience with the loss to which the imagination can be subject: the 'margin' (l. 20) of the 'untravelled world' (l. 20) 'fades' (l. 20) 'For ever and for ever' (ll. 20–1). Wordsworth's speaker accepts that the radiance that was once so bright has been lost, but settles for a compensatory 'Strength in what remains behind' (IV. x. l. 180). In 'Ulysses', the powerful finality of Wordsworth's 'for ever' is given added urgency by the twin presence of another iambic 'for ever', which together enact 'a falling and a rising cadence',[55] signalling how Ulysses' untravelled imaginative world is visible yet out of reach. His desire 'To sail beyond the sunset' (l. 60) in search of imaginative immortality is thwarted by the echo of the Ode's 'setting sun' (l. 196) that takes 'a sober colouring from an eye / That hath kept watch o'er man's mortality' (IV. xi. ll. 197–8); by default, immortality echoes mortality, but without the mediation of the 'Intimations' ode's replacement for imaginative loss to accompany it, the 'faith that looks through death' (IV. x. l. 185) and 'the human heart by which we live' (IV. xi. l. 200). Ulysses expresses a wish to move beyond the Wordsworthian setting sun, to move beyond the sunset, yet the Wordsworthian echoes within the poem pull him back to the losses the Wordsworthian imagination contains, but without a means by which to navigate them.

The lack of reparation for the Wordsworthian loss mediated in the text is exemplified by Ulysses' account of his previous 'transcendental' experience; the experience he recounts inhibits the 'experience' (l. 19) which is an arch through which 'Gleams that untravelled world' (l. 20). The text itemises Ulysses' achievements in life, how he has 'suffered greatly, both with those / That loved me, and alone; on shore, and when / Through scudding drifts the rainy Hyades / Vext the dim sea' (ll. 8–11). Ricks notes a confluence of Shelley, Milton and Pope in the 'vext' sea.[56] Ulysses' list of achievements is an inventory of the mind's transfiguration of the objects around it, an epiphanic moment stored in memory,[57] just as the gleams that shimmer alluringly through the arch of experience are a projection of possible future transcendence. But the sense of the mind's power of projection is nevertheless undermined by Ulysses' own telling: 'dim', in its *OED* sense of 'not shining brightly', both weakens Ulysses' epiphanic moment of transcendence – imaginative transcendence is 'dim' rather than 'luminous' – and acts as a predicate for his projection of possible future transcendence through the arch of experience. 'Dim' also carries a sense of indistinct or limited perception and this sense of indistinctness and limitation both defines Ulysses' past transcendental experience and inflects his projection of the transcendence he hopes to gain through his 'arch' of experience, as perception is a necessary marriage partner in the process of conception. The 'untravelled world' that gleams so becomingly through Ulysses' 'arch' of experience is thus inscribed, and prescribed, with a sense of limitation and faded transcendence from Ulysses' past, reinforced by the famously delayed rhythm of the lines.[58]

The limitations of the past also include the Wordsworthian past, as 'dim' also has a resonance in 'Tintern Abbey', where it is employed to evoke the mind's power to reinvigorate the 'dim and faint' into a revived and consoling image: 'And now, with gleams of half-extinguished thought, / With many recognitions dim and faint, / And somewhat of a sad perplexity, / The picture of the mind revives again' (ll. ll. 59–61). But, whereas the picture the mind produced in 'Tintern Abbey' allows that dimness to revivify, the reader is aware that this is a process with finite possibilities for the speaker: Dorothy may well 'forget / That on the banks of this delightful stream' (ll. l. 150–1) she and the speaker stood together. The echo of 'dim' in 'Tintern Abbey', with its sense of potential loss, feeds into 'Ulysses' and forfeits Ulysses' claim to past and future imaginative transcendence, inflecting the allusively Shelleyan 'dim sea', the cited source for the phrase.[59] Ulysses is made up of these past projected images – he is 'a part of all that [he has] met' (l. 18) – but his past epiphanic experience does not provide him with the capacity with which to recover from the visionary loss that has been introduced into the text through the intertextual process: the self has been fractured and the sublime ego with it. He will not be able 'to store and hoard' (l. 29) himself in the hope of producing future imaginative transcendence, to 'sail beyond the sunset' (l. 60) in a search for imaginative immortality, as he has no suitable store of transcendent experience on which to draw to furnish his journey.

Moreover, by repeating the term 'hoard', the text is also equating Ulysses with the 'savage race, / That hoard, and sleep, and feed' (ll. 4–5), a race, one would assume, whose savagery precludes them from achieving transcendental awareness.[60] In a continuation of the same agricultural imagery, Ulysses' voyage of discovery will not 'yield'

(l. 70) the imaginative immortality he seeks. There can be no recovery from visionary failure, as there is in the 'Intimations' ode, as there is no cohesive self on which to base such a revival: the past revives only broken images, which cannot sustain the self in the present or the future. This is the same disjunction between self and other that Wordsworth describes in 'Tintern Abbey'; yet, in 'Tintern Abbey', there is a synergy between these past and present selves, a stable identity or unity of self that can accommodate the shift in register.

And it is only on the self that Ulysses can rely: Wordsworth's texts, the 'Intimations' ode included, are based on an extreme individualism, where it is the self that 'creates' transcendence, and the self, by association, that recovers from transcendental loss. In 'Ulysses', the reliance on the priority of the self is seen to fail, and when the self fails, all fails. Through Ulysses' fractured epiphany, then, Tennyson exposes the overreliance on the self on which Wordsworthian visionary transcendence is premised. There can be no imaginative recompense in nature – in the equivalent 'meanest flower that blows' (IV. xi. l. 202), or in the tender 'human heart' (IV. xi. l. 200) – as the self here is incapable of assuaging its loss, as mind and heart fail to coalesce. As a result of the Wordsworthian borrowings in the text, Ulysses' journey is not one of personal growth through loss, but one inhibited by the self and essentially over before it has begun.

Similarly, the lake that glows like a 'burnish'd mirror' (I. l. 126) from Wordsworth's *An Evening Walk* also inflects Ulysses' desire not to 'rust unburnished' (l. 23) on the shore, dislocating the 'rusty mail' of *Troilus and Cressida* that is the suggested allusive source for the lines.[61] The 'burnish'd mirror' from *An Evening Walk* finds its way into 'The Lady of Shalott', polishing Lancelot's 'burnished hooves' (III. l. 101), but it has a place here too, freighting Ulysses' desire with an imaginative load. Yet, Wordsworth's speaker views the lake as it descends into the darkness of evening, prefiguring the poem's descent into its own imaginative darkness, and colouring Ulysses' desire not to rust with an unburnished imagination.

Ulysses' 'Gleams' (l. 20) through his arch of experience also evoke both the imaginary 'gleams' (I. l. 311) of the imagination's descent into darkness in *An Evening Walk* and, seemingly, its recovery from that same darkness. The presence of gleams in 'Ulysses' suggests the pattern of recovery in *An Evening Walk* is to be replicated, with the imagination redeemed from its precipitous decline, as 'gleams' functions as a verb in the text, disseminating a sense of 'shining brightly with reflected light' (*OED*). In Wordsworth, 'gleam' is often used as a noun, where it encapsulates a sense of loss, as it can only ever be a 'faint and brief light' (*OED*): the very gleams of 'Tintern Abbey''s 'gleams of half-extinguished thought' (II. l. 59) and the 'Intimations' ode's 'visionary gleam' (IV. iv. l. 56) contain an incipient loss, therefore, a loss which Wordsworth attempts to deflect through sublimation or displacement. Similarly, the imagination's loss of power in *An Evening Walk* is described as a 'gleam' that is 'sullen' (I. l. 209). In 'Ulysses', however, the borrowing of 'gleam' as a verb proposes that the loss at the heart of the Wordsworthian gleam has been overridden, with 'faintness' being replaced with a sense of 'shining brightly'. The use of the present tense in 'gleams' in the text also implies a sense of continuity, of an unbroken trajectory of imaginative transcendence running from past, to present, to future. Significantly, Wordsworth switches back from using gleam as a noun in *An Evening Walk*, when describing the imagination's descent into darkness, to using it as a verb at the close of the poem, where its sense of 'shining brightly' underpins the sense of recovery the speaker has undergone after his momentary loss of imaginative power: the 'azure tide' (I. l. 377) 'gleams' (I. l. 377) in the speaker's imagination.

However, the use of 'gleams', in its sense of 'shining brightly', is destabilised in 'Ulysses'. Confirmation of this comes with Ulysses' account of the start of his journey in search of imaginative immortality. Confidently, he says: 'There lies the port; the vessel puffs her sail: / There gloom the dark broad seas' (ll. 44–5). The phrase 'There gloom the dark broad seas', with its demonstrative (and deictic) 'There', indicates that this is an imaginative projection from Ulysses' own mind, but the phrase also carries intimations of darkness, of the 'dark passages' Keats observes in Wordsworth's poetry,[62] which implies that the projection is replete with the darkness to which the Wordsworthian imagination can be subject. Similarly, 'gloom' links the text to *An Evening Walk*'s darkness and temporary loss of imaginative power, 'The soft gloom deepening on the tranquil mind' (I. l. 335). This sense of 'gloom' feeds into Ulysses' imaginative projection, disrupting his projection of future imaginative transcendence with a sense of failing imaginative power.

However, in *An Evening Walk* there is a sense that the loss of power is temporary only or can be mitigated, emphasised here through the use of the adjective 'soft', but there is no such sense of redemption in 'Ulysses', underlined by the repetition of hard consonants in 'gloom', 'dark' and 'broad'. Equally, the use of assonance, and the substitution of spondaic for iambic feet in the line – as in 'dark broad' (l. 45) – creates a sense of slowness, which, rather than creating a beguiling, 'hypnotic rhythm',[63] helps to accentuate Ulysses' imaginative torpor and failing imaginative power. The use of 'gloom' as a verb in the text is also unsettled, as any sense of energy contained in the verb itself is inhibited by this sense of developing imaginative fatigue. Tennyson, in effect, rewrites *An Evening Walk*, as the use of 'gleams' and 'gloom' is transposed: in *An Evening Walk* imaginative gloom is replaced by active gleams of thought, which signal the recovery of the imagination and its primacy over nature; in 'Ulysses' the process is reversed, as Ulysses' expectant gleams are supplanted by imaginative 'gloom'. The recovery of the imagination's power over nature that takes place in *An Evening Walk* is superseded by an imagination that is losing its power: imaginative recovery is replaced with the loss of the transcendental imagination. Any hope of the self-growth that develops through Wordsworthian darkness is truncated.[64]

Significantly, in 'Ulysses' the 'eye' is suppressed, serving to underline the loss of imaginative power taking place in the text, as the eye is integral to the transcendental process: in 'Tintern Abbey', it is the eye and ear that produce thoughts that revive, and it is Dorothy's eyes in which Wordsworth hopes to see his moments of transcendence sustained: the speaker describes 'the mighty world / Of eye, and ear' (II. ll. 106–7), and the 'gleams' he hopes to catch from Dorothy's 'wild eyes' (II. l. 149). In *An Evening Walk* and the 'Intimations' ode, the eye is integral to the visionary process: the eye 'reposes' (I. l. 71) in *An Evening Walk*, for instance, and in the 'Intimations' ode, the speaker describes 'every common sight' (IV. i. l. 2), lamenting 'The things which I have seen I now can see no more' (IV. i. l. 9).

In 'Ulysses', the ear is acoustically manifest: the 'plains' of 'windy Troy' are ringing (l. 17); there are 'many voices' (l. 56) moaning in the deep. The emphasis on sound replicates the pattern in *An Evening Walk*, where sound comes to compensate for the temporary loss of sight.[65] It is the 'eye' which is significant by its absence in 'Ulysses', an absence which prevents the imaginative process from fully functioning. The ear's loss of its partner in conception underpins the failing power of the transcendental imagination, and the transcendental self on which that transcendence is based, effected in the text through the revisions of the 'Intimations' ode and *An Evening Walk*. At the same time, the ear is a reminder of the echo or borrowing at work in the poem, which through the transmission of words like 'Gleams' (l. 20) and 'gloom' (l. 45) creates its own patterning of assonantal and alliterative sound, complementing, or even subverting, Tennyson's own celebrated poetic 'ear'.[66]

Ulysses' loss of visionary power equates to Freud's notion of the lost 'love-object':[67] Ulysses can be seen to refuse the loss of the imagination and to absorb the lost love-object – the imagination – in the ego in defiance of its death or disappearance. According to Freud, the love-object is eaten in order to imprison it within the self: 'It may assimilate this object, and, in accordance with the oral or cannibalistic phase of libido development, may do so by eating it.'[68] Yet,

> the object, once incorporated, preys upon the subject in return until the latter is 'totally impoverished'. Thus the ego, like a healthy savage, gobbles up the object in one gulp, but the object behaves like the stealthy vampires of the *fin de siècle*, substituting nightly sucking for the cannibal's almighty bolt.[69]

The lost object takes over the ego, in an 'internal struggle' in 'which the ego attacks itself as a stand-in for the beloved object'.[70] However, 'in order to be lost the object must be looked for; it is the seeking that establishes its absence'.[71] Ulysses, from this perspective, goes in search, not of immortality, but of the lost object, which is the Wordsworthian imagination. He has eaten the object, emphasised by the text's copious food imagery and symbolised by his 'hungry heart' (l. 12). He is the consumed rather than the consumer, however, setting off in search of that which can never be found. The Freudian element here might confirm that the revisionary pattern at work in the poem thus far has been a Bloomian one, with Tennyson's revisions an example of Bloom's conflictual revisionism. But, however fruitful Tennyson's revisions have been in terms of allowing the later poet to defend and strengthen the monologue against the incursions of the precursor poet, Ulysses' journey in pursuit of a Wordsworthian imagination that the poem has itself defined as lost reveals a deep-seated desire to cleave to Wordsworth's imaginative processes rather than to supplant them. Rather than answering the 'Intimations' ode's 'Strength in what remains behind' with the need for going forward, as Tucker maintains, Tennyson's poem sets out to reactivate the 'strength' in what remains behind. Tennyson has not so much a need for going forward here as a need for going back.

Nevertheless, if 'Ulysses' rewrites Wordsworthian imaginative sublimation as loss, then it also confirms Wordsworthian imaginative plenitude as loss by confirming the incipient loss in the poem 'I WANDERED lonely as a Cloud' (1807). In Wordsworth, as with the other Romantics, 'epiphany and loss [are glimpsed] in the same moment of vision',[72] although this loss is often not foregrounded in Wordsworth. In 'I WANDERED lonely as a Cloud', the speaker is able to revive memories of the past to sustain him in the present: the daffodils he sees standing beside the lake are 'Continuous as the stars that shine / And twinkle on the milky way' (II. ll. 7–8) and 'For oft when on my couch I lie / In vacant or in pensive mood, / They flash upon that inward eye / Which is the bliss of solitude: / And then my heart with pleasure fills, / And dances with the Daffodils' (II. ll. 19–24). 'Twinkle' has a place in 'Ulysses', which would suggest a similar level of imaginative renewal: 'The lights begin to twinkle from the rocks: / The long day wanes: the slow moon climbs: the deep / Moans round with many voices. Come, my friends, / 'Tis not too late to seek a newer world' (ll. 54–7). Lights 'twinkle', the slow moon 'climbs', the deep 'moans' round, and a new world lies ahead. The lines pulsate with a buoyant (Wordsworthian) imaginative energy, as well as the 'languorous slowness' it offers in response to Shelley's 'rhythms of ardent impatience' in stanza LIII of *Adonais*.[73] Twinkling stars are also a reminder of Byron's *Childe Harold's Pilgrimage*, Cantos III and IV (1816–18), when the speaker-poet enters Rome and confronts both human power and its opposite, human 'dust':

> But when the rising moon begins to climb
> Its topmost arch, and gently pauses there;
> When the stars twinkle through the loops of time,
> And the low night-breeze waves along the air
> The garland-forest, which the gray walls wear,
> Like laurels on the bald first Caesar's head;
> When the light shines serene but doth not glare,
> Then in this magic circle raise the dead:
> Heroes have trod this spot – 'tis on their dust ye tread.[74]
>
> (IV. cxliv. ll. 1–9)

Yet these lines are themselves an echo of Wordsworth, in the poem's 'conversion' to a Wordsworthian philosophy of nature which Byron at other times saw fit to mock. The lines are a reminder too of Tennyson's somewhat specious perturbation at suggestions that he was imitating the work of others: '"They allow me nothing"', as he says.[75]

The possibility of imaginative renewal in 'Ulysses' is thwarted by Ulysses' 'dim sea' epiphany, however, which suggests that Ulysses is not able to muster images from the past to sustain him in the future in the way that Wordsworth's speaker can: the light that 'twinkles' is 'dimmed' by its own nexus of Wordsworthian phrasing in this way. The dimming of the imagination is underlined by Tennyson's allusion to *An Evening Walk*'s burnished lake, with its 'thousand, thousand twinkling points of light; / There, waves that, hardly weltering, die

away' (I. ll. 122–3). Wordsworth's lake dips into darkness, prefiguring the imagination's own dip into darkness. Yet, Tennyson's 'lights'
only 'begin to twinkle', unlike Wordsworth's lake with its 'thousand,
thousand twinkling points of light', suggesting that the imagination
can forestall its decline. But the use of assonance and spondaic feet
in the lines quoted prefigure the imagination's decline, as 'long day'
and 'slow moon' drag the rhythm of the speech, tangling any imaginative vitality they contain in belatedness. By contrast, the jaunty
iambic tetrameter of Wordsworth's poem complements the joyous
'wealth' (II. l. 18) of the imaginary process. The focus on 'eye' in
Wordsworth's poem – 'Ten thousand' daffodils at a 'glance' (II. l. 11)
'flash upon that inward eye' (II. l. 21) – places a spotlight on the
importance of perception to the process of conception, contrasting
sharply with the eye's absence in 'Ulysses'.

The failure of the imagination to shine and to renew itself is confirmed in the text by the echo of the word 'margin'. 'Margin' has a
primary role in 'I WANDERED lonely as a Cloud', where it is associated with the 'golden Daffodils' (II. l. 4), which 'stretched in never-
ending line / Along the margin of a bay' (II. ll. 9–10); the speaker's faith
in imaginative renewal and continuity is attendant upon the daffodils'
power over him, although 'margin' suggests limit, as if there were a
limit to the imaginative sustenance the speaker can expect. In 'Ulysses',
the sense of limit is foregrounded by the application of 'fades' to the
margin; 'fades' is weighted with an actual sense of fading, but also bears
the implications of imaginative loss from its linguistic imprints from
the 'Intimations' ode: 'The Youth, who daily farther from the East /
Must travel, still is Nature's Priest, / And by the vision splendid / Is on
his way attended; / At length the Man perceives it die away, / And fade
into the light of common day' (IV. v. ll. 71–6). The 'vision splendid'
may 'fade into the light of common day' once the Youth becomes a
Man, of course, as compensation can be found in the poem through
the process of personal maturation through loss. The transcription of
'fade' into 'fades' (l. 20) in 'Ulysses' – the 'margin' of Ulysses' 'untravelled world' 'fades' the more he moves – immerses Ulysses' hopes of
imaginative transcendence in, paradoxically, an active sense of fading,
of dying away, compromising both any hope of growth and his quest
to 'sail beyond the sunset' (l. 60). The pun on the use of 'margin' – as
in the margin of a text – emphasises that the revisionary project with
which the text is involved is also a textual one.[76]

Significantly, the poem inscribes notions of death from Wordsworth
in order to underwrite the sense of imaginative loss being established
in the text, which, in turn, confirm the suggested imaginative losses

in Wordsworth's poems themselves. Ulysses describes himself as 'this gray spirit yearning in desire / To follow knowledge like a sinking star, / Beyond the utmost bound of human thought' (ll. 39–41). The adjective 'sinking' has been coupled with 'star' in 'I WATCH, and long have watched, with calm regret' (1819), as it has with other planetary objects like the 'moon' in 'STRANGE fits of passion I have known' (1800), and the 'sun' in 'It is a beauteous Evening, calm and free' (1807). In each example, sinking is associated with death, and in 'STRANGE fits of passion I have known', specifically with the speaker's inability imaginatively to transcend the boundary between life and death. In 'I WATCH, and long have watched, with calm regret', for example, the speaker draws a direct analogy between the 'slowly-sinking Star' and human fate,[77] where 'We struggle with our fate, / While health, power, glory, pitiably decline, / Depressed; and then extinguished: and our state, / In this, how different, lost Star, from thine, / That no to-morrow shall our beams re-store!' (ll. 10–14). Wordsworth's sinking star here is able to recover from its fall and to have its power restored, whereas it is the fate of human health, power and glory to decline and then to be extinguished. Ulysses himself acknowledges his struggles with fate and declining power, conceding at the close of the poem that 'We are not now that strength which in old days / Moved earth and heaven; that which we are, we are; / One equal temper of heroic hearts / Made weak by time and fate, but strong in will' (ll. 66–9). Ulysses, nonetheless, wants 'To follow knowledge like a sinking star' (l. 31), unaware that such knowledge is a synonym for death; it is only the sinking star that can have its power restored. Ulysses may strive and seek, but he will find that the only thing that abides is death, unless he can rediscover the lost Wordsworthian imagination. In 'STRANGE fits of passion I have known', the sinking moon is also a symbol of death, acting as a luminous barrier between the mortal and immortal worlds,[78] and blocking the speaker's ability imaginatively to access the immortal:

And now we reached the orchard plot;
And as we climbed the hill,
Towards the roof of Lucy's cot
The Moon descended still.

In one of those sweet dreams I slept,
Kind Nature's gentlest boon!
And all the while my eyes I kept
On the descending Moon.

My Horse moved on; hoof after hoof
He raised, and never stopped:
When down behind the cottage roof,
At once, the bright Moon dropped.

What fond and wayward thoughts will slide
Into a Lover's head! –
'O mercy!' to myself I cried,
'If Lucy should be dead!'

(I. ll. 13–28)

The association with death is intimately linked with Ulysses' project of imaginative transcendence, as the 'As though to breathe' section of the poem, which contains the adjectival 'sinking', comes immediately after its principal moment of putative transcendence: 'sinking star' is thus wedded to Ulysses' 'arch' of imaginative transcendence. The 'untravelled world' that gleams through the 'arch' of experience is compromised by the mind's inability imaginatively to transcend death, making Ulysses' desire to follow the promise of transcendental knowledge like a 'sinking star' a projection of death itself. His 'sinking star' is also a 'sinking moon', blocking his journey in search of imaginative transcendence. In describing himself as 'like a sinking star' he performs the same function in the text as the sinking moon of Wordsworth's poem (as well, of course, as a fading celebrity, unable to recapture the status of the past), acting as a barrier between life and death rather than a journeyman setting out imaginatively to conquer mortality. Like Ulysses, the speaker of Wordsworth's poem is himself a wayfarer, underlining the intertextual connections between the poems.[79]

Ulysses' description of the scene around him as he starts on his journey in search of imaginative immortality is delimited by the continuing presence of 'STRANGE fits of passion I have known', with the text making an implicit play upon the latter's 'moon': the 'dropped' moon (I. l. 24) of Wordsworth's poem transforms into 'the slow moon [that] climbs' (I. l. 55), signifying that Tennyson's poem is forming a response to Wordsworth's; Ulysses' journey is predicated on a 'strange fit of passion' in this way. Both moons, whether dropping or climbing, act as barriers to the imagination. Any possibility of the barrier being partially withdrawn or halted – the moon is 'climbing' and so not yet fully in position – is negated by the pact of 'climbing' with dropping, however: the speaker of the poem climbs the hill only to be confronted with the sinking moon as it descends behind Lucy's cot (I. l. 15). 'Ulysses', in effect, provides an answer to the question posed at the end of 'STRANGE fits of passion I have known': the speaker of Wordsworth's poem describes his premonitory fear of Lucy's death, stimulated by the sudden dropping of the moon, but ends the poem asking what '"If Lucy should be dead!"' (I. l. 28). The line can obviously be read as a statement of fact: is Lucy dead? But its conditional 'If' can also be interpreted as a questioning of whether, if Lucy should indeed be dead, she will survive death in the speaker's imagination. Wordsworth's poem does not provide an answer to this question; rather, it displaces the question, suggesting that the issue raised does not need to be answered, as the speaker's fear occurred only 'once' (I. l. 4) and was one of his passing 'fits of passion' (I. l. 1), although the presence of the barrier moon can be said to provide its own answer.[80] By confirming the centrality of the sinking star and sinking moon, however, 'Ulysses' confirms that the imaginative barrier between life and death is more than a passing fit of passion.

A similar process is at work in Ulysses' description of himself as 'this gray spirit yearning in desire' (ll. 30–1), which reactivates the 'spirit' of 'A SLUMBER did my spirit seal', and indeed the lost Lucy of 'Lucy Gray' (1800). In 'A SLUMBER did my spirit seal', the speaker laments an unnamed 'She' (II. l. 3) or 'thing that could not feel / The touch of earthly years' (II. ll. 3–4). By the second stanza, the speaker comes to accept that the beloved 'She' is lost to his imagination, as she is 'Rolled round in earth's diurnal course, / With rocks and stones and trees!' (II. ll. 7–8), although she retains a vitality through the daily actions of the earth, nevertheless. 'Ulysses' cements the 'spirit' of 'A Slumber''s loss of imaginative power: the application of the adjective 'gray' to spirit, a carry-over from Ulysses' 'dim sea' epiphany, accentuates the fact that Ulysses is himself an attenuated imaginative essence, whose imaginative powers are enervated. This sense of imaginative depletion, in turn, is emphasised by the use of the third person in Ulysses' description of himself as 'this gray spirit', which serves to distance him from his already reduced imaginative capability.

Hallam's 'Vision' of His Own

If 'Ulysses' echoes Wordsworth, then it also echoes Hallam echoing Wordsworth; the continuum finds a resting place in Tennyson's poem. Tennyson frequently alludes to Hallam's prose and verse in his own poetry, including in *In Memoriam* and 'Ulysses'.[81] 'Ulysses' reveals, for instance, how Tennyson borrows from Hallam's Cambridge medal submission, 'Timbuctoo', and its own latent borrowings from Wordsworth.

Hallam's 'Timbuctoo' is heavily indebted to Wordsworth, although it carries Shelleyan influences, too. Richard Cronin suggests that Hallam 'owns two masters' in the poem, Wordsworth and Shelley:[82]

> Whenever he represents his ideal country 'decked in the bright colours of the thing to be', Hallam is Shelley's disciple. But the discovery of the lost city also figures for Hallam the contradictory and characteristically Wordsworthian truth that disillusion inevitably terminates all dreams of an ideal world, which is why he chose as its epigraph lines in which Wordsworth wryly acknowledges that Yarrow can remain a type of ideal beauty only for so long as he neglects to visit it.[83]

The epigraph from Wordsworth's 'Yarrow Unvisited' (1807), with its acknowledgement that dreams inevitably come undone, sets the tone for the poem as a whole, explicitly foregrounding its allusive dependency on Wordsworth: 'Be Yarrow stream unseen, unknown! / It must, or we shall rue it: / We have a vision of our own; / Ah! why should we undo it?'[84] Line 88 of the poem also alludes to the 'Intimations' ode, where the lines 'Lo! there hath past away a glory of Youth / From this our world' (ll. 88–9) are constructed from line 18 of the 'Intimations' ode and the 'glory' (II. l. 18) that hath passed away from 'the earth' (II. l. 18); similarly, line 194, '"In which the affections gently lead us on"', is lifted *verbatim* from Wordsworth's 'Tintern Abbey', line 42.

The speaker in Hallam's poem toys with the propensity of the transcendent imagination to fail. Describing the lost city of 'Timbuctoo', the speaker states: 'Imagination decked those unknown caves, / And vacant forests, and clear peaks of ice / With a transcendent beauty' (ll. 4–6). He then goes on to describe how:

> In the last days a man arose, who knew
>   That ancient legend from his infancy.
>   Yea, visions on that child's emmarvailed view
> Had flashed intuitive science; and his glee
>   Was lofty as his pensiveness, for both
>   Wore the bright colours of the thing to be!
> But when his prime of life was come, the wrath
>   Of the cold world fell on him; it did thrill
>   His inmost self, but never quenched his faith.

Still to that faith he added search, and still,
 As fevering with fond love of th' unknown shore,
 From learning's fount he strove his thirst to fill.
But always Nature seemed to meet the power
 Of his high mind, to aid, and to reward
 His reverent hope with her sublimest lore.
Each sentiment that burned; each falsehood warred
 Against and slain; each novel truth inwrought –
 What were they, but the living lamps that starred
His transit o'er the tremulous gloom of Thought?
 More, and now more, their gathered brilliancy
 On the one master Notion sending out,
Which brooded ever o'er the passionate sea
 Of his deep soul; but ah! too dimly seen,
 And formless in its own immensity!

             (ll. 40–63)

The sense of failing imaginative power achieved in the poem is underwritten by echoes of a number of Wordsworthian poems, which serve to underpin the loss of imaginative power taking place: 'tremulous' (l. 4, l. 109) and 'gloom' (l. 75, l. 177, l. 204, l. 318) have a parallel in *An Evening Walk*, where they are transmitters of the temporarily failing imagination, for instance. In *An Evening Walk*, the speaker's failing visionary power is emblematised through the 'gloom' of the forest, where the 'soft gloom' (I. l. 335) deepens on the 'tranquil mind' (I. l. 335); but the adjective 'soft' implies that the gloom can dissipate, or can be overcome, as indeed occurs. Of course, 'gloom' carries its own associations of darkness and diminishing power, which is accentuated by the definition of it as 'fading light' (*OED*). The poem also cites 'dimly', with its sense of being dimly, or faintly, seen: Nature's 'living lamps' that starred the speaker's transit over the tremulous gloom of thought are 'too dimly seen'. 'Dim', as has been established, has a particular resonance in Tennyson's own poem where it destabilises Ulysses' store of epiphanic memory, but beyond that it also has a resonance in 'Tintern Abbey', where 'recognitions dim and faint' (II. l. 60) are revived by the 'picture of the mind' (II. l. 62), if only for a finite time. The mediation of imaginative loss, or potential loss, echoes through Hallam's poem, underpinning the speaker's account of a stalling imaginative power.

 However, Hallam attempts to overwrite the sense of failing transcendent power that he himself establishes in the text: the speaker refers to how:

Last came the joy, when that phantasmal scene
  Lay in full glory round his outward sense;
  And who had scorned before in hatred keen
Refuged their baseness now: for no pretence
  Could wean their souls from awe; they dared not doubt
  That with them walked on earth a spirit intense.

(ll. 64–9)

He goes on to describe:

Thou fairy City, which the desert mound
  Encompasseth, thou alien from the mass
  Of human guilt, I would not wish thee found!
Perchance thou art too pure, and dost surpass
  Too far amid th' Ideas rangèd high
  In the Eternal Reason's perfectness,
To our deject, and most imbasèd eye,
  To look unharmed on thy integrity,
  Symbol of Love, and Truth, and all that cannot die.

(ll. 112–20)

This sense of a City of the imagination, created out of the 'fairy', or fanciful, imagination is displaced by the Wordsworthian echoes in the text, however, which continue the theme of failing power. 'Full glory', 'spirit intense' and the pureness of the City of the imagination are reminders of Wordsworth's imaginative losses in the threatened glory of the 'Intimations' ode, the spirit of 'A SLUMBER did my spirit seal' and the 'purer mind' (II. l. 30) and 'purest thoughts' (II. l. 110) of 'Tintern Abbey'. Each in turn chips away at the imaginative City Hallam's speaker so lovingly constructs.

    The poem ends with an exhortation for visionary imagination to continue to flourish:

So be it ever! Ever may the mood
  'In which the affections gently lead us on'
  Be as thy sphere of visible life. The crowd,
The turmoil, and the countenance wan
  Of slaves, the Power-inchanted, thou shalt flee,
  And by the gentle heart be seen, and loved alone.

(ll. 193–8)

Hallam's quotation of 'Tintern Abbey''s 'affections [that] gently lead us on' is intended to support the corralling of the imagination. But the affections may not gently lead us on, and if they do, then they may simply lead into a void, a nothingness. They may simply 'lead us' on.

It is this inflected doubt that 'Ulysses' borrows from Hallam's poem, as it confirms the loss at the heart of the Wordsworthian imaginative moment. Hallam's echoes and allusions – like 'tremulous', 'gloom' – are picked up by Tennyson and reworked. 'Ulysses' is echoing Hallam echoing Wordsworth and rewriting both, as Hallam's City of the imagination collapses. A prominent example of this is 'Ulysses''s use of 'gloom', which has a Wordsworthian provenance, as has been made clear, but which echoes through Hallam's text, too, in the 'tremulous gloom of Thought' (l. 58). 'Ulysses' makes 'gloom' an active verb in the text – 'There gloom the dark broad seas' (l. 45) – which, paradoxically, gives its meaning of fading light and darkness a sense of agency that is missing in Hallam's poem, where it is used as a noun. In this sense, 'Ulysses' is reactivating the imaginative failure which Hallam's poem has subsequently overwritten as imaginative recovery. The fact that this sense of agency is itself immured in imaginative torpor through the use of assonance and prosodic experimentation serves only to underline the imaginative failure that 'Ulysses' is writing into itself.

Significantly, Hallam's metaphor of the 'passionate sea' (l. 61) is reworked in 'Ulysses', where it becomes 'dim sea' (l. 11), replacing the earlier poem's use of it to evoke a sense of passionate energy with a film of dimness and failing power. Both uses of 'sea' – in 'Ulysses' and Hallam's 'Timbuctoo' – have a common denominator in the 'Intimations' ode's 'immortal sea / Which brought us hither' (IV. ix. ll. 163–4), where it is linked with the recompense the speaker finds in the 'truths that wake, / To perish never' (IV. ix. ll. 155–6). The imaginative recovery found in both Hallam and Wordsworth's poems is overridden in 'Ulysses', however, through a sea that remains resolutely 'dim'.

Conclusion

Tennyson's borrowings from Wordsworth allow him to question the strands on which Wordsworthian transcendence is based, including the priority of the self, and the growth of that self through the losses attendant upon the imaginative moment itself. In so doing, Tennyson strengthens the form of the monologue, which is predicated on distancing the subjectivity of the Romantic lyrical speaker. In breaking down the Wordsworthian imagination and the Wordsworthian self in this way, the echoes and borrowings allow Tennyson to consolidate the form of the poem, strengthening its capacity to work independently from the solipsistic Romantic lyric from which it stems. The poem does not follow Wordsworth in writing a narrative of imaginative loss as growth; rather, Tennyson implies that loss is too high a price to pay for the growth that customarily accompanies Wordsworthian imaginative transcendence. The transcendent self is disassembled in the text, making the growth of which Wordsworth writes unattainable. In revising Wordsworth, Tennyson is nonetheless depriving himself of a route to imaginative immortality; like Ulysses himself, he is left in search of that which can no longer be found. Paradoxically, Ulysses' continuing search for that which the text itself defines as lost reveals how Tennyson still yearns for the Wordsworthian imagination as a portal to immortality, despite the apparent freedom its 'death' affords him. By association, the linkage to Wordsworth in this way also reveals Tennyson as implicitly acknowledging the necessity of Wordsworth's imaginative process, and Wordsworth's language, to the poem: Wordsworth is the frame on which the poem hangs. The poem establishes itself as committed to preoccupations with the Wordsworthian imagination and its inability to redeem its own loss and, by association, the loss of Hallam through sustained imaginative connection and an imaginative transcendence of death.

Tennyson's revision of Wordsworth seemingly accords with Bloom's revisionary model, in that Tennyson positions himself in relation to his Romantic forebear, reducing Wordsworth's dominance in order to prioritise his own dramatic project. Ulysses' quest in search of the lost Wordsworthian imagination also confirms that the revisionary process at work in the poem is functioning at a deep, psychic level. And yet it cannot be said that this process is a defensive measure on Tennyson's part: the fact that Ulysses expresses a desire to go in search of that which is lost implies that Tennyson wants to (re)affiliate himself with Wordsworth as much as he wants to weaken his dominance.

Tennyson continues to test the Wordsworthian imagination and its ability to allow him imaginatively to connect with Hallam, in *In Memoriam* (1850), a poem begun in 1833, and which he compares unfavourably with 'Ulysses' in terms of how much of himself it contains.[85] *In Memoriam* returns compulsively and nostalgically to Wordsworth through repeated verbal echoes in the text, which result in Tennyson revealing more of himself than his comments on the later poem would suggest. Rather than shoring up a dramatic monologue like 'Ulysses', however, the Wordsworthian borrowings in *In Memoriam* allow Tennyson to move towards his accommodations with God, with science and with the death of Hallam, as well as allowing him to renegotiate the pastoral form.

Notes

1. Tennyson, *The Poems of Tennyson*, I, l. 19 (p. 616). All further references to the poem are to this volume and appear parenthetically in the text.
2. Tennyson, *The Poems of Tennyson*, I, p. 613. Hallam died on 15 September 1833; on 1 October Tennyson was sent the news. As Ricks emphasises, no event in Tennyson's life 'was of greater importance'. See Tennyson, *The Poems of Tennyson*, II, pp. 304, 305.
3. Tennyson, *The Poems of Tennyson*, I, p. 613. Ricks cites the comment as being made to James Knowles, *Nineteenth Century*, 33 (1893), p. 182.
4. Tennyson, *The Poems of Tennyson*, I, p. 613.
5. The poems are linked in other ways, too: both are classical monologues; Ulysses can be seen as refusing to die, while Tithonus yearns for death; and both 'poems take their occasion from the movement of the sun and might be read as heavily ironized blank verse Pindaric odes to Evening and to Morning, respectively'. See Rowlinson, *Tennyson's Fixations*, p. 182, n. 2.
6. Tennyson, *The Poems of Tennyson*, I, p. 614.
7. Decker, 'Tennyson's Limitations', p. 61.
8. Ricks, *Tennyson*, p. 125.
9. Tucker, *Tennyson and the Doom of Romanticism*, p. 228.
10. Sinfield, *Alfred Tennyson*, p. 53.
11. Tennyson, *The Poems of Tennyson*, I, p. 615, l. 5. Ricks maintains that *Hamlet* IV iv 33–9 'not only echoes "sleep and feed", but is also apt to the theme of the poem'.
12. Tennyson, *The Poems of Tennyson*, I, p. 616, l. 11. Ricks also notes an allusion to *Paradise Lost* i 305–6 here, 'with fierce Winds *Orion* arm'd / Hath vext the Red-Sea Coast'; and Pope's *Iliad* iii 5–6: 'When inclement Winters vex the plain / With piercing frosts, or thick-descending rain'. This 'sense is common in Shelley', he concludes.
13. Tennyson, *The Poems of Tennyson*, I, p. 617, l. 23. Ricks quotes Tennyson as citing the speech in *Troilus and Cressida* III iii 150–3 – 'Perseverance, dear my lord, / Keeps honour bright: to have done, is to hang / Quite out of fashion, like a rusty mail / In monumental mockery' – as one of '"the noblest things" in Shakespeare'.
14. Tennyson, *The Poems of Tennyson*, I, p. 616, ll. 10–11.

15. Tucker, *Tennyson and the Doom of Romanticism*, p. 225. The Words-worth quotation, absorbed from the line 'something far more deeply interfused' of 'Tintern Abbey', is taken from *The Poetical Works of William Wordsworth in Five Volumes*, II, l. 97 (p. 183). All subsequent references to Wordsworth's poems are to these volumes and appear parenthetically in the text unless otherwise stated. References are given by volume and line number.

16. Tucker, *Tennyson and the Doom of Romanticism*, p. 223.

17. Tucker, *Tennyson and the Doom of Romanticism*, p. 223.

18. Tucker, *Tennyson and the Doom of Romanticism*, p. 225.

19. Tucker, *Tennyson and the Doom of Romanticism*, p. 225.

20. Tucker, *Tennyson and the Doom of Romanticism*, p. 237.

21. O'Neill, 'The Wheels of Being', p. 193.

22. O'Neill, 'The Wheels of Being', p. 194.

23. Decker, 'Tennyson's Limitations', p. 75. Decker includes all of the poem's allusions in this, including the echo of Shelley's Count Cenci in line 43, where Ulysses says of his son, Telemachus, 'He works his work, I mine'. See Decker, 'Tennyson's Limitations', p. 70 and n. 17.

24. Hollander, *The Figure of Echo*, p. 88. Hollander reminds us how 'A single word or phrase . . . amplified or not by a phonetic scheme, may easily carry rumors of its resounding cave'. See *The Figure of Echo*, p. 95.

25. See Langbaum, *The Poetry of Experience*, p. 85.

26. For more on Tennyson's involvement in the development of the mono-logue, see Hughes, *The Manyfacèd Glass*.

27. Bloom, *The Anxiety of Influence*, p. 8.

28. Day, *Tennyson's Scepticism*, p. 8.

29. Day, *Tennyson's Scepticism*, p. 15.

30. Day, *Tennyson's Scepticism*, p. 15.

31. Stanley Cavell describes the ending of the 'Intimations' ode as finding fulfilment in 'an ordinariness which a new ordinariness must replace'. See Cavell, *In Quest of the Ordinary*, p. 71.

32. The term 'meanest' here may have a source in eighteenth-century poetry, where it carries a sense of 'humbleness' or 'modesty', as in Thomas Gray's unfinished Ode of 1754 or 1755, published 1775, '[Ode on the Pleasure Arising from Vicissitude]'. For more on the pos-sible eighteenth-century derivation of Wordsworth's 'meanest' in the 'Intimations' ode, see O'Neill and Tovey, 'Shelley and the English Tra-dition', p. 505.

33. O'Neill, *The All-Sustaining Air*, p. 21.

34. O'Neill, *The All-Sustaining Air*, p. 108.

35. Quoted in Tennyson, *The Poems of Tennyson*, I, p. 617, ll. 20–2.

36. Quoted in Tennyson, *The Poems of Tennyson*, I, p. 617, ll. 20–2.

37. Quoted in Tennyson, *The Poems of Tennyson*, I, p. 616, l. 19.

38. Douglas-Fairhurst, 'Tennyson', p. 604.

39. Cronin, 'Edward Lear and Tennyson's Nonsense', p. 269.
40. Keble, 'The Third Sunday after Epiphany', pp. 38–41.
41. See Hopkins, *The Poetical Works of Gerard Manley Hopkins*, ll. 2–3 (p. 31).
42. Landow, 'Rainbows'.
43. Landow, 'Rainbows'.
44. Landow, 'Rainbows'.
45. Landow, 'Rainbows'.
46. Landow, 'Rainbows'.
47. Landow, 'Rainbows'.
48. Landow, 'Rainbows'.
49. Landow, 'Rainbows'.
50. Landow, 'Rainbows'.
51. Landow, 'Rainbows'.
52. Wordsworth, 'Preface to the Second Edition', p. 382.
53. See Barthes, *Image-Music-Text*, p. 159.
54. Wordsworth writes: '– Fancy is given to quicken and to beguile the temporal part of our nature, Imagination to incite and to support the eternal. – Yet is it not the less true that Fancy, as she is an active, is also, under her own laws and in her own spirit, a creative faculty. In what manner Fancy ambitiously aims at a rivalship with the Imagination, and Imagination stoops to work with the materials of Fancy, might be illustrated from the compositions of all eloquent writers, whether in prose or verse; and chiefly from those of our own Country'. See 'Preface to the Edition published in 1815', pp. xxxvii–xxxviii.
55. McDonald, 'Tennyson's Dying Fall', p. 35.
56. See Tennyson, *The Poems of Tennyson*, I, p. 616, ll. 10–11, l. 11.
57. Tucker also views this as an epiphany, claiming 'the prosody and syntax of this passage at length slide together, so the dramatic speaker Ulysses merges in lyric epiphany with the poet, imagining an empowered scene that mingles vexation with remoteness, menace with allure'. See Tucker, *Tennyson and the Doom of Romanticism*, p. 216.
58. The delayed rhythm of these lines caused Matthew Arnold to declare that 'these three lines by themselves take up nearly as much time as a whole book of the *Iliad*'. See Arnold, 'On Translating Homer', p. 306.
59. See Tennyson, *The Poems of Tennyson*, I, p. 616, ll. 10–11.
60. Paul Maltby avers that Wordsworth's 'spot of time' is the most 'eloquent testimony' to the artistic sensibility. See Maltby, *The Visionary Moment*, p. 41.
61. Tennyson, *The Poems of Tennyson*, I, p. 617, l. 23.
62. Keats, *Selected Poems and Letters of Keats*, p. 52.
63. Shaw, *Tennyson's Style*, p. 87.
64. Hartman, *The Unremarkable Wordsworth*, p. 139.
65. Hartman, *Wordsworth's Poetry 1787–1814*, p. 97.

66. T. S. Eliot famously compliments Tennyson on his fine poetic 'ear'. See Eliot, *Selected Prose*, p. 239.

67. Freud, 'Mourning and Melancholia', p. 205.

68. Freud, 'Mourning and Melancholia', pp. 209–10.

69. Ellmann, 'Introduction', p. xxi.

70. Ellmann, 'Introduction', p. xxii.

71. Ellmann, 'Introduction', p. xxii.

72. O'Neill, 'Yeats, Stevens, Rich, Bishop: Responses to Romantic Poetry', p. 147.

73. O'Neill, 'The Wheels of Being', p. 193.

74. Byron, *The Poetical Works of Lord Byron*, IV. cxliv, ll. 1–9 (p. 246).

75. Tennyson, as reported in Page, *Tennyson: Interviews and Recollections*, p. 71.

76. Compare Tucker, 'Epiphany and Browning', p. 1210. Tucker sees in these lines from Wordsworth, for instance, 'a gentle pun on "passages" (as pathways and as texts) [which] implies that writing is the medium where otherwise volatile spirits stay put for contemplation', p. 1210.

77. Wordsworth, *The Miscellaneous Poems of William Wordsworth*, III, l. 2 (p. 145). Further references to the poem appear parenthetically in the text.

78. Hartman, 'Retrospect 1971', in *Wordsworth's Poetry 1787–1814*, p. xix.

79. Hartman, 'Retrospect 1971', in *Wordsworth's Poetry 1787–1814*, p. xix.

80. O'Neill suggests that Wordsworth's poems present 'both a question and an answer, but the answer is given in such a way that troubling aspects of the question are never wholly banished or repressed'. See O'Neill, *Romanticism and the Self-Conscious Poem*, p. 47.

81. Ricks, *Allusion to the Poets*, pp. 181–2 and Tennyson, *The Poems of Tennyson*, I, p. 620, ll. 66–9.

82. See Cronin, *Romantic Victorians*, p. 150. Aidan Day also suggests Samuel Taylor Coleridge as an influence in the poem. See Day, *Tennyson's Scepticism*, p. 12.

83. Cronin, *Romantic Victorians*, p. 151.

84. Hallam, *The Poems of Arthur Henry Hallam*, p. 17. All subsequent references to the poem will appear parenthetically in the text.

85. See Tennyson, *The Poems of Tennyson*, I, p. 613.

Chapter 3

'The dead man touched me from the past':[1] Tennyson's *In Memoriam* and Wordsworth

In Memoriam, written in lament for Arthur Henry Hallam, dead from a brain haemorrhage at twenty-two, is concerned with absence, or rather with making an absence present. The poem, an elegy, published anonymously in 1850, the year that saw the posthumous publication of Wordsworth's *The Prelude*, as well as Tennyson's appointment as Poet Laureate,[2] combines private grief with public expression, as it explores faith, God and science in its attempt to come to terms with Hallam's unexpected loss, and ends with the speaker's ostensible accommodation with all three. Elegy, alongside monologue, one of the major forms of Victorian poetry, behoves Tennyson to make public his thoughts on the death of Hallam, although the public, communal voice and the private experience did not cohere, a fact Tennyson openly acknowledges, saying to James Knowles, friend and co-founder of the Metaphysical Society, 'It's too hopeful, this poem, more than I am myself'.[3] Tennyson's speaker makes clear his struggles to articulate his private thoughts in public form, stating: 'I sometimes hold it half a sin / To put in words the grief I feel; / For words, like Nature, half reveal / And half conceal the Soul within' (V. ll. 1–4). Dealing in halves, the speaker admits that such words can only 'half' reveal what he feels, while acknowledging that he holds it 'half' a sin to put into words his grief, leaving open the possibility that the disjunction between private grief and public expression can be bridged, a bridge that extends beyond the 'numbing' (V. l. 8), narcotic effect of its mere iteration.

Wordsworth forms 'the most important Romantic presence' within Victorian elegy,[4] which emerges at a 'specific, late Romantic moment',[5] and this chapter argues that Tennyson borrows Wordsworth's words and phrases as an aid to the writing of the poem. It explores how

Tennyson's borrowings from Wordsworth help the later poet to work towards finding his own form of consolation, however tenuous this consolation subsequently proves to be, and therefore to make his accommodations with his faith – 'a poor thing', as T. S. Eliot says[6] – and with the claims of nineteenth-century science and religion, and thus with the loss of Hallam himself. But it also examines how Wordsworth helps Tennyson both to stabilise his 'public' voice and to develop the pastoral elements of elegy; *In Memoriam* forms part of a long pastoral tradition, where death is regarded as 'somehow intended by, or implicated within, a persisting natural order'.[7] Tennyson borrows the gifts that Wordsworth's language has to offer, and in drawing on Wordsworth in this way, Tennyson is drawing on a poet who is able to articulate his grief and to move towards finding a form of consolation. Many of the Wordsworthian poems from which Tennyson borrows are themselves elegies – Tennyson returns to a site of loss (the elegy itself) and gains strength from it, turning Wordsworth's losses into a gain or at least a difference. *In Memoriam* totters unsteadily towards consolation, faltering where it should firmly tread; Tennyson borrows liberally from Wordsworth's elegies as poetic models, as poems that do articulate grief and do work towards consolation, even if this consolation is elided as in the 1807 'Elegiac Stanzas: Suggested by a Picture of Peele Castle, in a Storm, Painted by Sir George Beaumont' (hereafter cited as 'Elegiac Stanzas'). As the chapter will argue, Tennyson acknowledges the disjunction between mind and nature that occurs in 'Elegiac Stanzas', but draws on the resources of the poem to work towards his own form of consolation. Robert Douglas-Fairhurst notes how 'So many of *In Memoriam*'s literary echoes emerge from contexts of loss (the splintered remains of earlier elegies that rise unpredictably to the surface of Tennyson's verse, like the debris of shipwrecks)';[8] as the following discussion reveals, Wordsworth's elegies do not randomly rise to the surface of *In Memoriam* and nor do they lie inert like the debris of abandoned shipwrecks; rather, Tennyson borrows from Wordsworth's elegies to help him conceive and write the poem, weaving their language and phrasing into new configurations and connections; the poem's trajectory towards the 'one far-off divine event, / To which the whole creation moves' ('Epilogue', ll. 143–4) is facilitated by Wordsworth's language in this sense. The borrowings from Wordsworth form a chamber of echoes that Tennyson harnesses, reworks, reconfigures, replays in a different context and in a different time; but sometimes the later poet is unable fully to transfigure and rework Wordsworth's language, but is constrained, limited, inhibited by it, and these effects make themselves manifest in the poem too.

Wordsworth's presence in the poem seemingly questions Tennyson's claim to originality and creative autonomy. Tennyson, as has been established, was sensitive to the suggestions by critics that he borrowed similes and expressions from other writers, taking the suggestion as an imputation of carelessness at best or, at worst, unimaginativeness or unoriginality.[9] Yet, if Tennyson's borrowings from Wordsworth do compromise his claims to originality, they also allowing him to self-originate, to remodulate and restyle Wordsworth's language. *In Memoriam* forms a version of *The Prelude*, 'the product of the egotistical vision on trial', according to Patricia M. Ball:[10] whereas Wordsworth's poem charts the poet's 'ordered experience',[11] Tennyson 'is not engaged in demonstrating assimilated and ordered experience but in making the initial effort to master the near-chaos of self, emotion and event'.[12] But the borrowings from Wordsworth allow Tennyson to steer a course through the crisis of self, emotion and event, helping him both to express this crisis and at times to explore and mitigate it. The echoes and allusions in the poem thus create a pattern of both independence from and dependence on Wordsworth, a desire for unity and filiation with the older poet, alongside a desire to re-engender and reinvent.

In Memoriam alludes often and liberally to other writers and poets, including William Shakespeare, on whose sonnet sequence the poem is claimed to be, in part, based.[13] Christopher Ricks writes persuasively of the way in which the highly allusive echoes of previous poets in *In Memoriam* offer Tennyson 'the company of dear, dead poets';[14] Tennyson in the poem, according to Ricks, enters a 'creative relationship',[15] or 'loving masterdom',[16] which is 'the art of allusion'.[17] Such creative alliances include Tennyson's allusion in 'On the bald street breaks the blank day' in Section VII of the poem, which, as Ricks points out, furnishes the later poet with the word '"blank" as a shield against misgivings; "Blank misgivings of a Creature. . ." [from Wordsworth's 'Intimations' ode]'.[18] Other well-known allusions to Wordsworth in the poem include the description of the Wye in Section XIX;[19] the Arcadian walks in XXII and XXIII, which recall Wordsworth and Dorothy's walks together in 'Tintern Abbey';[20] and the 'living soul' from 'Tintern Abbey' in Section XCV, line 36. The allusive usage in the poem widens out to include other Wordsworthian poems, however, like the 'Intimations' ode (1807), which is found in the 'forgetting' of XLIV, line 3,[21] as well as in the 'blank' of VII, as Ricks suggests, while yet other allusions pick up the 'iron' of Wordsworth's *Guilt and Sorrow or Incidents upon Salisbury Plain* (1842) in CVII, line 12,[22] or 'they shape themselves and go' in CXXIII, line 8, from *The White Doe of Rylstone* (1815).[23] The latter allusion to the 'clouds [that] shape themselves and go' (CXXIII. l. 8) describes hills that shimmer into insubstantiality like Wordsworth's dark pool in *The White Doe of Rylstone*, where 'night insects in their play' (IV. iv. l. 30) disturb the garden pool's dark surface, causing it to break into 'A thousand, thousand rings of light / That shape themselves and disappear / Almost as soon as seen' (IV. iv. ll. 32–4). The section of the poem from which these lines are taken is prefaced by 'Ah! who could think that sadness here / Hath any sway? or pain, or fear?' (IV. iv. ll. 25–6). Through the lines Tennyson imports a sense of how an imaginative connection to the earth can mitigate emotional loss, although the paralepsis at work here hints at the opposite, of course. Tennyson's poem captures the potential imaginative mutability contained within Wordsworth's lines – 'The hills are shadows, and they flow / From form to form, and nothing stands; / They melt like mist, the solid lands, / Like clouds they shape themselves and go' (ll. 5–8) – and the later poet adds a response in lines 9–10 of CXXIII, with the speaker asserting, 'But in my spirit will I dwell, / And dream my dream, and hold it true'; in his spirit will he dwell rather than the hills, which are but shadows that melt like mist.

Ricks suggests that Tennyson's allusions often 'embody a contrariety between a malign force and a benign solidarity'.[24] Malignity gives rise to thoughts of Harold Bloom's conflictual model of intrapoetic influence and the desire for '*priority*'.[25] But Tennyson does not appear to be working at the level of deep impulse and self-protection in the poem, although there is evidence that Tennyson's recalibration of Wordsworth is at times competitive or anxious, or driven by compositional fear and therefore working at a psychic level. The processes at work in the poem generally operate on a linguistic, literary, surface level, however, the level of poetic practice that Bloom eschews;[26] nor can anxiety be said to be an analogue of the creative process in the poem.[27] The literary echoes that sound through the poem are not always self-protecting and defensive or conflictual, but expansive and sympathetic, holistic and communitarian, unifying and identificatory. Bloom's model is inadequate in explaining the complex, and at times contradictory, processes at work in the text.

Tennyson wrote the lyrical sections of the poem incrementally over a seventeen-year period, beginning immediately after the death of Hallam in 1833. The poet describes the process of writing the poem thus:

The sections were written at many different places, and as the phases of our intercourse came to my memory and suggested them. I did not write them with any view of weaving them into a whole, or for publication, until I found that I had written so many.[28]

Tennyson's use of 'weaving' draws attention to the process of inter-textual echo taking place in the text. Roland Barthes reminds us that 'etymologically, the text is a tissue, a woven fabric',[29] an arrangement of words that are *'already read'*;[30] this arrangement, Barthes makes clear, gives rise to a *'stereographic plurality'* of meanings,[31] none of which is managed by the author. The countless references to weaving in the poem are therefore a reminder of the poem's construction, of how it employs the traditional tropes of elegy – 'crucial images of weaving, of creating a fabric in the place of a void',[32] as Peter M. Sacks puts it – and of how it weaves intertexts, words that are *'already read'*, into its fabric.

The discussion begins with an analysis of Section XCV and its borrowings and echoes from Wordsworth, including Tennyson's reworking of Wordsworth's own borrowing of classical material and the role of public voice in elegy, before moving on to discuss the Wordsworthian borrowings in other sections of the poem that deal directly with faith, such as Section XXXVI. It then goes on to discuss the effects of Tennyson's borrowings from Wordsworth on the pastoral elements of the poem as seen in Section XIX, for instance, and on the poem's exploration of nature in Section LVI. It concludes with a discussion of the way in which Wordsworth's echoing presence in the poem helps Tennyson to make his accommodations with both his faith and with the demands of nineteenth-century science, and, ultimately, with the loss of Hallam.

'A trance stricken through with doubt'

Section XCV of *In Memoriam* describes the speaker's momentary communion, both with the past and with the dead Hallam. The section can be read as encapsulating a numinously transcendent moment, although the moment of connection is nonetheless tentative, as is the faith that underpins it. Tennyson repeatedly borrows from Words-worth to support the speaker's fleeting communion with Hallam, augmenting the divine with the pantheistic. Specific borrowings from Wordsworth include those from 'Tintern Abbey' (1798), the 'Inti-mations' ode (1807) and a range of Wordsworthian elegies, some of which pivot on Wordsworth's own borrowings from classical sources.

However tentative, another level of reality is reached in Section XCV, an effect facilitated by language borrowed from Wordsworth's poetry; the words that make up the section are themselves 'silent-speaking' in this sense (XCV. l. 26). The section borrows from Wordsworth's 1807 'A WHIRL-BLAST from behind the hill', for instance, a poem that was occasioned by Wordsworth and his sister Dorothy being caught in hail shower while on an early morning walk. The start of Wordsworth's poem captures the immediacy and joyous transformational power of the hailstorm:

> A WHIRL-BLAST from behind the hill
> Rushed o'er the wood with startling sound:
> Then – all at once the air was still,
> And showers of hailstones pattered round.
> Where leafless Oaks towered high above,
> I sat within an undergrove
> Of tallest hollies, tall and green;
> A fairer bower was never seen.
> From year to year the spacious floor
> With withered leaves is covered o'er,
> And all the year the bower is green.
>
> (I. ll. 1–11)

There are clear allusions to Wordsworth's poem in Section XCV, as evidenced in the phrase 'all at once', for instance, a phrase that also appears in Tennyson's autograph corrections and additions to 'Œnone' in *Poems* (1833):[33]

> So word by word, and line by line
>   The dead man touched me from the past,
>   And all at once it seemed at last
> The living soul was flashed on mine,
>
> And mine in this was wound, and whirled
>   About empyreal heights of thought,
>   And came on that which is, and caught
> The deep pulsations of the world.
>
> (XCV. ll. 33–40)

Tennyson borrows Wordsworth's 'WHIRL-BLAST' to furnish his speaker's own moment of sudden transformation, as he is 'whirled / About empyreal heights of thought' (XCV. ll. 37–8). Like Wordsworth, the speaker in Tennyson's poem comes startlingly 'on that which is' (I. l. 39). The later poem echoes Wordsworth's sense of immediacy and surprise too, of how 'all at once' the air was still; in Tennyson, 'all at once' the living soul was flashed on the speaker's own. Yet there are differences: Wordsworth moves from whirl to stillness; Tennyson from stillness to frenzy to stillness, as Wordsworth's animistic trance is converted into a fleeting moment of numinous connection.

Nonetheless, if it is the language of the written word,[34] the language of 'those fallen leaves which kept their green, / The noble letters of the dead' (XCV. ll. 23–4), which 'line by line' (XCV. l. 33) and 'word by word' (XCV. l. 33) touch the speaker from the past, then this language partly belongs to Wordsworth. The intertextual link with Wordsworth's language is further emphasised through the play of 'green' in the text. The 'fallen leaves' keep 'their green' in Tennyson; in Wordsworth, the 'tallest hollies' are 'tall and green' (I. l. 5); 'the spacious floor / With withered leaves is covered o'er / And all the year the bower is green' (I. ll. 9–11). Wordsworth's fallen leaves are 'withered'; it is the tallest hollies that ensure that the bower remains green all year round. Tennyson, by contrast, echoes Wordsworth's green to suggest the continuing life of the 'noble letters of the dead' (XCV. l. 24), 'those fallen leaves which kept their green' (XCV. l. 23). Withered leaves in Wordsworth are transfigured into the perennial leaves of the dead in Tennyson.

Wordsworth's poem is underpinned by a motion and a spirit that informs all things, and Tennyson draws on this motion to give a sense of the whirling empyreal heights of thought, of being '"whirled up and rapt into the Great Soul"',[35] creating his own trance from Wordsworth's 'trance'. In Wordsworth, deep pulsations roll through all thinking things, a pattern made clear in 'Tintern Abbey': in this poem, Wordsworth writes of how there is 'A Motion and a spirit, that impels / All thinking things, all objects of all thought, / And rolls through all things' (I. ll. 101–3). A similar spirit rolls through 'A WHIRL-BLAST from behind the hill' in the rushing whirl-blast itself and pattering hailstones. Tennyson harnesses these Wordsworthian pulsations to help create the sense of catching the 'deep pulsations of the world' (XCV. l. 40).

'Deep' is also closely aligned with 'Tintern Abbey' in Section XCV, however, through its syntactical connection to 'world'. The 'deep pulsations of the world' (XCV. l. 40) vibrate with the rhythm of 'Tintern Abbey''s 'sense sublime / Of something far more deeply interfused' (II. ll. 96–7), which induces in the speaker a love 'of all the mighty world' (II. l. 106). *In Memoriam*'s 'deep pulsations of the world' therefore also embody 'A motion and a spirit, that impels / All thinking things' (ll. 101–2) of Wordsworth's world of mind and nature. Pulsation feeds into this sustaining rhythm, as it links to the sensations in 'Tintern Abbey' that are 'Felt in the blood, and felt along the heart' (II. l. 29), replicating the arterial beat of sensation of the former poem. Pulsations, too, create an echoing beat and these vibrations act as a reminder of how 'echo' is a metaphor for the transmission of language taking place in the text.[36]

But if Tennyson is borrowing 'Tintern Abbey''s pulsating energy of 'Tintern Abbey' in Section XCV, then he also draws on its arbitrariness, too, as the section echoes with the doubt that 'Tintern Abbey' contains over the sustainability and durability of the moment of transcendence. It is the language of Wordsworth's speaker's 'former heart' (ll. l. 118), a language that describes a process that the speaker is struggling to recapture, which catches hold in the poem. Yet consolation remains nebulous in Wordsworth's poem, with the speaker straining to control his gains. The rhyme of 'thought' with 'caught' in lines 38–9 emphasises the connection to 'Tintern Abbey', foregrounding the sense of strain, as 'thought' in Wordsworth's poem is simultaneously associated both with imaginative communion and its possible forfeiture. The rhyme of 'thought' with 'caught' in lines 38–9 emphasises the connection to 'Tintern Abbey' and foregrounds this process, as 'thought' in Wordsworth's poem is simultaneously associated both with imaginative communion and its possible forfeiture: the speaker has 'pleasing thoughts / That in this moment there is life and food / For future years' (ll. ll. 64–6), yet this 'food' for future years may not sustain the years that extend beyond the speaker's death. Seamus Perry confirms how *In Memoriam*'s

> verse entwines a moment of confirmation (in its middle couplet) with a lingering return (in its outer rhyme), so that each verse, whatever the sense of purpose with which it sets out, ends acoustically haunted by the thought with which it began.[37]

Here that confirmatory couplet endorses the rhyme of 'thought' and 'caught', locking them into cycles of imaginative loss and gain. But the echoes carry a sense of the loss at the heart of the deep pulsations in 'Tintern Abbey'; these will eventually beat no more, despite the speaker's investment in Dorothy as custodian of his memories. Tennyson's Wordsworthian borrowings transport this loss into the heart of Section XCV's moment of transcendence, confirming that it too has a vacancy at its heart. Tennyson draws on the earlier poem's tentativeness to create his own numinous vulnerability, to give a sense that the moment of transcendence has a pulsating feel but that it nonetheless has an in-built obsolescence; the poem's speaker makes this point explicit, pointing out that 'At length my trance / Was cancelled, stricken through with doubt' (XCV. ll. 43–4). Wordsworth's moments of transcendence lead to the possible sense of growth through loss; there is ostensibly 'abundant recompense' (ll. l. 89) to be found in the speaker's loss, in the 'still, sad music of humanity' (ll. l. 92) and 'sense sublime / Of something far more deeply interfused' (ll. ll. 96–7).

Tennyson mediates Wordsworth's arbitrariness, then, but without mediating Wordsworth's means of possible recompense, a fact neatly confirmed by the full stop with which Tennyson ends the speaker's acknowledgement that his trance is stricken through with 'doubt' (XCV. l. 44). Yet in Tennyson endings are themselves often arbitrary acts of deferral.[38] The bb rhyme of 'Chance' and 'trance' inflects the definitive full stop that closes the stanza, opening up a route to possible recompense, of loss leading to personal growth. The rhyme also cancels out the finality of Death in the middle of the stanza and the caesural full stop which seemingly confirms it.[39] Even so, the implicit sense of hope, the desire for unity and completion brought into the text through Wordsworth's language, is compromised by the stanza's return to where it began, mechanically casting itself back on the word 'out'.

The sense of arbitrariness mediated in the section via Wordsworth's language involves the presence of the verb 'seemed', the word on which the vulnerability of the moment of numinous connection ostensibly rests. The Tennysonian flash is tentative, stricken through with doubt, and the later poet draws on Wordsworth to emphasise the moment's uncertainty through his borrowing of 'seemed'. Lines 34–6 read: 'The dead man touched me from the past, / And all at once it seemed at last / The living soul was flashed on mine'. The 'living soul' to which the speaker refers is regarded by critics (Tucker, Rapf and others) as an allusion to 'Tintern Abbey', where through 'that serene and blessed mood' (ll. l. 42) we 'are laid asleep / In body, and become a living soul' (ll. ll. 46–7). Wordsworth's vaulting pantheism is absorbed into the poem, with Tennyson affording the 'living soul' a sense of universality through the replacement of the original 'his' living soul with 'the' living soul.[40] 'Seemed' is a specific Wordsworthian borrowing, as Wordsworth insists that 'the appropriate business of poetry . . . is to treat of things . . . not as they exist in themselves, but as they *seem* to exist to the *senses* and to the *passions*'.[41] In borrowing Wordsworth's sense of things as they seem to exist to the senses, Tennyson thus helps to create his own sense of the living soul as only 'seemingly' flashed on the speaker's.

Tennyson's echoing of 'flashed' evokes a similar tentativeness, as it recalls 'I WANDERED lonely as a Cloud' (1807) and that poem's 'flash upon that inward eye / which is the bliss of solitude' (ll. ll. 21–2). Wordsworth's flash mediates an alternative concept of continuity and renewal into the text, and suggests that the flash of 'the living soul' has sparked, and will continue to spark, on the speaker's memory. However, Wordsworth's poem is based on imaginative impression rather than imaginative projection, something Wordsworth himself openly acknowledges, saying: "'the subject of these Stanzas is rather an elementary feeling and simple impression (approaching to the nature of an ocular spectrum) upon the imaginative faculty, than an *exertion* of it'".[42] Paradoxically, then, the flash of 'the living soul' in Section XCV resonates with the notion of a 'casual' impression upon the speaker's soul,[43] compounding the moment of communion's arbitrariness: the current, and any future, flash will occur only through chance impression during a moment of 'vacant or . . . pensive mood', as in 'I WANDERED lonely as a Cloud' (II. l. 20). Such randomness dilutes the universal applicability that the poet introduces into the poem through the syntactical shift from the possessive adjective 'his' to the definite article in 'the living soul' itself, aided by the use of the passive 'was flashed'.

Tennyson's echoings and borrowings from Wordsworth in Section XCV also include the later poet's own borrowing from classical sources. Duncan Wu writes of how the thrice-waved hand in 'The Vale of Esthwaite' – 'Now as we wandered through the gloom / In black Helvellyn's inmost womb / The Spectre made a solemn stand, / Slow round my head thrice waved his [hand], / And cleaved mine ears then swept his [lyre] / That shriek'd terrific, shrill an[d] [dire]'[44] – carries 'the same inscrutable logic as Aeneas' three attempts to embrace his dead father, Anchises, when he descends into the underworld in the *Aeneid* Book VI'.[45] 'Hand' here signals a departure but also acts as a metonym for the embrace that is to follow. More concretely, in the blank verse draft passage of the Solitary's 'impassioned apostrophe to his dead daughter', 'The Tuft of Primroses', in *The Excursion*,[46] touching and embracing are directly associated, and both offer, 'for a moment, the possibility of reclaiming the dead':[47] the departing Child 'That never never more shall be displaced / By the returning Substance, seen or touchd, / Seen by mine eyes or clasped in my embrace –'.[48] As Wu makes clear in his comments on the poem,

> it can be no accident that clasping in his arms is precisely what Orpheus had wanted to do with Eurydice, a desire painfully faithful to bereavement as it oscillates between incredulity at loss and the vain hope that the dead are not gone forever.[49]

Wordsworth's use of classical models, such as Orpheus' wish to return Eurydice to life, speaks 'powerfully of the desire to resuscitate the dead through the power of primitive, elemental forces in nature';[50] Virgil's tale itself is embedded within the tale of Aristaeus and his attempt to bring his bees back to life, an effect 'intensified by the pantheism that pervades his view of the natural world'.[51] In Section XCV 'touch' carries a sense of touching as in being touched by something (the speaker is reached, as in touched, by the letters, word by word), and a sense of being touching, as in something being moving or poignant. But it also implies touch in a tactile sense, as in by hand through an embrace. Hands feature frequently in the poem, as has often been noted. For Perry, hands signal Hallam's bodily presence;[52] for Sacks, they are 'similar to the demand for empirical knowledge'.[53] The stress of the iambic tetrameter in line 34 of Section XCV, however – 'dead', 'touched', 'from', 'past' – underlines the act of touching the dead through time that is taking place: 'dead touched from past'. The speaker and the dead Hallam in Section XCV 'touch' in the underworld, achieving the contact Aeneas can attempt only in his triple wave of the hand; they touch hands through time. In 'Nutting' (1800), too, 'touch' is concerned both with the return of nature and the return of the dead: 'Then, dearest Maiden! move along these shades / In gentleness of heart; with gentle hand / Touch – for there is a spirit in the woods' (II. ll. 54–6). 'Touch' suggests that there is a spirit, a shade or ghost, in the woods of Section XCV, glimmering among the white kine, quietly hinting at the return of the dead. This spirit is sacred, a *Numen in est*,[54] but it is also the spirit that is Hallam awaiting his return. The 'living soul' (l. 36) also bears resemblance to the 'living man' of 'The Tuft of Primroses': 'Her cheek to change its colour was conveyed / From us to regions inaccessible / Where height or depth admits not the approach / Of living man though longing to pursue' (ll. 24–7). As Wu again makes clear, 'The living man who longs to pursue the dead is familiar from Wordsworth's classical education at Hawkshead, an echo of Aeneas and Orpheus'.[55] The positions of the living and the dead are reversed in Tennyson's text, though, as the pursued becomes the pursuer: the dead, or rather 'living', man, Hallam, touches the speaker from the past, actively seeking out a connection with the present, answering the speaker's imprecation in LXXX, 'Reach out dead hands to comfort me' (l. 16).

The classical connections here mirror that of Eliot's *Four Quartets*, where in 'Little Gidding II' the speaker 'caught the sudden look of some dead master',[56] as if he, the dead master, were alive, which, of course, he is if we accept that he is in the underworld. Sarah Annes Brown, for instance, suggests that Eliot's use of allusion in the poem is itself classical and is derived from the 'ancient epic motif of *katabasis* . . . [whereby] a hero visits the dead and recognises former comrades, unearthing buried memories',[57] the '*locus classicus*' for which is Homer's account of Odysseus' descent to the underworld, where Odysseus meets a succession of 'shades', starting with 'Elpenor'.[58] The time of day – night, before the doubtful dawn (l. 49) breaks – in which the touching takes place in Section XCV encapsulates the way in which *katabasis* is a 'Night Journey':[59] the reaching of hands through time takes place in the dark, lit only by the flash of 'the living soul'. However, as Wu points out, Wordsworth's classical models are 'tragic',[60] as the dead may be 'revisited' but not necessarily reclaimed:[61] 'Aeneas and Orpheus descend into the underworld so as to re-experience loss'.[62] Significantly, in 'The Tuft of Primroses' restoration of the dead is 'impossible', and the 'consolation of an afterlife' denied:[63] all we have is 'the finality of death'.[64] In *In Memoriam*, too, the dead man touched the speaker from the past, linking hands through time, but he can remain only lost in time, revisited but not reclaimed. Tennyson borrows from Wordsworth here to reveal how Wordsworth himself acknowledges that the dead cannot be reclaimed; all that can be done is that they can be (re) visited endlessly. The echoic pattern at work thus feeds and supports the poem, but also constrains it: the dead man can only ever be lost in time, touched but never present. Ian H. C. Kennedy sees Section XCV as inverting classical elegy by separating Hallam from the speaker: the former is a 'dead' man.[65] Yet, the speaker is not separated as such from the dead man, but is caught in a continuous process of revisiting a loss or absence, emblematised by the cyclical return of the stanza itself. If Wordsworth facilitates Tennyson's tentative moment of communion, then, he also denies the later poet the full spiritual or physical unity he seeks. The effect here is more of the myth of Echo herself, or more accurately Orpheus, rather than Bloomian *apophrades*, however; rather than being 'back in the later poet's flooded apprenticeship', Tennyson, like Orpheus, is simply perpetually confined to nothing but a 'backward glance'.[66]

Significantly, Tennyson moves from borrowing from Wordsworth to achieve his sense of tenuous communion, both through the numinous moment of communion itself and the process of touching, to drawing on Wordsworth to give a sense of how grief can be healed or at least managed. Lines 15–16 and 51–2 are repetitions of each other in the section and confirm this sense of return and reclamation, or at least suggest its possibility: 'The white kine glimmered, and the trees / Laid their dark arms about the field'. 'Glimmering' alludes to Wordsworth's *An Evening Walk* (1793), where it is associated with the grief of loss but also with the possible loss of imaginative connection with nature: music steals round 'the glimmering deeps' (I. l. 320), yet 'Lost in the thicken'd darkness, glimmers hoar' (I. l. 329). Ricks, in his gloss to *In Memoriam*, notes how the setting and mood of Section XCV suggest Thomas Gray's 'Elegy Written in a Country Churchyard' (1751).[67] Allusions to Gray feel their way through lines 15–16 and 51–2: 'Now fades the glimmering landscape on the sight, / And all the air a solemn stillness holds'.[68] The remembrance of Gray, however, blends with that of *An Evening Walk*, which itself replicates Gray with its 'thickened darkness'. 'Glimmers' in *An Evening Walk* occurs in a section of the poem where the imagination is temporarily lost to the darkness: the speaker assuages his guilt, however, and is imaginatively reunited with his lost loved one.

'Glimmering' also contains echoes of Wordsworth's 'THERE was a Boy' (1800), where 'many a time, / At evening, when the earliest stars began / To move along the edges of the hills, / Rising or setting, would he stand alone, / Beneath the trees, or by the glimmering lake' (II. ll. 2–6), which provides parallels of the loss of Tennyson's own 'boy', Hallam. This poem, too, is concerned with loss and grief, but, like *An Evening Walk*, finds mitigation for it in the imagination, this time in the 'silent memorial of the nameless protagonist';[69] grief here is not 'destructive', but evidence of 'creativity and imagination' and a symbol of the continuing life of the dead as an inspirational force,[70] an 'articulation' found in the first of the 'Essays upon Epitaphs' in 1810, but also in an unfinished epitaph of 1788.[71] Tennyson draws on Wordsworth here to give a sense that the dead, if not locatable via classical sources, are at least a source of creativity and imagination and an inspirational force. They 'continue' in this way, if not literally.

The lines also echo another Wordsworth poem concerned with grief, 'Sonnet, Written at Evening', which was first published in the *Morning Post*, 13 February 1802, and later included in revised form in *Poems, in Two Volumes* in 1807 as 'Written in very early Youth'.[72] This poem is again concerned with the imagination and its capacity, in its relationship with nature, to alleviate loss: 'On the [ ] village Silence sets her seal, / And in the glimmering vale the last lights die; / The kine, obscurely seen, before me lie / Round the dim horse that crops his later meal / Scarce heard'.[73] The scene described produces a 'timely slumber' (l. 5), which in turn produces 'a strange harmony, / Home-felt and home-created' (ll. 7–8) that 'seems to heal / That grief for which my senses still supply / Fresh food' (ll. 8–10). Grief is healed through the imagination, through that 'strange harmony' where the speaker is temporarily 'at peace' (l. 11), but the poem also implicitly restores 'what has been taken'.[74] Section XCV, interestingly, echoes Wordsworth's poem linguistically and syntactically, allowing Tennyson to borrow its healing of grief, that sense of restoring what has been lost: the kine are obscurely seen in Wordsworth's poem; Tennyson's glimmer in and out of view; the 'i' from Wordsworth's 'glimmering', 'light', 'die' and 'lie' are transcribed into 'white kine glimmered', encapsulating a sense of trembling possibility. The repetition of 'i' also produces a slowing effect, replicating the sense of silence and stasis in Wordsworth's poem. These effects occur in the lines that act as a frame to the moment of communion in Section XCV – lines 15–16 and 52–3 – suggesting that nature holds the key to the restoration of the dead. As in 'Nutting' there is a suggestion that there is a spirit or shade in the woods, this time glimmering among the white kine, quietly hinting at the return of the dead. The spirit is sacred, a *Numen in est*, but it is also the spirit that is Hallam silently awaiting his return. Tennyson echoes Wordsworth's nature in an attempt to restore what is lost; his grief can possibly be healed and Hallam restored, albeit tentatively. The play of light and dark in the luminously glimmering kine and the 'dark arms about the field' (XCV. l. 52) unsettle this idea, however, as the 'dark arms' contain echoes of the hands that reach through time, placing the text back in the position of revisiting a *katabatic* loss. Tennyson is thus both nourished by Wordsworth here and constrained by him; the momentary communion the later poet describes is fed by Wordsworth's language but can end only in quivering, faltering uncertainty.

Tennyson's borrowing from Wordsworth in the section extends to the speaker's sense of grasping at memory through language. The speaker describes his own struggles to account for his moment of transcendence as 'Vague words! but, ah how hard to frame / In matter-moulded forms of speech, / Or even for intellect to reach / Through memory that which I became' (XCV. ll. 45–8). Tennyson's poem echoes 'Tintern Abbey' here and its speaker's own struggles with the dichotomy that exists between language and experience. Wordsworth's speaker reaches through memory to grasp at a former self: it is 'with many recognitions dim and faint' (II. l. 60) and 'gleams of half-extinguished thought' (II. l. 59) that Wordsworth's speaker struggles to remember his own moments of transcendence, for instance. And the intellect that struggles to reach through memory echoes Wordsworth's 'recognitions dim and faint'. Wordsworth acknowledges in his poem that he could not 'paint' (II. l. 76) 'What then [he] was' (II. l. 77), and this recognition echoes through Tennyson's speaker's own acknowledgement of how hard it is to frame in language 'that which [he] became' (XCV. l. 48), enabling him to bridge the gulf that exists between language and lived experience.

The 'touch of earthly years'

Tennyson borrows Wordsworth's language and phrasing in other sections of the poem, specifically those that continue to engage with faith or the separation occasioned by death and the role that faith plays in either perpetuating or mitigating such division. In Section XXXVI the speaker writes of the durability of Christian faith, a faith possibly readable to those who bind the sheaf or build the house or dig the grave, but seemingly beyond the capacity of those who live in rudimentary societies:

> And so the Word had breath, and wrought
>   With human hands the creed of creeds
>   In loveliness of perfect deeds,
> More strong than all poetic thought;
>
> Which he may read that binds the sheaf,
>   Or builds the house, or digs the grave,
>   And those wild eyes that watch the wave
> In roarings round the coral reef.
>
> (XXXVI. ll. 9–16)

Tennyson draws from Dorothy's 'wild eyes' in 'Tintern Abbey' (II. l. 149) to suggest the 'wild eyes' of the Pacific Islanders who watch the wave in roarings round the coral reef,[75] turning eyes that are lit with the spark of a transcendent nature into eyes that are seemingly wild with ignorance about the coral reef on which they gaze and the Word that has 'wrought / With human hands the creed of creeds' (XXXVI. ll. 9–10).

Tennyson also borrows from Wordsworth to help him explore the separation that now exists between Hallam and the speaker. In XL the speaker acknowledges that he is alienated from the deceased Hallam by his Christian faith, which places them in separate spheres: 'My paths are in the fields I know, / And thine in undiscovered lands' (XL. ll. 31–2). Ricks finds an allusion both to Shelley's *Alastor* (1816) here and to *Hamlet* III i 79–80, that 'undiscovered country, from whose bourn / No traveller returns'.[76] Yet, Hallam has 'turned to something strange' (XLI. l. 5), and the speaker has 'lost the links that bound / Thy changes; here upon the ground, / No more partaker of thy change' (XLI. ll. 6–8). He wishes that this separation could be healed, 'That I could wing my will with might / To leap the grades of life and light, / And flash at once, my friend, to thee' (XLI. ll. 10–12).

The 'something strange' and 'flash' draw from the 'strange harmony' (l. 7) of 'Written in very early Youth' and the 'something far more deeply interfused' (II. l. 96) of 'Tintern Abbey', as well as the casual 'flash' (II. l. 21) of 'I WANDERED lonely as a Cloud'. Tennyson borrows Wordsworth's language to help him express his desire to 'flash' to his friend, leaping over the grades of life and light, although flash is linked with 'will' rather than mind. 'Flash' contains an arbitrariness that cannot be suppressed, however, weakening the connection the speaker wishes to make. The language with which the speaker summarises the separation between Hallam and himself serves only to widen the gulf further by closing down the possibility of the imaginative communion such 'flashing' seeks, however. Tennyson's speaker says:

> Ay me, the difference I discern!
>   How often shall her old fireside
>   Be cheered with tidings of the bride,
> How often she herself return,
>
> And tell them all they would have told,
>   And bring her babe, and make her boast,
>   Till even those that missed her most
> Shall count new things as dear as old:
>
> But thou and I have shaken hands,
>   Till growing winters lay me low;
>   My paths are in the fields I know,
> And thine in undiscovered lands.
>
> (XL. ll. 21–32)

'Ay me, the difference I discern' (XL. l. 21), with its echoes of 'SHE dwelt among the untrodden ways' (1800) and the speaker's acknowledgement that Lucy is 'in her Grave, and, oh, / The difference to me!' (I. ll. 11–12), exposes how the divide between life and death is imaginatively unbridgeable. Tennyson's speaker, in acknowledging that 'My paths are in the fields I know, / And thine in undiscovered lands' (XL. ll. 31–2), implicitly draws on Wordsworth to confirm that the divide that he wants to bridge is nevertheless unbridgeable. Ricks notes in his three-volume edition of the poem that the Trinity manuscript of *In Memoriam*'s Section XL ends with lines that acknowledge the bitterness that such separation occasions: 'But ah the bitter difference / That knowledge here is left to hope / And that imaginative scope / That seeks for truths beyond the sense'.[77] Tennyson borrows from 'SHE dwelt among the untrodden ways' here too to create a sense that the imaginative hope of bridging the divide between life and death is closed down – Lucy is beyond imaginative contact, as is Hallam.

However, if Tennyson draws on Wordsworth's inability to express lived experience in Section XCV, then he also draws on what Perry deftly describes as Wordsworth's 'expressive power of inarticulacy'.[78] The speaker's 'accomplished public voice falters beneath a private pressure' in 'SHE dwelt among the untrodden ways',[79] as the poem demonstrates its reluctance to 'yield up [its] innermost privacies':[80] 'She *lived* unknown, and few could know / When Lucy ceased to be' (ll. 9–10; emphasis Perry's own).[81] A similar reticence, or reluctance to yield up inner privacies, permeates Section XXVI of Tennyson's poem. Here, the speaker longs 'to prove / No lapse of moons can canker Love, / Whatever fickle tongues may say' (ll. 2–4), but 'if that eye which watches guilt / And goodness, and hath power to see / Within the green the mouldered tree' (ll. 5–7) or 'Oh, if indeed that eye foresee / Or see (in Him is no before) / In more of life true life no more / And Love the indifference to be' (ll. 9–12), then might he find 'That shadow waiting with the keys, / To shroud [him] from [his] proper scorn' (ll. 15–16). The later poet acknowledges his own poetic incapacity here, admitting his inability to see or write beyond those conditional 'ifs': that shadow will be waiting with the keys to shroud him from his proper scorn only if, in more of life, there is true life no more and if the eye foresees Love to be indifferent. The Wordsworthian echoes of 'SHE dwelt among the untrodden ways' – 'And Love the indifference to be' – reprises both the earlier poem's 'difference to me' and its 'When Lucy ceased to be', underscoring the poem's implicit acknowledgement of the power of the inexpressible. The speaker's imprecation at the start of the stanza, 'Oh', echoes the 'oh, / the difference' (I. ll. 11–12) of Wordsworth's poem too. *In Memoriam* acknowledges its own inarticulacy, its inability to match thought and feeling to language, as does Tennyson himself: the poem is but 'this poor flower of poesy' (VIII. l. 19), and can only 'half reveal / And half conceal' (V. ll. 3–4) what is within; it is too hopeful, says the poet of his poem. Yet in drawing from Wordsworth's reticent public voice, Tennyson finds a way to heal the wound in his own public inarticulacy by acknowledging that the inexpressible has its own expressibility and power. In embracing Wordsworth's poetic incapacity in this way, Tennyson also collapses the distance that exists between himself and Wordsworth as public poets, however. The agonistic competition or rivalry that Bloom maintains exists between poets therefore also collapses, as Tennyson becomes a beneficiary of Wordsworth's own 'weakness'.

The speaker of *In Memoriam* avers that the dead are 'happy' (XLIV. l. 1), but this is conditional on whether 'Sleep and Death be truly one' (XLIII. l. 1), that the dead '"sleep in Jesus"'.[82] The Wordsworthian echo in the section from which these lines are taken suggests that the two are not as indivisible as the speaker would like: if 'every spirit's folded bloom / Through all its intervital gloom / In some long trance should slumber on' (XLIII. ll. 2–4), then this 'slumber' draws from Wordsworth's 'A SLUMBER did my spirit seal'. Tennyson borrows the slumber of Wordsworth's poem to suggest the long trance in which the dead, like Wordsworth's loved one, are absorbed. In Wordsworth's poem it is the speaker who is in a slumber. But in echoing Wordsworth's 'slumber', Tennyson raises the possibility that to sleep in Jesus is nonetheless to be rolled round with rocks and stones and trees: while the speaker of Wordsworth's poem slumbers, his beloved 'She' is caught in a cosmic flurry. The Wordsworthian echo here in Tennyson feeds into the broader question of whether the slumber of the dead equates to sleep. Ricks draws attention to the arguments undertaken during the Renaissance as to whether or not the dead sleep. He points out that there was ample scriptural authority for the belief that they do – for example, 1 *Thessalonians* iv 13–15 – but goes on to suggest that the issue still excited controversy in Tennyson's time.[83] In drawing from Wordsworth's poem in the way that he does, Tennyson implies that the dead do not in fact sleep; a return to earth brings with it only a ceaseless round of activity. The echo, with its intimations of cosmic upheaval, therefore does nothing to assuage either Tennyson's separation anxiety or Hallam's unawareness of the silent traces of the past: sleep and death are not truly one and seemingly never can be.

Tennyson again borrows from 'A SLUMBER did my spirit seal' in Section XCVII of the poem to furnish his account of 'the relation of one on earth to one in the other and higher world':[84] 'My love has talked with rocks and trees; / He finds on misty mountain-ground / His own vast shadow glory-crowned; / He sees himself in all he sees' (XCVII. ll. 1–4). The text returns again here to Wordsworth's 'A SLUMBER did my spirit seal', with its love rolled round with rocks and stones and trees, but also to 'Tintern Abbey', with its 'misty mountain winds' (ll. l. 137):

> Therefore let the moon
> Shine on thee in thy solitary walk;
> And let the misty mountain winds be free
> To blow against thee: and, in after years,
> When these wild ecstasies shall be matured

Into a sober pleasure; when thy mind
Shall be a mansion for all lovely forms,
Thy memory be as a dwelling-place
For all sweet sounds and harmonies; oh! then,
If solitude, or fear, or pain, or grief,
Should be thy portion, with what healing thoughts
Of tender joy wilt thou remember me,
And these my exhortations!

(II. ll. 135–47)

Tennyson draws on Wordsworth's language again here to create a sense of Hallam's vast shadow as 'glory-crowned'; Hallam, in 'seeing himself' in all he sees, also shadows the Romantic, Kantian form of transcendence, where the mind 'half-creates' what it sees: Kant sees the mind as actively imposing its own forms on the objects of perception, in that we can 'know *a priori* of things only what we ourselves put into them'.[85] Tennyson's speaker confirms that his 'love' has talked with rocks and trees, giving him an agency, unlike Wordsworth's speaker who can only simply acknowledge how his love 'is' rolled round in 'earth's diurnal course' (l. 7).

In Section XCVII, Tennyson's speaker also compares how he and Hallam are 'Two partners of a married life' (l. 5) – 'I looked on these and thought of thee / In vastness and in mystery, / And of my spirit as of a wife' (ll. 6–8). The married-life analogy in the section borrows from Wordsworth's desire to be remembered by his sister Dorothy in 'Tintern Abbey – 'wilt thou remember me' (II. l. 146) – transposing sister for 'wife'. There is also a sense that Wordsworth's relationship with Dorothy is replicated in the remainder of the section, where Tennyson's speaker goes on to describe how

She knows but matters of the house,
And he, he knows a thousand things.

Her faith is fixt and cannot move,
She darkly feels him great and wise,
She dwells on him with faithful eyes,
'I cannot understand: I love.'

(XCVII. ll. 31–6)

Ricks records how Tennyson says of the section:

'The spirit yet in the flesh but united in love with the spirit out of the flesh resembles the wife of a great man of science. She looks up to him – but what he knows is a mystery to her'.[86]

There is a sense here that Tennyson is borrowing from Wordsworth's Dorothy, who perhaps does not understand the 'mysteries' that have been entrusted to her, or at least is not allowed a voice with which to discuss them in the text. The female figure in 'masculine' Romanticism is erased from discourse:[87] 'almost all of Wordsworth's women are dead, either literally (as in the cases of Lucy, Margaret and Martha Ray) or figuratively (they are mad, or allowed to live only vicariously through the words and experiences of male narrators)'.[88] So:

> Dorothy remains a silenced auditor in *Tintern Abbey*, a less conscious being whose function is to mirror and thus to guarantee the truth of the poet's development and perceptions, even as the poem itself acknowledges the existence of an unbridgeable gap between the poet's forever-lost past subjectivity and his present self.[89]

In borrowing from both 'A SLUMBER did my spirit seal' here and 'Tintern Abbey', Tennyson attenuates Wordsworth's placing of the female as merely the mirror and guarantor of the poet's development and perceptions. Tennyson's 'She' does not speak; 'She' has no 'understanding'; she 'knows but matters of the house' and can only feel, dwell and love. Tennyson's borrowings thus fail to challenge Wordsworth's male-centric subjectivity; rather, they perpetuate and intensify it as here.

The separation anxiety caused by faith runs through Section XLIV, where the speaker laments Hallam's forgetfulness of his past life:

> How fares it with the happy dead?
>   For here the man is more and more;
>   But he forgets the days before
> God shut the doorways of his head.
>
> The days have vanished, tone and tint,
>   And yet perhaps the hoarding sense
>   Gives out at times (he knows not whence)
> A little flash, a mystic hint;
>
> And in the long harmonious years
>   (If Death so taste Lethean springs),
>   May some dim touch of earthly things
> Surprise thee ranging with thy peers.
>
> If such a dreamy touch should fall,
>   O turn thee round, resolve the doubt;
>   My guardian angel will speak out
> In that high place, and tell thee all.

(XLIV. ll. 1–16)

For the Victorians, the afterlife was 'seen as a place of individual spiritual progress and unceasing activity, rather than static worship of God'.[90] The speaker voices his doubts over this theology, fearing that spiritual progress for Hallam in the afterlife means a forgetting of the past in general and him in particular. The language of Wordsworth's 'Intimations' ode is allusively employed to suggest that 'Our birth is but a sleep and a forgetting' (IV. v. l. 58), that there is 'yet perhaps the hoarding sense' (l. 6) of the 'days that have vanished' (l. 5). Tennyson once more draws on Wordsworth to achieve his effects: Wordsworth's 'flash' becomes mystical here. Like the flash of soul on soul in Section XCV, the 'little flash' or 'mystic hint' is 'littler' still through its association with Wordsworth's 'I WANDERED lonely as a Cloud', while the 'dim touch of earthly things' rings to the sound of 'A SLUMBER did my spirit seal' and the 'She' that 'seemed a thing that could not feel / The touch of earthly years' (II. ll. 3–4). The 'touch of earthly years' is transfigured into the 'touch of earthly things' in Tennyson's poem, reworking the suggestion of imaginative reconnection contained in the first stanza of the earlier poem. Tennyson transfigures Wordsworth, hoping that Hallam will in heaven feel the touch of earthly things, surprising him when he is ranging with his peers. The echo brings with it the suggestion of imaginative connection from the first half of Wordsworth's poem. The hint of imaginative possibility raised in the text is potentially foreclosed, however, by the lines that follow these: 'If such a dreamy touch should fall, / O turn thee round, resolve the doubt' (XLIV. ll. 13–14) confirms that Hallam, like the 'She' of Wordsworth's poem, is 'Rolled round in earth's diurnal course' (II. l. 7), well beyond a dreamy touch, and imaginatively lost to the speaker. Tennyson transfigures the touch into a dreamy one, acknowledging its insubstantiality, calling on Hallam to turn himself round, although this is prefigured by a conditional 'if'. Wordsworth's poem ends with the acknowledgement that a connection with the dead cannot be made; Tennyson's with the belief that this hope is still alive, albeit tentatively.

Wordsworthian echoes and resonances reverberate through the speaker's projection of Hallam as a Christ-like figure in Section CIII. The speaker, in his dream, envisions 'A statue veiled' (CIII. l. 12) – an image of weaving again – that 'though veiled, was known to me, / The shape of him I loved, and love / For ever: then flew in a dove / And brought a summons from the sea' (CIII. ll. 13–16). That 'For ever' resonates with 'the radiance which was once so bright / Be now for ever taken from my sight' (IV. x. ll. 175–6) of the 'Intimations' ode. Hallam has been taken 'for ever' from Tennyson's sight, a 'radiance

that was once so bright', but the echo also brings with it the strength
Wordsworth finds in what remains behind after the radiance has gone:

> Though nothing can bring back the hour
> Of splendour in the grass, of glory in the flower;
>   We will grieve not, rather find
>   Strength in what remains behind;
>   In the primal sympathy
>   Which having been must ever be;
>   In the soothing thoughts that spring
>   Out of human suffering
>   In the faith that looks through death
> In years that bring the philosophic mind.
>
> (IV. x. ll. 181–90)

Tennyson draws on Wordsworth's loss here to communicate his own
loss, but 'for ever' contains within it a residue of strength, which also
transmits itself through Tennyson's text; there are soothing thoughts
to be had that spring out of human suffering. Similarly, in CXII the
speaker states:

> But thou, that fillest all the room
>   Of all my love, art reason why
>   I seem to cast a careless eye
> On souls, the lesser lords of doom.
>
> For what wert thou? some novel power
>   Sprang up for ever at a touch,
>   And hope could never hope too much,
> In watching thee from hour to hour,
>
> Large elements in order brought,
>   And tracts of calm from tempest made,
>   And world-wide fluctuation swayed
> In vassal tides that followed thought.
>
> (CXII. ll. 5–16)

The senses are transposed here: the radiance is taken for ever from
Wordsworth's sight, but Tennyson finds that some novel power
springs up for ever at a touch. But sight returns, as Tennyson, in
watching Hallam 'from hour to hour', finds 'Large elements in order
brought / And tracts of calm from tempest made'. And sight returns
in Wordsworth, too: it is in the faith 'that looks through death' that

the speaker finds strength. Rather than betraying the anxiety of composition here, then, Tennyson's borrowings reveal the gratitude of
compensation.[91]

Shore Deep

If Tennyson draws on Wordsworth's language when discussing
questions of faith, then he also calls on Wordsworth's language to
help him engage with the elegy's pastoral mode,[92] an exploration
that reaches its apotheosis in Section CXXX, which sees Hallam's
voice become part of the 'rolling air' (l. 1). The return to the pastoral in the poem has been claimed as a 'sad mechanic exercise',[93]
whereby Tennyson 'recognizes the deep fallacy of the old [pastoral]
conventions'.[94] Intriguingly, if Tennyson returns to Wordsworth's
pastoralism in this section, then he also borrows from those Wordsworthian elegies in which, for Wordsworth, the pastoral mode has
itself become a sad mechanic exercise, where the link between mind
and nature has been broken. In Section XIX of *In Memoriam* lines
1–8 read:

> The Danube to the Severn gave
>   The darkened heart that beat no more;
>   They laid him by the pleasant shore,
> And in the hearing of the wave.
>
> There twice a day the Severn fills;
>   The salt sea-water passes by,
>   And hushes half the babbling Wye,
> And makes a silence in the hills.

The 'darkened heart' beats with the pulse of 'Tintern Abbey''s
'sensations sweet, / Felt in the blood, and felt along the heart'
(ll. ll. 28–9); Tennyson, famously, had visited Tintern Abbey in
the autumn of 1834.[95] He notes, almost perfunctorily: '"After the
burial [of Hallam] these thoughts come"'.[96] But the section alludes
to other Wordsworth poems, including some of the elegies, such
as 'Elegiac Stanzas: Suggested by a Picture of Peele Castle, in a
Storm, Painted by Sir George Beaumont' (1807; hereafter 'Elegiac
Stanzas'). Wordsworth had explored the disconnection between
mind and nature in the 'Intimations' ode, but the link between the
two finally breaks in 'Elegiac Stanzas'. 'Shore' is a resonant word

in Wordsworth that echoes throughout the elegies and is associated with loss, either of the imagination or directly of a loved one, as in 'To the Daisy' (1815), another of the 'Elegiac Stanzas', written for Wordsworth's brother John, lost in a drowning accident: John 'Sleeps by his native shore' (IV. l. 7) in his 'senseless grave' (IV. l. 71). England's 'shore' (IV. l. 7) also features in the 1807 'I TRAVELLED among unknown men', where it symbolises the speaker's nostalgic affiliation with the lost Lucy of the poem. The 'Intimations' ode too harbours a compensatory admiration for 'the Children [that] sport upon the shore' (IV. x. l. 166), with their ability to embody eternal truths. Tennyson makes his shore 'pleasant', although implicitly 'native'. Susan Shatto and Marion Shaw note here a Keatsian influence from '*Hyperion* ii 262: "a pleasant shore"'.[97] But the phrase also appears in an early Wordsworth poem, which Wordsworth began in 1800, finished in 1802 and published in 1815: 'WHEN, to the attractions of the busy World'. According to Ernest de Selincourt, Wordsworth's lines 1–83 were 'probably written on August 29, 30, 1800; the remainder in 1802, while John W. [Wordsworth's brother] was absent on a voyage to China from which he returned in September of that year'.[98] Wordsworth adds a note at the close of the poem, recording how the speaker's earnest wish to meet 'A second time, in Grasmere's happy Vale' (III. l. 109) did not come to fruition: 'the lamented Person not long after perished by shipwreck, in discharge of his duty as Commander of the Honourable East India Company's Vessel, the Earl of Abergavenny'.[99] Wordsworth's speaker describes the feelings occasioned by his brother's departure, when the latter left Esthwaite's 'pleasant shore':

> When thou hadst quitted Esthwaite's pleasant shore,
> And taken thy first leave of those green hills
> And rocks that were the play-ground of thy Youth,
> Year followed year, my Brother! and we two,
> Conversing not, knew little in what mould
> Each other's minds were fashioned; and at length,
> When once again we met in Grasmere Vale,
> Between us there was little other bond
> Than common feelings of fraternal love.
> But thou, a School-Boy, to the sea hadst carried
> Undying recollections; Nature there
> Was with thee; she, who loved us both, she still
> Was with thee; and even so didst thou become
> A *silent* Poet; from the solitude

Of the vast sea didst bring a watchful heart
Still couchant, an inevitable ear,
And an eye practised like a blind man's touch.

(III. ll. 66–82)

The laying of Hallam by the 'pleasant shore', in the 'hearing of the wave', echoes in its shore, silence and sense of brotherhood the sounds and influences of Wordsworth's own melancholic, wistful account of his brother's dangerous life at sea: John Wordsworth was a '*silent* Poet'. Tennyson's speaker can hear a darkened heart that beat 'no more' (XIX. l. 2); in Wordsworth's 'Intimations' ode, the speaker laments 'The things which I have seen I now can see no more' (IV. i. l. 9). Wordsworth laments the finality of that which can be seen 'no more'; Hallam too can be seen 'no more' in an echo of the earlier poem's spondaic finality. Interestingly, Tennyson echoes the same phrase in CVI, this time directly associating it with seeing, or rather with not seeing: 'Ring out the grief that saps the mind, / For those that here we see no more' (ll. 9–10). The phrase appears again in Section VII of *In Memoriam*. Tennyson writes of the

Dark house, by which once more I stand
　Here in the long unlovely street,
　Doors, where my heart was used to beat
So quickly, waiting for a hand,

A hand that can be clasped no more –
　Behold me, for I cannot sleep,
　And like a guilty thing I creep
At earliest morning to the door.

(VII. ll. 1–8)

Ricks reminds us that Tennyson's guilty thing possibly owes its origin to Shakespeare's *Hamlet* and Wordsworth's 'Intimations' ode.[100] But Tennyson borrows from Wordsworth's Ode here in the hand that can be clasped no more. The phrase 'no more' is evidence too of Tennyson's own predilection for self-repetition, echoing, for instance, resoundingly through Tennyson's 'Tears, Idle Tears' (1847) in the speaker's lament to the 'days that are no more' (ll. 5, 10, 15, 20). The phrase also appears in one of Tennyson's very early pieces of juvenilia, 'No More' (1830), where it contains decidedly Wordsworthian resonances:

Oh sad *No More!* Oh sweet *No More!*
Oh strange *No More!*
By a mossed brookbank on a stone

I smelt a wildweed-flower alone;
There was a ringing in my ears,
And both my eyes gushed out with tears.
Surely all pleasant things had gone before,
Lowburied fathomdeep beneath with thee, NO MORE![101]

Tennyson struggles to express his thoughts in the poem, which contains little of the poet's later facility with language and sound. But the poem nonetheless draws significantly on Wordsworth's 'Intimations' ode to render the evanescence of beauty and pleasure: the speaker's acknowledgement that 'Surely all pleasant things had gone before' (l. 7) evokes the Ode and its things that can be seen 'no more'; the 'Lowburied fathomdeep' resonates with the Ode's 'Thoughts that do often lie too deep for tears' (IV. l. 203). The allusions to the Ode's 'no more' that run through *In Memoriam* can be seen therefore to have a specific source in Tennyson's very early writing and its reworking of Wordsworth's intimations of immortality, although for Tennyson's speaker there is little intimation of immortality when faced with the stark reality of Hallam's body returning to the pleasant shore.

If Section XIX draws from the Ode, however, then it also draws from Wordsworth's poem of grief and estrangement from nature, the 'Elegiac Stanzas', which, like 'To the Daisy', was written in response to the death of Wordsworth's brother. 'Elegiac Stanzas' confirms the speaker's imaginative separation from nature; the poem repeats much of the vocabulary of Wordsworth's earlier poems, as it pushes towards severing the sustaining link between mind and nature. 'Shore' is again important among this vocabulary, as is 'deep'. 'Deep', so resonant in 'Tintern Abbey' and the 'Intimations' ode, renews itself in the poem, like grief itself, and encapsulates the speaker's movement from imaginative connection to disconnection, and is intimately linked to 'shore' through its association with the sea. At the start of Wordsworth's poem, in his memory-image of Peele Castle, the speaker fulsomely describes the imaginative affiliation with nature he once possessed:

So pure the sky, so quiet was the air!
So like, so very like, was day to day!
Whene'er I look'd, thy Image still was there;
It trembled, but it never pass'd away.

How perfect was the calm! it seem'd no sleep;
No mood, which season takes away, or brings:
I could have fancied that the mighty Deep
Was even the gentlest of all gentle Things.[102]

The Deep is mighty, as is the speaker's imaginative ability to connect with, and subdue, nature: he 'could have fancied', with the play here, in the Wordsworthian sense, on fancy as a supportive faculty to imagination,[103] that 'the mighty Deep / Was even the gentlest of all gentle Things'. As the poem progresses and the speaker moves on to describe Beaumont's actual painting of Peele Castle, the speaker also describes the disintegration of this imaginative ability, where 'deep' is again central to the process, developing its connections with the 'mighty Deep' into an expression of imaginative failure: 'I have submitted to a new controul: / A power is gone, which nothing can restore; / A deep distress hath humanized my Soul' (ll. 35–6). Tennyson draws freely on 'Elegiac Stanzas''s 'deep' in Section XIX, which, in its transmission into the later text, through Tennyson's use of superlative and comparative adjectival forms, intensifies into 'deepest grief' (XIX. l. 10) and 'deeper anguish' (XIX. l. 15). In Wordsworth's poem, this 'deep distress' feeds back into 'shore', continuing 'deep''s affiliation with the sea in the poem.[104] After admitting that he has submitted to a new control, Wordsworth's speaker confirms:

> Not for a moment could I now behold
> A smiling sea and be what I have been:
> The feeling of my loss will ne'er be old;
> This, which I know, I speak with mind serene.
>
> Then, Beaumont, Friend! who would have been the Friend,
> If he had lived, of Him whom I deplore,
> This work of thine I blame not, but commend;
> This sea in anger, and that dismal shore.
>
> (ll. 37–44)

Deep distress turns to anger; the shore becomes dismal. Through the borrowings at work in the poem, Section XIX's 'pleasant shore' not only contains echoes of 'WHEN, to the attractions of the busy World' but also contains 'Elegiac Stanzas''s 'dismal shore' and 'deep distress' within its midst, which themselves store the cumulative losses of 'shore' and 'deep' from Wordsworth's earlier poems. In borrowing the language of 'Elegiac Stanzas', Tennyson reactivates a lost trope (Wordsworth himself acknowledges that the link between mind and nature is broken), simultaneously confirming both that the form is a sad mechanic exercise and that it acts as a template for Tennyson's own sad mechanic exercise – the poem itself. The 'eye, and ear' (II. l. 107) of 'Tintern Abbey' are now 'blind' (l. 56); the 'gleams / Of past existence' (II. ll. 149–50) become 'the light that never was' (l. 15). In the 'Character of the Happy Warrior' (1807), which like 'Elegiac Stanzas' is concerned with the drowning of John Wordsworth (rather than the death of Nelson),[105] the mind is able to exercise an imaginative power in the face of grief,[106] but this imaginative power is lost in 'Elegiac Stanzas'. Wordsworth suggests, rather, that there is no imaginative transcendence over death and that loss must be 'born [sic]' (l. 58). The poem moves towards an acceptance of faith in a divine power; God is not named in the poem, but there is a sense that the speaker 'as in the elegies composed the previous year . . . strives to inculcate a proper humility towards a divine order he cannot understand, but which has demonstrated the centrality of pain in human life'.[107] 'Elegiac Stanzas' might be a sad mechanic exercise on which Tennyson draws as a standard for the sad mechanic exercise that the pastoral has become, but he also draws on its God who is not named; 'Elegiac Stanzas' therefore steers Tennyson towards healing his 'crisis' or anxiety of faith.

Section CXXX of *In Memoriam* sees Hallam as 'mixed with God and Nature' (l. 11). In positioning Hallam as part of nature, Tennyson once more draws on Wordsworth's poetry: 'Tintern Abbey' and 'The Solitary Reaper' (1807) echo through the section, mixing Hallam with God and a Wordsworthian pantheistic Nature. In 'Tintern Abbey', the speaker hopes that in 'thy voice' (II. l. 117), that is, Dorothy's voice, he will 'catch / The language of [his] former heart' (II. ll. 117–18). Tennyson echoes the earlier poem's 'Thy voice' in the opening line of the section, inspiring him with the hope that he too can catch the language of his former heart in Hallam's voice. The allusion to 'Tintern Abbey' is underpinned by the 'rolling air' of line 1, which recalls 'Tintern Abbey''s sense sublime that 'rolls through all things' (II. l. 102). Ricks, in his gloss to the poem, notes the section's affiliation to Hallam's own poem to Tennyson's sister Emily, *Lady, I Bid Thee* 6: '"Old Dante's voice encircles all the air"'.[108] He also notes an allusion to Shelley's *Adonais* lines 370–87, beginning: '"He is made one with Nature: there is heard / His voice in all her music"'.[109] But 'Tintern Abbey''s 'thy voice' both opens and closes the section, 'circling' Hallam in their embrace:

Thy voice is on the rolling air;
   I hear thee where the waters run;
   Thou standest in the rising sun,
And in the setting thou art fair.

What art thou then? I cannot guess;
   But though I seem in star and flower
   To feel thee some diffusive power,
I do not therefore love thee less:

My love involves the love before;
   My love is vaster passion now;
   Though mixed with God and Nature thou,
I seem to love thee more and more.

Far-off thou art, but ever nigh;
   I have thee still, and I rejoice;
   I prosper, circled with thy voice;
I shall not lose thee though I die.

                              (CXXX. ll. 1–16)

Lawrence Kramer points out that 'star and flower' in CXXX, line 6, is an allusion to 'SHE dwelt among the untrodden ways', a seemingly appropriate phrase as the citation 'belong[s] to the mourning poet's state of mind before death has intruded on it'.[110] Death has intruded on Tennyson's speaker's mind here, however, but the presence of Wordsworth's pantheism nevertheless allows him to 'prosper', circled as he is by Hallam's, or rather, Dorothy's voice. Another intertext is also at work in these lines too, as 'Far-off' (CXXX. l. 13) recalls Wordsworth's 'The Solitary Reaper' (1807) and the Reaper's cyclical pattern of revisiting old, unhappy, far-off things: 'Will no one tell me what she sings? / Perhaps the plaintive numbers flow / For old, unhappy, far-off things, / And battles long ago' (III. ll. 17–20). Hallam is a far-off thing, but paradoxically 'ever nigh'.

In giving his account of a terroristic nature in Section LVI, Tennyson calls on 'thy voice' from 'Tintern Abbey' 'to soothe and bless' the futile and frail life of modern science as represented in Charles Lyell's second volume of the *Principles of Geology*, with its suggestion that both the individual and species must perish:[111] 'O life as futile then as frail! / O for thy voice to soothe and bless! / What hope of answer, or redress? / Behind the veil, behind the veil' (LVI. ll. 25–8). These sections of the poem can themselves be seen as the culmination of an alien Wordsworthian nature. 'Elegiac Stanzas' makes manifestly clear a nature that is alienated from the mind that observes it. Correspondences abound between the earlier poem and Tennyson's poem in terms of a nature that is alien and indeed violent. 'Nature, red in tooth and claw' (LVI. l. 15) is red with anger and rage, as well as blood, and this is adumbrated in 'Elegiac Stanzas', with its sea in 'anger' (l. 44), which is a 'passionate Work!' (l. 45); similarly, the swell of the sea in the poem is 'deadly' (l. 47), the sky 'rueful' (l. 48), making for 'a pageantry of fear!' (l. 48); the wind is 'fierce' and the waves trample (l. 52).

Curiously, the famous closing lines of LVI – 'Behind the veil, behind the veil' – also borrow from Wordsworth, building on the Shelleyan and Coleridgean influences already at work.[112] In a late poem of 1833, one of his 'Itinerary Poems', Wordsworth ponders the role of 'Imaginative faith' in relation to 'Science' and 'Reason':

> DESIRE we past illusions to recall?
> To reinstate wild Fancy would we hide
> Truths whose thick veil Science has drawn aside.
> No, – let this Age, high as she may, install
> In her esteem the thirst that wrought man's fall,
> The universe is infinitely wide,
> And conquering Reason, if self-glorified,
> Can nowhere move uncrossed by some new wall
> Or gulf of mystery, which thou alone,
> Imaginative Faith! canst overleap,
> In progress toward the fount of Love, – the throne
> Of power, whose ministering Spirits records keep
> Of periods fixed, and laws established, less
> Flesh to exalt than prove its nothingness.[113]

Wordsworth's poem has an implicit influence on Tennyson's text, in its validation of 'Imaginative Faith' and its ability to protect 'Truth'. 'Truth' remains accessible, despite its thick veil being drawn aside by 'Science', as there is no 'new wall / Or gulf of mystery' that 'Imaginative Faith' (not 'wild Fancy') cannot surmount in support of it.[114] In urging his readers to 'Look behind the veil', Tennyson thus reprieves Wordsworth's 'faith' in the imagination and its ability to discover truth, a truth that is able to resist the encroachments of evolutionary science, as it makes its progress towards the 'fount of Love'; the 'universe is infinitely wide', as Wordsworth's speaker says, allowing for the co-existence of both 'Imaginative Faith' and 'Reason'. When Tennyson's speaker asks 'What hope of answer, or redress?', then the answer to this question is already provided in the text by Wordsworth's 'Imaginative Faith' and its conduit to 'Truth'. Tennyson was not antithetical to science. Writing to Tennyson's son, Hallam, Lord Tennyson, Professor Henry Sidgwick, the utilitarian philosopher and economist, confirms that for Tennyson,

> the physical world is always the world as known to us through physical science: the scientific view of it dominates his thoughts about it; and his general acceptance of this view is real and sincere, even

when he utters the intensest feeling of its inadequacy to satisfy our deepest needs.[115]

Sidgwick goes on to discuss feeling itself in relation to science or reason as it appears in Section CXXIV of *In Memoriam*:

> If e'er when faith had fallen asleep,
>   I heard a voice 'believe no more'
>   And heard an ever-breathing shore
> That tumbled in the Godless deep;
>
> A warmth within the breast would melt
>   The freezing reason's colder part,
>   And like a man in wrath the heart
> Stood up and answered 'I have felt.'
>
> No, like a child in doubt and fear:
>   But that blind clamour made me wise;
>   Then was I as a child that cries,
> But, crying, knows his father near.
>
> (CXXIV. ll. 9–20)

Sidgwick claims that:

> At this point, if the stanzas had stopped here ['I have felt'], we should have shaken our heads and said, 'Feeling must not usurp the function of Reason. Feeling is not knowing. It is the duty of a rational being to follow truth wherever it leads.'
>   But the poet's instinct knows this; he knows that this usurpation by Feeling of the function of Reason is too bold and confident; accordingly in the next stanza he gives the turn to humility in the protest of Feeling which is required (I think) to win the assent of the 'man in men' at this stage of human thought.[116]

Sidgwick recognises how in Tennyson spiritual feeling comes not to override reason but to work in its 'proper' place alongside it. Wordsworth's 'Imaginative Faith' is closely aligned with 'feeling' – for Wordsworth, poetry is 'the spontaneous overflow of powerful feelings'.[117] But in Wordsworth, imaginative power is also closely linked to feeling: Michael O'Neill reminds us, for instance, that

> Romantic epiphanies often reveal to the poet an inner imaginative power, states in which, in Wordsworth's phrase, 'We have had

deepest feeling that the mind / Is lord and master, and that outward sense / Is but the obedient servant of her will' (*The Prelude*, 1805, ll. 271–3).[118]

Wordsworth's 'Imaginative Faith' in Section LVI in this way forms a bridge to Section CXXIV, allowing Tennyson also to claim that he has 'felt'. Wordsworth's 1833 poem also acts as a template for Tennyson in its successful alignment of (imaginative) faith and reason, allowing Tennyson to make an alignment between his own spiritual faith or feeling and that of reason.

'That friend of mine who lives in God': Endings and Beginnings

The co-existence of faith and reason in Section LVI prepare the speaker for his accommodation with faith and science at the close of the poem, that 'combination of evolutionism and spiritual hope'.[119] 'Regret is dead, but love is more' ('Epilogue', l. 17). Wordsworth forms a presence in the Epilogue as much as he does in any other part of the poem. The Epilogue ends with the marriage of a 'daughter of our house' ('Epilogue', l. 7), sealing the accommodations the text is making with God and science into an emblem of domesticity and fraternity. The speaker gives a description of the bride: 'O when her life was yet in bud, / He too foretold the perfect rose. / For thee she grew, for thee she grows / For ever, and as fair as good' ('Epilogue', ll. 33–6), and again, 'Now waiting to be made a wife, / Her feet, my darling, on the dead; / Their pensive tablets round her head, / And the most living words of life / Breathed in her ear' ('Epilogue', ll. 49–53). Tennyson borrows from Wordsworth's 'Intimations' ode once more, with the perfect rose that grows 'For ever'; what was forever lost is now forever found. The 'living' words, too, suggest the 'living soul' of 'Tintern Abbey', infused with joy and the power of seeing into the life of things; and also perhaps the 'living man', longing to pursue the dead. Similarly, the speaker addresses the moon:

> And rise, O moon, from yonder down,
>   Till over down and over dale
>   All night the shining vapour sail
> And pass the silent-lighted town,

> The white-faced halls, the glancing rills,
>   And catch at every mountain head,
>   And o'er the friths that branch and spread
> Their sleeping silver through the hills;
>
> And touch with shade the bridal doors,
>   With tender gloom the roof, the wall;
>   And breaking let the splendour fall
> To spangle all the happy shores
>
> By which they rest, and ocean sounds,
>   And, star and system rolling past,
>   A soul shall draw from out the vast
> And strike his being into bounds,
>
> And, moved through life of lower phase,
>   Result in man, be born and think,
>   And act and love, a closer link
> Betwixt us and the crowning race.
>
> ('Epilogue', ll. 109–28)

The touch of shade echoes Section XCV with its touching of 'shades' from the classical past, suggesting here that Tennyson is continuing to try to connect with Hallam. The moon that is invoked to 'catch at every mountain head' and 'To spangle all the happy shores' evokes Wordsworth's 'Elegiac Verse', 'In Memory of My Brother, John Wordsworth' (1842), where the speaker finds the consolation he seeks in the 'Meek Flower!',[120] 'Spangling a cushion green like moss' (l. 57), which he finds once he has crossed the 'mountain' (l. 60). As Sacks makes clear, the consolation in Wordsworth's poem is found once the speaker has crossed the mountain, crossed over into death, and is derived from a 'scarcely transformed sexual impulse toward the mother earth'.[121] In spangling all the happy shores, Tennyson thus feeds on the Christian consolation to which Wordsworth moves in his poem. Wordsworth allows Tennyson finally to embrace God, after guiding him to God via the 'Elegiac Stanzas'.

The poem ends with the speaker explicitly acknowledging his commitment to both Christian faith and contemporary science, simultaneously making Hallam into a semi-divine creature:

> Of those that, eye to eye, shall look
>   On knowledge; under whose command
>   Is Earth and Earth's, and in their hand
> Is Nature like an open book;

No longer half-akin to brute,
  For all we thought and loved and did,
  And hoped, and suffered, is but seed
Of what in them is flower and fruit;

Whereof the man, that with me trod
  This planet, was a noble type
  Appearing ere the times were ripe,
That friend of mine who lives in God,

That God, which ever lives and loves,
  One God, one law, one element,
  And one far-off divine event,
To which the whole creation moves.

('Epilogue', ll. 129–44)

The open book is in the hand of those who look to scientific knowledge; as Ricks points out, the metaphor of the open book 'was invigorated by its geological aptness'.[122] Likewise, 'That God, which ever lives and loves / One God, one law, one element, / And one far-off divine event' evoke the Book of Revelation and Hallam's *On the Picture of the Three Fates*.[123] Not surprisingly, given Tennyson's borrowing of Wordsworth's words and phrases throughout the poem, the section is inflected with Wordsworth's language; the hand that holds Nature like an open book bears an imprint of the hand that reaches into the underworld looking for the lost loved one; the 'one far-off divine event' evokes Wordsworth's Reaper and her revisiting of 'old, unhappy, far-off things' (III. l. 19). Ricks suggests that there is a 'loving companionship' with James Thomson here, from whom Tennyson 'inherited the right kind of gloom',[124] a 'solidarity with the unterrible muse of Thomson against the terrible Muses'.[125] Likewise, he maintains that the poem here 'reaches a hand through time to catch the far-off interest of Shakespeare's tears',[126] and well they might do. But in echoing the phrase 'far-off' the poem begins and ends with Wordsworth. If there is an investment in tears to be had, as Section I promises and the poem makes manifest through its movement towards the one divine event towards which the whole creation moves, then this investment is achieved in the poem with the help of the Wordsworthian language that transects it. Even so, in a paradoxical movement consonant with many of the Wordsworthian effects in the poem, the echo reminds us that this investment cannot fully shake off its associations with 'old, unhappy, far-off things'.

Conclusion

Tennyson has echoed and borrowed Wordsworth's language and phrasing throughout the poem – to unravel the complexities of his faith; to make communion with Hallam; to secure a public voice; to investigate nature; to make an accommodation between faith and reason. Wordsworth limits Tennyson at times, but limitation turns to nourishment in part, as in the case of the 'Elegiac Stanzas', where the disjunction between mind and nature itself becomes enabling. If the poem is transected by Wordsworthian affiliations and connections, then this fine network or web becomes an intricate scaffolding of support. The presence of Wordsworth's language in the text allows Tennyson to define himself and his poetry in relation to his Romantic past and both to express the crisis of self and to work towards mitigating that crisis. A complex pattern of echo and allusion is at work in the poem. Tennyson is not flooded by Wordsworth's poetry; rather, Tennyson benefits from his precursor's presence, even Wordsworth's 'difficulty' in articulating a public voice. The echoic pattern is overwhelmingly productive rather than overwhelming, supporting the Ricksian model of benign influence; a community of 'poets' is created. In drawing on Wordsworth in the way that he does, Tennyson validates Wordsworth's later poetry, stabilising Wordsworth's 'Victorian' reputation, mediating Wordsworth's public voice, and validating Wordsworth's move away from the transcendent in the 'Elegiac Stanzas'. At the same time, Wordsworth's presence assuages Tennyson's poetic and religious anxiety. Tennyson's echoing of Wordsworth is not made up of impulsive, defensive gestures that 'weaken' the earlier poet, but small, incremental acts of affiliation and reinvention that allow Tennyson to achieve form.

Tennyson published a number of occasional poems in the slip-stream of *In Memoriam*, including 'To the Queen' (1851), his first publication as Poet Laureate, 'Ode on the Death of the Duke of Wellington' (1852), 'Will' (1855) and 'To the Rev. F. D. Maurice' (1855). Other poems published during this period include 'The Daisy' (1855), a poem written to Tennyson's wife Emily, remembering their Italian tour of 1851.[127] 'To the Queen' pays express homage to Wordsworth as Tennyson's predecessor as Laureate – 'This laurel greener from the brows / Of him that uttered nothing base' (ll. 7–8) – and some of the poems themselves reiterate Wordsworthian themes, and, indeed, language. 'The Daisy', for instance, despite its Horation metre, draws on the Wordsworthian trope of the self in time, of a 'plucked' (l. 88) daisy, that 'told of England then to me, / And now it tells of Italy' (ll. 89–90). The daisy, crushed and dry and pressed into the pages of a book, becomes the 'nurseling of another sky' (l. 98) and another self: the speaker is 'ill and weary, alone and cold' (l. 96) in his 'dark city' (l. 95) here tonight. Despite the power of the daisy to transform the speaker's present, the past remains unrecoverable: he can only dream his wife still beside him and his fancy fled to the South again. Or, rather the daisy elucidates how the self changes ineluctably with time, while, paradoxically, remaining constant. The poem, typically, draws directly from Wordsworth's language for its exploration of loss: 'The gloom that saddens Heaven and Earth' (l. 102), for instance, acts as a reminder of Wordsworth's 'Epitaph for Jemima Quillinan' (written in 1822), where 'These Vales were saddened with no common gloom'.[128] The gloom that saddened Wordsworth's vales widens out in Tennyson to include 'Heaven and Earth, / The bitter east, the misty summer / And gray metropolis of the North' (ll. 102–4).

In 1855 Tennyson published *Maud*, a poem that engages with Wordsworth in a more complex way than any of the occasional poems listed above. *Maud*, the subject of the next chapter, is experimental, said to be in Oedipal conflict with Wordsworth,[129] and one of Tennyson's favourites – his '"pet bantling"',[130] as he affectionately terms it.

Notes

1. Tennyson, *The Poems of Tennyson*, II, XCV. l. 34 (p. 413). All future references to *In Memoriam* are to this volume and appear parenthetically in the text, as do references to other Tennyson poems in the chapter unless otherwise stated.
2. Tennyson was appointed Poet Laureate on the basis of Prince Albert's admiration for *In Memoriam A. H. H. OBIIT MDCCCXXXIII*. See Ricks, in Tennyson, *The Poems of Tennyson*, II, p. 463, quoting from *Alfred, Lord Tennyson: A Memoir*, I, p. 334. Please note, the shorter title of the poem will be used in the chapter, as it is throughout the book.
3. See Tennyson, *The Poems of Tennyson*, II, p. 312.
4. Perry, 'Elegy', p. 118.
5. Perry, 'Elegy', p. 117.
6. Eliot, *Selected Prose*, p. 245.
7. Perry, 'Elegy', p. 116.
8. Douglas-Fairhurst, *Victorian Afterlives*, p. 261.
9. Page, *Tennyson: Interviews and Recollections*, p. 71.

10. Ball, 'Tennyson and the Romantics', p. 11.
11. Ball, 'Tennyson and the Romantics', p. 11.
12. Ball, 'Tennyson and the Romantics', p. 11.
13. Ricks cites Shakespeare's sonnet sequence as 'an important source for *In Memoriam*'. See Ricks, *Tennyson*, p. 214.
14. Ricks, *Allusion to the Poets*, p. 188.
15. Ricks, *Allusion to the Poets*, p. 188.
16. Ricks, *Allusion to the Poets*, p. 188.
17. Ricks, *Allusion to the Poets*, p. 188.
18. Ricks, *Allusion to the Poets*, p. 195. The 'Intimations' ode quotation is taken from *The Poetical Works of William Wordsworth in Five Volumes*, IV, l. 144 (p. 353). All subsequent references to this, and other, Wordsworth poems appear parenthetically in the text and are to these volumes unless otherwise stated. References are given via volume and line number.
19. See Ricks' note to lyric XIX, in *The Poems of Tennyson*, II, p. 338.
20. Kramer, 'Victorian Sexuality and "Tintern Abbey"', pp. 405–6.
21. See Ricks, in *The Poems of Tennyson*, II, pp. 361–2, xliv 4.
22. See Ricks, in *The Poems of Tennyson*, II, p. 429, cvii 11.
23. See Ricks, in *The Poems of Tennyson*, II, p. 443, cxxiii 8.
24. Ricks, *Allusion to the Poets*, p. 199.
25. Bloom, *The Anxiety of Influence*, p. 64.
26. Bloom, *The Anxiety of Influence*, pp. 7, 31.
27. Hollander, 'The Anxiety of Influence'.
28. See Ricks, in *The Poems of Tennyson*, II, p. 312.
29. Barthes, *Image-Music-Text*, p. 159.
30. Barthes, *Image-Music-Text*, p. 160.
31. Barthes, *Image-Music-Text*, p. 159.
32. Sacks, *The English Elegy*, p. 18.
33. Tennyson annotates the sixth line of 'Œnone' in *Poems*, p. 51. Moxon's published line describes 'A path thro' steepdown granite walls below / Mantled with flowering tended twine' (ll. 5–6). Tennyson, however, handwrites the phrase 'all at once' above the published line 6, positing 'all at once' as an alternative to 'flowering tended twine', which would allow the line to read 'Mantled with flowers all at once'. The phrase is excluded from subsequent published editions of the poem, but Tennyson's annotation to the 1833 version echoes Wordsworth's 1807 poem with its fair 'bower' (l. 8), echoes that reappear in Section XCV of *In Memoriam*. See *Poems*, with autograph additions and corrections, Fitzwilliam Museum, Cambridge.
34. See, for instance, Rapf, '"Visionaries of Dereliction"', p. 378, and Perry, *Alfred Tennyson*, p. 141. Rapf claims 'that it is language', the speaker's reading of Hallam's letters, that 'leads to the perception of another level of reality' in Section XCV; Perry suggests that 'the poem comes nearest to the *peripeteia* of classical elegy in Section XCV, which describes a numinous communion while Tennyson is reading Hallam's letters'.

35. See Ricks, in Tennyson, *The Poems of Tennyson*, II, p. 413, xcv 36.
36. Hollander notices the way in which poems seem 'to echo prior ones for the personal aural benefit of the poet, and . . . whichever poetic followers can overhear the reverberations'. See 'Preface', in *The Figure of Echo*, p. ix.
37. Perry, 'Elegy', p. 119.
38. See Douglas-Fairhurst, 'Tennyson', pp. 613–14, for more on endings in Tennyson.
39. Ricks offers an allusion in the middle lines of the stanza here to Milton, *On Time* 22, in these lines: 'Triumphing over Death, and Chance, and thee O Time'. See Ricks, in *The Poems of Tennyson*, II, p. 413, n. xcv 42–3.
40. See Ricks, in Tennyson, *The Poems of Tennyson*, II, p. 413, xcv 36, for more on Tennyson's quibbles over the possessive adjective 'his'.
41. Wordsworth, 'Essay, Supplementary to the Preface', p. 358. Michael O'Neill points out how the word '"seems" [is the] catalyst of many Romantic epiphanies'. See O'Neill, *The All-Sustaining Air*, p. 50.
42. Quoted in Hartman, 'Retrospect 1971', in *Wordsworth's Poetry 1787–1814*, p. xiv.
43. Hartman describes Wordsworth's encounter with the daffodils in 'I WANDERED lonely as a Cloud', as 'casual' and a 'mild seizure or ecstasy'. See Hartman, *The Unremarkable Wordsworth*, p. 23.
44. I quote Wu's version of the poem here. See *Wordsworth: An Inner Life*, ll. 242–7 (p. 22). Wu himself draws from *Early Poems and Fragments*.
45. Wu, *Wordsworth: An Inner Life*, p. 22.
46. Wu, *Wordsworth: An Inner Life*, p. 306.
47. Wu, *Wordsworth: An Inner Life*, p. 307.
48. Wu, *Wordsworth: An Inner Life*, p. 306. The lines from 'The Tuft of Primroses' are quoted from Wu's book; the draft itself never made it into print. See ll. 42–4 (pp. 306–7). Subsequent quotations from this edition are given in the chapter.
49. Wu, *Wordsworth: An Inner Life*, pp. 307–8.
50. Wu, *Wordsworth: An Inner Life*, p. 24.
51. Wu, *Wordsworth: An Inner Life*, p. 25.
52. Perry, *Alfred Tennyson*, p. 33.
53. Sacks, *The English Elegy*, p. 172.
54. Hollander, 'The Anxiety of Influence'.
55. Wu, *Wordsworth: An Inner Life*, p. 306.
56. Eliot, 'Little Gidding II', in *Collected Poems: 1909–1962*, l. 39 (p. 204).
57. Brown, *A Familiar Compound Ghost*, p. 180.
58. Brown, *A Familiar Compound Ghost*, p. 180.
59. Hartman, *Wordsworth's Poetry 1787–1814*, p. 123.
60. Wu, *Wordsworth: An Inner Life*, p. 199.
61. Wu, *Wordsworth: An Inner Life*, p. 24.

62. Wu, *Wordsworth: An Inner Life*, p. 199.
63. Wu, *Wordsworth: An Inner Life*, p. 308.
64. Wu, *Wordsworth: An Inner Life*, p. 308.
65. Kennedy, '*In Memoriam* and the Tradition of Pastoral Elegy', p. 362.
66. See Decker, 'Tennyson's Limitations', p. 73, n. 22. Decker's discussion of Orpheus' backward glance relates to Tennyson's 'Ulysses', but his reading of allusion as 'simultaneously an act of taking possession and a sign of irrevocable loss and separation' has an applicability with my own reading here.
67. See Ricks, in Tennyson, *The Poems of Tennyson*, II, p. 412, xcv 18: 'The setting and mood suggest Gray's *Elegy* 1–4: ". . . And leaves the world to darkness and to me"'.
68. Gray, *The Complete Poems of Thomas Gray: English, Latin and Greek*, ll. 5–6 (p. 37).
69. Wu, *Wordsworth: An Inner Life*, p. 32.
70. Wu, *Wordsworth: An Inner Life*, p. 32.
71. Wu, *Wordsworth: An Inner Life*, p. 32.
72. See Wu, *Wordsworth: An Inner Life*, p. 57.
73. I quote from Wu's version of the text. See *Wordsworth: An Inner Life*, ll. 1–5 (p. 57) and pp. 57–8, n. 31.
74. Wu, *Wordsworth: An Inner Life*, p. 61.
75. The Macmillan Eversley edition of the poem, edited by Hallam, Lord Tennyson, glosses the Pacific Islanders as 'barbarian'. See 'Notes' to *In Memoriam*, in *The Works of Tennyson*, III, p. 234, n. 76.
76. Ricks, in Tennyson, *The Poems of Tennyson*, II, p. 358, xl 32.
77. Ricks, in Tennyson, *The Poems of Tennyson*, II, p. 358, xl 21–32.
78. Perry, 'Elegy', p. 118.
79. Perry, 'Elegy', p. 118.
80. Perry, 'Elegy', p. 118.
81. Perry, 'Elegy', p. 118.
82. Wheeler, *Heaven, Hell, and the Victorians*, pp. 23–5, quoted in Cole, 'The Recovery of Friendship', p. 54.
83. See Ricks, in Tennyson, *The Poems of Tennyson*, II, p. 360, xliii.
84. See Ricks, in Tennyson, *The Poems of Tennyson*, II, p. 415, xcvii.
85. Kant, *Critique of Pure Reason*, p. 23.
86. See Ricks, in Tennyson, *The Poems of Tennyson*, II, pp. 415–16, xcvii.
87. Mellor, *Romanticism and Gender*, p. 19.
88. Mellor, *Romanticism and Gender*, p. 19.
89. Mellor, *Romanticism and Gender*, p. 19.
90. Cole, 'The Recovery of Friendship', p. 54.
91. Decker, 'Tennyson's Limitations', p. 66.
92. Perry, 'Elegy', p. 122.
93. Perry, 'Elegy', p. 122.

94. Perry, 'Elegy', p. 122.

95. See Ricks, in Tennyson, *The Poems of Tennyson*, II, p. 338, xix.

96. See Ricks, in Tennyson, *The Poems of Tennyson*, II, p. 338, xix.

97. Tennyson, *The Poems of Tennyson*, II, p. 338, xix 3; and Shatto and Shaw, *In Memoriam*, p. 182, l. 3.

98. Selincourt, in *The Poetical Works of William Wordsworth*, p. 120, n.1.

99. See *The Poetical Works of William Wordsworth in Five Volumes*, III, p. 100, 'Note'.

100. Ricks, in Tennyson, *The Poems of Tennyson*, II, p. 326, vii 7.

101. See Tennyson, *The Poems of Tennyson*, I, p. 175. Ricks records how the poem, written in 1826, was published in October 1830 in *The Gem* for 1831, but not reprinted. He also notes that the poem acts as the germ of 'Tears, Idle Tears'. Subsequent references to the poem appear parenthetically in the text.

102. Wordsworth, *Poems, in Two Volumes*, II, ll. 5–12 (p. 141). All subsequent references to this poem appear parenthetically in the text.

103. See Wordsworth, 'Preface to the Edition Published in 1815', pp. xxxvii–xxxviii.

104. 'Deep' is often synonymous with the sea in Tennyson's poetry. In 'The Kraken' (1830), for instance, the Kraken sleeps 'Below the thunders of the upper deep'. See *The Poems* of *Tennyson*, I, l. 1 (p. 269).

105. Wu, *Wordsworth: An Inner Life*, p. 14.

106. Wu, *Wordsworth: An Inner Life*, p. 14.

107. Wu, *Wordsworth: An Inner Life*, p. 249.

108. See Ricks, in Tennyson, *The Poems of Tennyson*, II, p. 450, cxxx i.

109. See Ricks, in Tennyson, *The Poems of Tennyson*, II, p. 450, cxxx i.

110. Kramer, 'Victorian Poetry/Oedipal Politics', p. 359.

111. See Ricks, in Tennyson, *The Poems of Tennyson*, II, p. 372, lvi.

112. See Ricks, in Tennyson, *The Poems of Tennyson*, II, p. 374, lvi 28. Ricks points out that 'veil' was a favourite word of Shelley's and quotes John Beer's note on how the phrase 'behind the veil' appears in Coleridge's *Aids to Reflection*.

113. Wordsworth, *Yarrow Revisited; and Other Poems*, p. 199.

114. See note 103 above on Wordsworth and 'fancy'.

115. Tennyson, '*In Memoriam*, Introduction by the Editor', pp. 201–2.

116. Tennyson, '*In Memoriam*, Introduction by the Editor', p. 202.

117. Wordsworth, 'Preface to the Second Edition', p. 382.

118. See O'Neill, '"Infinite Passion"', p. 185.

119. Day, *Tennyson's Scepticism*, p. 138.

120. Wordsworth, *Poems, Chiefly of Early and Late Years*, l. 52 (p. 62).

121. Sacks, *The English Elegy*, p. 33.

122. See Ricks, in Tennyson, *The Poems of Tennyson*, II, p. 458, E 132.

123. See Ricks, in Tennyson, *The Poems of Tennyson*, II, pp. 458–9, E 141–4.

124. Ricks, *Allusion to the Poets*, p. 213.
125. Ricks, *Allusion to the Poets*, p. 213.
126. Ricks, *Allusion to the Poets*, p. 198.
127. Ricks, in Tennyson, *The Poems of Tennyson*, II, p. 494.
128. Line 1 from the 'Epitaph for Jemima Quillinan' is quoted from *Last Poems, 1821–1850*, p. 27.
129. Shires, '*Maud*, Masculinity and Poetic Identity', p. 280, as quoted in Pease, '*Maud* and its Discontents', p. 102.
130. Tennyson, *Alfred Lord Tennyson: A Memoir*, I, p. 468.

Chapter 4

Monodrama and Madness: *Maud* and the Shrieking of the Wainscot Mouse

Maud was published in 1855, just five years after *In Memoriam*. Originally titled *Maud or the Madness*, the poem was developed from the germ of the lyric 'Oh! that 'twere possible', written in 1833–4, shortly after the death of Arthur Henry Hallam.[1] The division into Parts I and II was made in 1859; the division into Part III in 1865; and the subtitle, *A Monodrama*, was added in 1875. The monodrama has eighteenth-century roots, although as Christopher Ricks points out in his gloss on the poem, the 'term *monodrama* was commonly used of any dramatic performance intended for a single actor . . . It was used where we would use the term *dramatic monologue*'.[2] The poem was met with sustained criticism, not least because of its 'innovatory' form, a fact Tennyson defensively acknowledges even towards the end of his life, saying to Henry van Dyke in 1892:

> You must remember always, in reading it, what it is meant to be – a drama in lyrics. It shows the unfolding of a lonely, morbid soul, touched with inherited madness . . . The things which seem like faults belong not so much to the poem as to the character of the hero.[3]

The 'faults' to which Tennyson refers include his seeming inability to master both lyric and narrative, the double strand of his 'drama in lyrics'. T. S. Eliot, in a stinging critique, describes what he regards as Tennyson's almost congenital inability to master narrative; his poems are 'always descriptive, and always picturesque; they are never really narrative . . . But for narrative Tennyson had no gift at all'.[4] Yet Eliot concedes that in *Maud* Tennyson turns such limitation to good account: '*Maud* consists of a few very beautiful lyrics . . . around which the semblance of a dramatic situation has been constructed with the greatest metrical virtuosity.'[5] Carol T. Christ too notes how 'the disjunction of the lyrics in *Maud* mirrors the hero's psychological disjunction',[6] and how 'this way of structuring the long poem' also offers the poet 'a way of transforming [his] difficulty in sustaining dramatic action to expressive opportunity'.[7]

Describing the poem as a '"Drama of the Soul" . . . The "antiphonal voice to *In Memoriam*", which is the "Way of the Soul"',[8] Hallam Tennyson gives a fuller account of the poem's 'peculiarity', however, drawing attention to the poem's innovation:

> This poem of *Maud or the Madness* is a little *Hamlet*, the history of a morbid, poetic soul, under the blighting influence of a recklessly speculative age. He is the heir of madness, an egoist with the makings of a cynic, raised to a pure and holy love which elevates his whole nature, passing from the height of triumph to the lowest depth of misery, driven into madness by the loss of her whom he has loved, and, when he has at length passed through the fiery furnace, and has recovered his reason, giving himself up to work for the good of mankind through the unselfishness born of a great passion. The peculiarity of this poem is that different phases of passion in one person take the place of different characters.[9]

Tennyson, speaking to James Knowles in 1870–1, also emphasises the innovatory nature of his dramatic achievement: '"No other poem (a monotone with plenty of change and no weariness) has been made into a drama where successive phases of passion in one person take the place of successive persons. It is slightly akin to *Hamlet*"'.[10] For many of the poem's critics, however, there was indeed too much change and not enough weariness.

But there are many voices to which *Maud* is slightly akin, not only *Hamlet*, including Shakespeare's *Romeo and Juliet*, Sir Walter Scott's *Bride of Lammermoor*, Charles Kingsley's *Alton Locke* (1850),[11] the Spasmodic School, with its depictions of extreme subjectivity,[12] Keats' 'Isabella' (1820), Thomas Hood's 'The Dream of Eugene Aram, the Murderer' (1929; 1831), Persian poetry and Edward Bulwer-Lytton's first novel, *Falkland* (1827).[13] The monodrama is also indebted to Tennyson's earlier monologues, 'Ulysses', 'Tiresias' and 'St Simeon Stylites'.[14] The poem, too, is replete with autobiographical references: as Susan Shatto confirms, *Maud* was to Tennyson what *David Copperfield* was to Dickens, his favourite child;[15] Ricks, drawing on R. W. Rader, claims that the poem sees Tennyson pulling

> together all the strands of his early life – the hero's father and his rage, the lonely mother, the old man ('of the wolds'), the politician son, and above all the love for Rosa Baring – though Maud herself blends Rosa, Sophy Rawnsley and T[ennyson]'s wife Emily.[16]

Likewise, the passages of the poem that deal directly with the Crimean War are gleaned from Tennyson's reading of newspapers and periodicals.[17] The myth of Narcissus and Echo, 'with variations, is one of the subtexts of *Maud*', although not one that Tennyson wished particularly to surface.[18] Echo herself, confined only to repeat the words of another, stands as a neat metaphor for the processes at work in the poem.

If *Maud* displays a variety of influences, however, it also displays a variety of metrical forms, in its attempt to render the speaker's successive stages of passion; these include ballad, heroic couplet, alexandrines and epithalamion. As Richard Cronin observes: 'The speaker's struggle to win or to retain his sanity is acted out within the verse line.'[19] But the voices in the poem also include that of Wordsworth; it is this chapter's contention that Wordsworth has a far bigger part to play in the poem than previously recognised, traceable through the borrowings and echoes of words and phrases in the poem. These borrowings operate alongside the well-established echo-chamber of voices the poem is known to contain, such as those cited above. The presence of this borrowed language creates a multiplicity of effects: some borrowings allow Tennyson to remodulate Wordsworth, allowing him to define himself in relation to his predecessor; others define him in turn, controlling the trajectory of the poem and questioning its narrative form; others allow Tennyson to address issues which the poem ostensibly avoids; yet others allow Tennyson to question his role as a public poet and as a poet of sensation. The poem is thus challenged, deflected, supported, sustained and questioned by the Wordsworthian language it contains. Linda M. Shires claims that the poem's intertextuality is evidence of a poetic identity buttressed by the male poetic tradition.[20] According to Shires *Maud* 'records the strain of adhering to a patriarchal code and of achieving the stable, unified poetic voice for which it so yearns'.[21] In exploiting Wordsworth's language, Tennyson does indeed draw on yet another series of male, canonised intertexts, yet the effect of Wordsworth's presence cannot simply be defined by the strain of Tennyson adhering to a patriarchal code.

It has also been claimed that *Maud*, Tennyson's first non-occasional poem as Laureate, is the result of an Oedipal rivalry with Wordsworth, on the basis of Wordsworth not only as Tennyson's poetic-father but also as the poet from whom Tennyson inherited the Laureateship in 1850, which, it has been suggested, induced in the later poet a crisis of authority and identity.[22] Certainly, *Maud* asserts its difference from its precursor, with its speaker sharing the 'subjectivity and the reciprocation of the imagination with the world' of the Wordsworthian speaker;[23] he is 'considered inoperative because of that very subjectivity',[24] descending into alienating and catastrophic madness. The poem also acts as a critique of the poetry of sensation – of the 'potentially distorting effects of viewing the world from the perspective of unhealthy preoccupations with one's own feelings'.[25]

The chapter acknowledges Harold Bloom's theory of influence, but suggests that his somewhat monolithic model cannot fully explain the processes at work in the text, which work at the linguistic level rather than the level of psychic disturbance; if there is evidence of Oedipal rivalry, then this is hedged and revised by the effects of the language itself within the poem. The borrowings are not working at the level of deep impulse or defensiveness, then, but more at the level of deep pragmatism. The chapter accepts in this respect that there is a level of poetic anxiety at work, but proposes that this anxiety is more compositional than defensive; drawing from Wordsworth affords Tennyson comfort, solidarity, community and company, assuaging his creative isolation and fear. Moreover, the chapter, in line with the main thrust of the monograph, does not locate Tennyson's creativity in anxiety,[26] nor does it accept that the poem exclusively treads upon the 'dark and daemonic ground' that is the 'anxiety of influence'.[27]

Breaking a Slumber

Wordsworth's echoing presence is clearly heard in the Maud who appears in the speaker's slumber-breaking vision in Part I of Tennyson's poem:

> Cold and clear-cut face, why come you so cruelly meek,
> Breaking a slumber in which all spleenful folly was drowned,
> Pale with the golden beam of an eyelash dead on the cheek,
> Passionless, pale, cold face, star-sweet on a gloom profound;
> Womanlike, taking revenge too deep for a transient wrong
> Done but in thought to your beauty, and ever as pale as before

Growing and fading and growing upon me without a sound,
Luminous, gemlike, ghostlike, deathlike, half the night long
Growing and fading and growing, till I could bear it no more
But arose, and all by myself in my own dark garden ground,
Listening now to the tide in its broad-flung shipwrecking roar,
Now to the scream of a maddened beach dragged down by the wave,
Walked in a wintry wind by a ghastly glimmer, and found
The shining daffodil dead, and Orion low in his grave.[28]

The description of Maud here recalls the early poems on Rosa
Baring, which Tennyson composed in 1835–6, 'I linger'd yet awhile
to bend my way', 'Ah, fade not yet from out the green arcades',
and 'How thought you that this thing could captivate?':[29] line 13
of 'How thought you that this thing could captivate?' – 'A perfect-
featured face, expressionless' – is heard, for instance, in Maud's 'cold
and clear-cut face'.[30] The shining 'daffodil' owes a debt to Wordsworth, which Tennyson openly acknowledges to his friend James
Henry Mangles.[31] But there are other, subtle Wordsworthian echoes
in this passage, including from Wordsworth's collection of 'Lucy'
poems such as 'A SLUMBER did my spirit seal' (1800) and 'SHE
dwelt among the untrodden ways' (1800). Wordsworth's collection
of poems – five in total – were added to the second edition of *Lyrical
Ballads* in 1800, except for 'I TRAVELLED among unknown men',
which was published only in a reissued edition of 1807.[32] Written on
a tour of Germany, the poems, or 'requiems',[33] are experiments not
only in what Wordsworth calls, in the 'Preface to the Second Edition'
of *Lyrical Ballads* (1800), 'the real language of men',[34] but also with
prosodic form, using the strict 'Common Measure', a form he used
in few other pieces;[35] the strict ballad form was eventually to prove
an 'uncongenial medium' for the poet, however.[36] In the second of
the ballads, 'SHE dwelt among the untrodden ways', Wordsworth
describes the isolated maid whom there were none to praise, it seems,
except the poem's speaker:

SHE dwelt among the untrodden ways
    Beside the springs of Dove,
    A Maid whom there were none to praise
And very few to love:

A Violet by a mossy stone
    Half hidden from the eye!
    – Fair as a star, when only one
Is shining in the sky.

> She lived unknown, and few could know
>   When Lucy ceased to be;
> But she is in her Grave, and, oh,
>   The difference to me!³⁷

Tennyson borrows from Wordsworth's description of Lucy in his account of Maud as 'star-sweet on a gloom profound'; but where Lucy is fair as a 'star' when only one is 'shining' in the sky, the vision of Maud forces the speaker into his garden ground where he finds the 'shining daffodil' dead. W. E. Buckler notes that the myth of Echo and Narcissus, with variations, forms a subtext in *Maud*, remarking how 'sweet Narcissus' changes in the published edition of the poem to the 'shining daffodil dead':[38] Tennyson may have made the switch, Buckler suggests, '"to keep his subtext from surfacing too obviously"'.[39] In keeping one subtext at bay, however, Tennyson allows another – Wordsworth's – to surface.

In Wordsworth, feeling is intimately linked to imagination, which is lord and master: '"We have had deepest feeling that the mind / Is lord and master, and that outward sense / Is but the obedient servant of her will" (*The Prelude*, 1805, ll. 271–3)'.[40] In Tennyson's *Maud*, the mind is ostensibly no longer lord and master; it has lost control, unable to unite subject and object and in thrall to passion. Outward sense is no longer the obedient servant of the mind's will, nature no longer in benign operation with the speaker's mind. The imaginative connection inherent in Wordsworth's daffodils, which 'flash upon that inward eye' (II. l. 21), is thwarted in Tennyson's poem: the glimmer becomes ghastly, the wind wintry, the beach maddened to a scream, the tide a shipwrecking roar. Nature itself has become alienated, a fact Tennyson explicitly acknowledges in the poem, drawing on passages of Robert Chambers' *Vestiges of the Natural History of Creation* (1844), as noticed by W. R. Rutland and John Killham:[41] 'So many a million of ages have gone to the making of man: / He now is first, but is he the last? is he not too base?' (I. IV. vi. ll. 136–7). The lines here also carry a reminder of Samuel Taylor Coleridge's 'Dejection: An Ode' (1802), where the separation between inner and outer states manifests in the wind 'Which long has raved unnoticed. What a scream / Of agony by torture lengthened out / That lute sent forth!'[42] The 'Mad Lutanist' (l. 104) 'Mak'st Devil's Yule, with worse than wintry song' (l. 106). Significantly, 'Dejection', in its first incarnation as 'Letter to Sara Hutchinson', was Coleridge's 'immediate response' to the imaginative loss charted in the first four stanzas of Wordsworth's 'Intimations' ode, read aloud to him by Dorothy

Wordsworth on 4 April 1802.[43] In the 'Preface to the Second Edition' of *Lyrical Ballads*, Wordsworth famously describes poetry as 'the spontaneous overflow of powerful feelings: it takes its origins from emotion recollected in tranquillity'.[44] But Wordsworth also confirms in his note to 'The Thorn' the condition that 'Poetry is passion; it is the history or science of feelings'.[45] Feeling is central to *Lyrical Ballads*, where it is intimately linked to sympathy; the Romantics, as Michael O'Neill says, channel 'processes of sympathy', riding the 'currents of associationist theories and a new stress on elective affinities'.[46] It is linked too '"with high objects, with eternal things" . . . with what Wordsworth ennobles as "A grandeur in the beatings of the heart"'.[47] 'SHE dwelt among the untrodden ways' exemplifies Wordsworth's elevation of feeling, with the speaker describing in minute detail how he feels about Lucy's death.[48] Lucy takes on a generalised status, representing all of the lost, insignificant Lucys in England.[49] Maud, with her courtly status, seemingly has little in common with the low-status Lucy. What she does have in common, however, is that she is the object of the speaker's intense feeling. Moreover, the speaker of 'SHE dwelt among the untrodden ways', as in the *Lyrical Ballads* generally, has a 'character-narrator' with an identity distinct from that of the poet. Wordsworth's

> character-narrators . . . attempt to represent incidents, situations, epi-sodes, experiences, etc. that have occurred in a fictionally realized past, although they may be based on actual events just as the narrator may be some refraction of the poet's identity or his autobiographical self.[50]

In his intense feeling for Maud the speaker thus functions as an extenuation of Wordsworth's speaker-characters in *Lyrical Ballads*, a speaker-narrator that may also be a refraction of Tennyson's identity or autobiographical self.

As well as drawing from 'SHE dwelt among the untrodden ways' to furnish his description of Maud, Tennyson also borrows from or echoes Wordsworth's 'A SLUMBER did my spirit seal' here to render the speaker's 'feeling'. Like 'SHE dwelt among the untrodden ways', 'A SLUMBER did my spirit seal' pivots on the speaker's 'feeling' or passion for Lucy, as he confronts the reality of her loss. But there are differences. Most obviously, Tennyson's speaker breaks a slumber, whereas in Wordsworth a slumber seals the speaker's spirit, preventing him from forming an imaginative connection with Lucy. The speaker of Wordsworth's poem is denied a vision of Lucy through his slumber, in fact, with the implicit criticism that this occasions; the speaker 'implicitly rebukes himself for having allowed such "slumber" to "seal" his "spirit", and yet to regard it as a state in which he might have been vouchsafed a true vision of Lucy's identity'.[51] Equally, the occasion for imaginative connection is lost in the hiatus between the two stanzas; 'Lucy's death or the thought of her death . . . occurs in the blank between the stanzas', as Geoffrey H. Hartman notes:[52]

> A SLUMBER did my spirit seal;
>   I had no human fears:
> She seemed a thing that could not feel
>   The touch of earthly years.
>
> No motion has she now, no force;
>   She neither hears nor sees;
> Rolled round in earth's diurnal course,
>   With rocks and stones and trees!

Unlike Wordsworth's speaker, however, Tennyson's speaker's slumber is broken, allowing him to achieve a vision of Maud; but the vision that comes on him is a nightmarish one of a cold, clear-cut face, cruelly meek, breaking a slumber in which all spleenful folly had previously been drowned. The vision is born in memory, with the speaker recalling Maud's 'provocative' ride past the speaker in her carriage, with her 'cold and clear-cut face' (I. II. l. 78). *Maud* in a sense fulfils the thwarted expectation of Wordsworth's poem, providing the vision of 'Lucy' denied to the speaker through his mistimed slumber, appearing ghostlike and deathlike but nevertheless 'clear-cut'. If the Lucy of 'A SLUMBER did my spirit seal' is rolled round with rocks and stones, here those rocks and stones are transfigured into gemlike luminosity. And yet Maud replicates Lucy's inability to hear or see, growing and fading upon the speaker without a sound. The phrase 'too deep' alludes directly to the 'Intimations' ode: in the Ode, the speaker describes thoughts that are 'too deep for tears' (IV. xi. l. 203), yet finds recompense for his early visionary losses in both 'the human heart by which we live' (IV. xi. l. 200) and the philosophic mind (IV. x. l. 186). Tennyson's speaker could bear the vision that grows and fades upon him 'no more' – a phrase that resonates through Tennyson's work from his juvenile poetry onwards, as we saw in Chapter 3,[53] but which is also found in Wordsworth's 'Intimations' ode; at the start of Wordsworth's poem the speaker bemoans 'The things which I have seen I now can see no more' (IV. i. l. 9). The phrase echoes in Tennyson's speaker's memory, as he remembers the 'Dead perfection, no more' (I. II. l. 83) of Maud as she passes in her carriage. Maud is charged by the speaker with exacting revenge too deep for a slight 'innocently' done in thought to her beauty; the nightmarish vision of Maud is 'womanlike', taking revenge much too deep for a transient wrong. Wordsworth's commitment to the human heart in the Ode is twisted into a female heart intent on revenge, seemingly uninflected by philosophic thought: in the Ode, by contrast, the imaginative loss that accompanies adulthood is compensated for by a combination of the thoughts that lie too deep for tears and the human heart by which we live. Tennyson's borrowings from Wordsworth enable Maud's speaker's distorted solipsism; the fact that Maud is 'luminous' emphasises the visionary heritage of his nightmarish vision. The delicate balance of feeling and memory in Wordsworth's 'A SLUMBER did my spirit seal' is exaggerated into madness and hallucination, distortion and blame, with Tennyson both drawing from his source and hyperbolising it. O'Neill notices how Wordsworth's mad mothers such as Martha Ray in 'The Thorn' inform Tennyson's Mariana, sitting alone in her 'dreamy' house (l. 65) and wishing she were dead,[54] but here the 'Lucy' poems form a prototype for *Maud* and the speaker's descent into madness, as Tennyson takes Wordsworth's expressions of passion to extremes. 'A SLUMBER did my spirit seal' suggests that the route to imaginative connection has been lost or ignored, blocking union with the lost Lucy herself; compensation for loss is found in the 'Intimations' ode, however, through the conduit the poem offers. *Maud* is an extenuation, or, more accurately, a completion, of 'A SLUMBER did my spirit seal' in this sense; Tennyson's speaker becomes a version of Wordsworth's speaker, offered the vision that Wordsworth was denied or that was forfeited when his slumber was sealed, or at least a vision as imagined by Tennyson in his own version of Wordsworthian 'feeling'.

It is possible that Tennyson's revisionary reading of Wordsworth here involves him in Bloomian-style agonistic rivalry, with the revision taking place at the level of deep, psychic impulse, especially as *Maud* is Tennyson's first poem since his inheritance of the Laureateship from Wordsworth in 1850. In these terms, there is possibly a sense of the second of Harold Bloom's revisionary ratios, *tessera*, at work, as though Tennyson were completing his precursor 'but in another sense',[55] or 'swerving' away from Wordsworth in a *clinamen* in the Maud who appears to the speaker with a clear-cut face.[56] The Lucy of Wordsworth's poems takes revenge for a wrong too deep for tears; from this perspective silent, objectified Lucy is taking her revenge for her lost, half-hidden status. But if Maud is a reactionary Lucy, then she is as confined by Tennyson's poetics as she is by Wordsworth's, rolled round in a hallucinatory vision rather than with rocks and stones and trees: Tennyson makes Maud 'passionless', acting as a foil to the impassioned speaker, voiceless, powerless, an object or projection of desire like Wordsworth's Lucy herself, sitting beside the springs of Dove; it is the speakers of each poem who are inflamed by passion or feeling. Similarly, if she is enacting revenge, then she chooses the wrong target; it is Wordsworth, after all, who affords Lucy the status she has otherwise been denied. Likewise, 'A SLUMBER did my spirit seal', in signalling that the object of the speaker's affections is lost, rolled round with rocks and stones and trees, also signals the loss of Maud later in the poem. Maud's 'paleness and dumbness denotes the absence which is death';[57] that sense of death and inarticulacy is rooted in Wordsworth's 'Lucy' poems, as Tennyson's borrowing in the section makes clear. The presence of 'SHE dwelt among the untrodden ways' and 'A SLUMBER did my spirit seal' adumbrate how Maud will soon be in her grave, while the last two sections of the poem dramatise 'the difference' this makes to Tennyson's speaker. Tennyson's poem, however, is an example of Wordsworth's powerful overflow of feeling taken to extremes, linked not with high objects and higher things, but to war, madness, death and destruction, and the 'distortion' of Lucy in Section I. Tennyson subverts Wordsworth's aggrandisement of the passions and feelings, reducing passion to its basest rather than its highest object. If Tennyson is completing Wordsworth in a Bloomian sense, then he is also simultaneously drawing on Wordsworth to 'complete' the trajectory of *Maud*; revisionary 'completion' has to be balanced here by revisionary dependency, reinvention with affiliation and unity.

Yet, in its engagement with passion, Tennyson's poem nevertheless participates in Wordsworth's concept of poetry: *Maud* is a display of the history and science of feelings, of different phases, or fits, of passion, even though these phases have loosened their connection to tranquil emotion, sympathy or the grandeur of the heart. Tennyson, in a sense, is reinventing the 'Lucy' poems, and to some extent the 'Preface to the Second Edition' of *Lyrical Ballads*, unmooring the poem from Wordsworth's affiliation of passion with morality, sympathy and emotion recollected in tranquillity. Robert Langbaum emphasises that in the dramatic monologue the 'sympathy which we give the speaker for the sake of the poem and apart from judgment makes it possible for the reader to participate in a position, to see what it feels like to believe that way, without having finally to agree';[58] hence in *Maud* the reader's sympathy for the speaker is continually set against moral judgement. The speaker of *Maud* is trapped within his own ego, unable to feel for others, least of all Maud: she is reduced merely to an object of desire on which he can project feelings of love as opposed to the subject of a 'pure and holy love', as Hallam Tennyson has it. The reader may sympathise with Tennyson's speaker, experience what it feels like to be part of his world, without having finally to agree with his subject position. Yet the reader does nevertheless sympathise with Maud, charged intemperately with the crime of taking out revenge for a wrong too deep, and trapped within the cosmic whirl of Tennyson's poetics. In reimagining Wordsworth's Lucy, Tennyson thus both perpetuates Wordsworth's influence and attenuates it, securing the reader's sympathy for Maud in her role as the Lucy of *Lyrical Ballads* and attenuating it through a continually negotiated sympathy for the speaker. Even so, Wordsworth's *Lyrical Ballads* are themselves subversive or at least experimental, eliding the division between author, speaker and reader and displacing and testing the reader's power of sympathy.[59] Tennyson's poem is, in this way, developing a pattern already at work in Wordsworth.

Strange Fits and Carved Stone

Wordsworth's 'Lucy' poems continue to be heard in other sections of Part I, as here:

> She came to the village church,
> And sat by a pillar alone;
> An angel watching an urn
> Wept over her, carved in stone;
> And once, but once, she lifted her eyes,
> And suddenly, sweetly, strangely blushed
> To find they were met by my own;
> And suddenly, sweetly, my heart beat stronger
> And thicker, until I heard no longer
> The snowy-banded, dilettante,
> Delicate-handed priest intone;
> And thought, is it pride, and mused and sighed
> 'No surely, now it cannot be pride.'
>
> I was walking a mile,
> More than a mile from the shore,
> The sun looked out with a smile
> Betwixt the cloud and the moor,
> And riding at set of day
> Over the dark moor land,

Rapidly riding far away,
She waved to me with her hand.
There were two at her side,
Something flashed in the sun,
Down by the hill I saw them ride,
In a moment they were gone:
Like a sudden spark
Struck vainly in the night,
Then returns the dark
With no more hope of light.

(I. VIII–IX. ll. 301–29)

Wordsworth's 'STRANGE fits of passion I have known' (1800), another of the five 'Lucy' poems, resonates through the above section:

STRANGE fits of passion I have known:
And I will dare to tell,
But in the Lover's ear alone,
What once to me befel.

When she I loved was strong and gay
And like a rose in June,
I to her cottage bent my way,
Beneath the evening Moon.

Upon the Moon I fixed my eye,
All over the wide lea;
My Horse trudged on – and we drew nigh
Those paths so dear to me.

And now we reached the orchard plot;
And as we climbed the hill,
Towards the roof of Lucy's cot
The Moon descended still.

In one of those sweet dreams I slept,
Kind Nature's gentlest boon!
And all the while my eyes I kept
On the descending Moon.

My Horse moved on; hoof after hoof
He raised, and never stopped:
When down behind the cottage roof,
At once, the bright Moon dropped.

What fond and wayward thoughts will slide
Into a Lover's head! –
'O mercy!' to myself I cried,
'If Lucy should be dead!'

Wordsworth writes of 'What once to me befel', which echoes through Tennyson's insistent 'And once, but once' here, replicating Wordsworth's simplicity of diction in the 'real language of men';[60] simplicity cuts through the richness of the language of sensation. But other echoes circulate. There is an echo of the earlier poem's balladic rhythm in the second stanza of Tennyson's section, for instance, with its abab rhyme and jaunty iambic trimeter/tetrameter metre. Adela Pinch writes of how Wordsworth draws on the 'cliché-ridden' aspects of the ballad form in 'STRANGE fits of passion' to convey the speaker's feelings:[61] '"moon"', for instance, cosily rhymes with '"June"';[62] the semi-chivalric lover, bending his way beneath an evening moon, 'travels along well-worn "paths"'.[63] Peter McDonald, in his account of the 'self-aware' use of rhyme in nineteenth-century poetry,[64] confirms that the finite number of possibilities in rhyme 'threaten poets with a limiting series of options for development of thought and expression';[65] rhyme, as he makes clear, has a 'pre-determined nature'.[66] In *Maud*, Tennyson borrows Wordsworth's predetermined balladic clichés, confirming the limit to the degree of self-consciousness to which McDonald refers: Tennyson writes of how 'the sun looked out with a smile', for instance, and the section features a semi-chivalric lover, although the position of the chivalric knight is transposed in Tennyson, as he walks 'a mile from the shore', watching the lovers riding 'rapidly' away. The rhyme scheme also fulfils a predetermined pattern, as in Wordsworth's 'STRANGE fits of passion', with a sustained abab rhyme scheme in the second stanza, a pattern broken only by the half-rhyme of sun/gone, allowing the poet to emphasise the speaker's disorientation at the lovers' disappearance in a blaze of sunlight. But *Maud*'s speaker is also the inheritor of Wordsworth's speaker's anxiety: Tennyson draws on the anxiety of the speaker in Wordsworth's poem that Lucy should be dead, turning the fear of death into one of jealousy, a jealousy accentuated by the almost bathetic dip into darkness at the close of the poem and the lovers' summary disappearance over the hill. The lovers' disappearance occurs in a 'sudden flash', as if by optical illusion. The moon in Wordsworth's poem disappears by an optical illusion caused by the speaker's 'own desirous motion up the hill'.[67] It is *Maud*'s speaker's own desirous motion, walking earnestly more than a mile, however, that sees the lovers disappear in 'a sudden spark'.

The presence of Wordsworth's 'STRANGE fits of passion' also adumbrates the speaker and Maud's fate; as Pinch confirms, in 'STRANGE fits of passion' 'love equals death; or rather, that the intentionality of romantic clichés can be deadly'.[68] Tennyson might transpose some of the elements of 'STRANGE fits of passion' here, but the ballad has a self-fulfilling prophecy: love equals death. The presence of Wordsworth's language in the section thus acts to confirm that the speaker's feelings originate 'in words and in literary form',[69] as well as in the pit where the speaker's father dashed himself down (or in inherited madness, as Tennyson himself attests in his comments about the poem).[70] The Wordsworthian echoes in this section therefore foreshadow the trajectory of *Maud*, consolidating the prefigurative pattern already established through the presence of 'A SLUMBER did my spirit seal' and 'SHE dwelt among the untrodden ways'; 'Echo' does indeed answer 'Death' to 'whatever is ask'd her' (I. I. i. l. 4). If Tennyson is hyperbolising Wordsworthian solipsism in *Maud*, then he is also, somewhat paradoxically, drawing on a traditional source as mediated via Wordsworth in support of that project. The later poet is keen to emphasise that in portraying the speaker's phases of passion he is developing a new form, but in so doing he is unable to break away from Wordsworth, relying on his predecessor to shape and structure his poem. In addition, Wordsworth's ordered rhythms here also make the poem more readable, offering pleasure rather than excitement,[71] soothing both the reader's and the speaker's passions. Wordsworth's restraining rhythms act discordantly with the speaker's inflamed feelings in this respect, confirming how rhythms are often at odds with meaning in *Maud*.[72]

The phrase 'carved in stone' is sourced in Wordsworth's *The White Doe of Rylstone* (1815). Conceived in the 'wake of Scott's *The Lay of the Last Minstrel* (1805) and inevitably challenging comparison with it through its origin in the ballad *The Rising in the North*',[73] Wordsworth's *The White Doe of Rylstone* reimagines the uprising of the Catholic Nortons against the Protestant Elizabeth I, setting the rebellion of Norton and eight of his sons against 'the sufferings of the two Protestant siblings [Francis and Emily] who stand apart from the rebellion'.[74] *The White Doe of Rylstone*'s revisionary methods, 'moving ballad, with its emphasis on action, ever more toward lyric',[75] bear some comparison with Tennyson's own lyric-narrative purpose in *Maud*. In the first section of the poem, Wordsworth's speaker describes the eponymous white doe's return every Sabbath day to Emily's grave, a return that forms the primary locus of the poem.[76] On her return,

> – She sees a warrior carved in stone,
> Among the thick weeds, stretched alone
> A warrior, with his shield of pride
> Cleaving humbly to his side,
> And hands in resignation prest,
> Palm to palm, on his tranquil breast;
> Methinks she passeth by the sight,
> As a common creature might:
> If she be doomed to inward care,
> Or service, it must lie elsewhere.
>
> (IV. Canto I. ll. 127–36)

Tennyson draws directly on Wordsworth's description of the warrior 'carved in stone' to describe the angel 'carved in stone' who looks over Maud as she sits in the village church, transforming the warlike into the angelic. In Wordsworth, the doe disregards the warrior, as her service lies elsewhere; 'saintly' (IV. Canto I. l. 104), she lies 'down in peace, and lovingly' (IV. Canto I. l. 148), committed to her weekly service to her mistress. She herself is flecked with angelic as well as saintly associations: she is 'spotless, and holy, and gentle, and bright; / And glides o'er the earth like an angel of light' (IV. Canto I. ll. 243–4). The doe's heavenly inflections are appropriated by Tennyson and applied to the 'angel' carved in stone who protects Maud as she sits in the local church.

The description of carved stone echoes elsewhere in Tennyson's poem, however: in I. XIV. ii, for instance, the speaker describes Maud's room thus:

> Maud's own little oak-room
> (Which Maud, like a precious stone
> Set in the heart of the carven gloom,
> Lights with herself, when alone
> She sits by her music and books
> And her brother lingers late
> With a roystering company) looks
> Upon Maud's own garden-gate.
>
> (I. XIV. ii. ll. 497–504)

Wordsworth's 'stone' and 'carved' are transformed by Tennyson here into precious stone and carven gloom, as Maud sits like a precious stone, set in the heart of her own little oak-room. Maud becomes Wordsworth's 'carved warrior' in this sense. In the same section the speaker says of himself:

> And I thought as I stood, if a hand, as white
> As ocean-foam in the moon, were laid
> On the hasp of the window, and my Delight
> Had a sudden desire, like a glorious ghost, to glide,
> Like a beam of the seventh Heaven, down to my side,
> There were but a step to be made.
>
> (I. XIV. ii. ll. 505–10)

The hand as white as ocean-foam in the moon is a reminder of the white doe in *The White Doe of Rylstone*: 'So beautiful the spotless Thrall, / (A lovely Youngling white as foam,) / That it was brought to Rylstone-hall; / Her youngest Brother led it home, / The youngest, then a lusty Boy, / Brought home the prize – and with what joy!' (IV. Canto VII. ll. 256–61). The doe is a spotless Youngling, white as foam; in Tennyson this transforms into a ghostly hand on the hasp of the window that is as white as ocean-foam in the moon. The 'ghostly' echoes with *The White Doe of Rylstone* continue through Tennyson's description of how his speaker's 'Delight' is like a glorious, gliding ghost. Wordsworth's white doe wanders like a gliding ghost in a glorious sunset:

> Most glorious sunset! – and a ray
> Survives – the twilight of this day;
> In that fair Creature whom the fields
> Support, and whom the forest shields;
> Who, having filled a holy place,
> Partakes, in her degree, heaven's grace;
> And bears a memory and a mind
> Raised far above the law of kind;
> Haunting the spots with lonely cheer
> Which her dear Mistress once held dear:
> Loves most what Emily loved most –
> The enclosure of this Church-yard ground;
> Here wanders like a gliding Ghost,
> And every Sabbath here is found;
> Comes with the People when the Bells
> Are heard among the moorland dells,
> Finds entrance through yon arch, where way
> Lies open on the Sabbath-day;
> Here walks amid the mournful waste
> Of prostrate altars, shrines defaced.
>
> (IV. Canto VII. ll. 321–60)

The doe that 'wanders like a gliding ghost' in a 'glorious sunset' is transfigured in Tennyson into the speaker's 'Delight', which has a sudden desire, 'like a glorious ghost, to glide, / Like a beam of the seventh Heaven, down to my side'. The white doe that, in Wordsworth, wanders like a gliding ghost in a glorious sunset, in Tennyson intensifies into a glissade of consonantal repetition, 'glorious ghost, to glide', to personify the speaker's 'Delight'. Further, Maud is definitively associated with the doe in Tennyson's poem; the doe in Wordsworth is described as 'milk-white' (IV. Canto I. l. 205); Maud a 'milkwhite fawn' (I. IV. x. l. 158). Interestingly, in 'Lucy Gray' (1800), Lucy is described as a 'fawn at play' (I. l. 9). The associations with *The White Doe of Rylstone* are intensified still further in *Maud*, however; Tennyson's 'milkwhite fawn' 'wanders', just like Wordsworth's doe:

> Ah Maud, you milkwhite fawn, you are all unmeet for a wife.
> Your mother is mute in her grave as her image in marble above;
> Your father is ever in London, you wander about at your will;
> You have but fed on the roses and lain in the lilies of life.
>
> (I. IV. x. ll. 158–61)

Like the 'milk-white doe' Maud 'wanders' around at her will; Maud wanders after being fed a life of luxury, a life of roses, while the doe haunts the spots that her mistress held dear. In being described as milk-white, Maud shares the attributes of Wordsworth's doe, becoming a ghostly presence. In *Maud* the narrator does not make clear whether Maud is alive or dead (or indeed a product of the speaker's imagination). She is described explicitly in ghostly or otherworldly terms: she is 'ghostlike' (I. III. l. 95); a 'ghastly Wraith' (II. I. i. l. 32); a 'dreary phantom' (III. VI. iii. l. 36) that arises and flies 'Far into the North, and battle, and seas of death' (III. VI. iii. l. 37). Similarly, Maud's mother is as mute in her grave as her image in marble above, echoing the 'grave' of the doe's beloved mistress, Emily:

> And floors encumbered with rich show
> Of fret-work imagery laid low;
> Paces softly, or makes halt,
> By fractured cell, or tomb, or vault;
> By plate of monumental brass
> Dim-gleaming among weeds and grass,
> And sculptured Forms of Warriors brave:
> But chiefly by that single grave,
> That one sequestered hillock green,

The pensive Visitant is seen.
There doth the gentle Creature lie
With those adversities unmoved;
Calm Spectacle, by earth and sky
In their benignity approved!
And aye, methinks, this hoary Pile,
Subdued by outrage and decay,
Looks down upon her with a smile,
A gracious smile, that seems to say –
'Thou, thou art not a child of Time,
But Daughter of the Eternal Prime!'

(IV. Canto VII. ll. 342–61)

In her return to her Mistress' grave, the white doe transcends time, becoming daughter of the 'Eternal Prime', blending both the natural and the eternal. Maud, too, in taking on the attributes of the doe becomes eternal. In affiliating Maud with the white doe, then, Tennyson confirms the coadunation of the human, natural and divine that drives Wordsworth's poem,[77] opening up the poem to notions of immortality, a topic thought merely to be reduced to comedic level in the poem or excluded by its overt 'antiphonal' status to *In Memoriam*.[78] Yet *Maud* exerts its difference from *The White Doe of Rylstone*, replacing the sense of community feeling that the doe's return to the grave engenders with the community of war;[79] it is only in war that the speaker can feel 'one with [his] kind' (III. VI. v. l. 58). Equally, *The White Doe of Rylstone*'s exploration of the transitory action – a step, a blow – that ultimately evolves into harmony and peace, as the verse epigraph added to the poem in 1836 has it,[80] is replaced in Tennyson by 'the Christless code, / That must have life for a blow' (II. I. i. ll. 26–7). Tennyson's speaker wonders to himself at his action after the death of Maud's brother – '"The fault was mine, the fault was mine"' (II. I. i. l. 1) – but does not find that 'through that darkness' (infinite though it seem / And irremoveable) gracious openings lie' (ll. 7–8).

The *White Doe of Rylstone* echoes through *Maud*, however, underpinning the later poem's associations with Wordsworth's text. Maud's speaker describes himself as

A wounded thing with a rancorous cry,
At war with myself and a wretched race,
Sick, sick to the heart of life, am I.

(I. X. ii. ll. 363–5)

These lines too owe a debt to Wordsworth's *The White Doe of Rylstone*. The speaker in Wordsworth's poem quotes Norton describing the failed assault on Barnard's Towers:

'This night yon haughty Towers must yield,
Or we for ever quit the field.
– Neville is utterly dismayed,
For promise fails of Howard's aid;
And Dacre to our call replies
That he is unprepared to rise.
My heart is sick; – this weary pause
Must needs be fatal to the cause'.

(IV. Canto IV. ll. 193–200)

Ricks suggests that Tennyson's lines are suggestive of George Crabbe's *The Old Bachelor*: 'But is not man, the solitary, sick / Of his existence, sad and splenetic?'[81] But the play of war and heart sickness in Tennyson is also coloured by Wordsworth's poem, echoes from which blend with the existential ennui of Crabbe's lines. Tennyson's speaker describes himself as a wounded thing, sick, sick to the heart of life, and at war with both himself and a wretched race, echoing the heart sickness of Wordsworth's poem. Wordsworth's speaker is sick to the heart with potentially failed purpose; Tennyson's sick with life itself. The Wordsworthian echo becomes transformed in Tennyson into one of subjectivity, mirroring the speaker's estrangement from himself and between subject and object, the root cause of his disturbed subjectivity.

The White Doe of Rylstone also plays a part in the epithalamion I. XVIII. viii; Tennyson's speaker here asks, in one of his calmer 'phases':

Is that enchanted moan only the swell
Of the long waves that roll in yonder bay?
And hark the clock within, the silver knell
Of twelve sweet hours that past in bridal white,
And died to live, long as my pulses play;
But now by this my love has closed her sight
And given false death her hand, and stolen away
To dreamful wastes where footless fancies dwell
Among the fragments of the golden day.
May nothing there her maiden grace affright!
Dear heart, I feel with thee the drowsy spell.
My bride to be, my evermore delight,

My own heart's heart, my ownest own, farewell;
It is but for a little space I go:
And ye meanwhile far over moor and fell
Beat to the noiseless music of the night!
Has our whole earth gone nearer to the glow
Of your soft splendours that you look so bright?
I have climbed nearer out of lonely Hell.
Beat, happy stars, timing with things below,
Beat with my heart more blest than heart can tell,
Blest, but for some dark undercurrent woe
That seems to draw – but it shall not be so:
Let all be well, be well.

(I. XVIII. viii. ll. 660–83)

The Keatsian resonances are evident here, with the 'drowsy spell' a reminder of the 'drowsy numbness' that dulls the speaker's senses in the 'Ode to a Nightingale'.[82] But Wordsworthian echoes circulate here too, harmonising with the borrowings from Keats. It is for 'a little space' that Tennyson's speaker says farewell to *Maud*. Tennyson is self-echoing here too – the phrase appears in 'The Lady of Shalott', when Lancelot 'mused a little space' (l. 168) after the death of the Lady herself. In *The White Doe of Rylstone*, Wordsworth describes the grave of Francis Norton:

Apart, some little space, was made
The grave where Francis must be laid.
In no confusion or neglect
This did they, – but in pure respect
That he was born of gentle Blood;
And that there was no neighbourhood
Of kindred for him in that ground;
So to the Church-yard they are bound,
Bearing the Body on a bier
In decency and humble cheer;
And psalms are sung with holy sound.

(IV. Canto VI. ll. 165–75)

The associations in *Maud* with death, graves, blood and gentility link 'a little space' intimately with *The White Doe of Rylstone*. But Wordsworth also uses the same phrase in Book VII of *The Prelude*: 'Yet, undetermined to what course of life / I should adhere, and seeming to possess / A little space of intermediate time / At full command, to London first I turned'.[83] It is both for a little space and a little time

that the speaker leaves Maud, suggesting that Tennyson is specifically harnessing his resources from Wordsworth's 1850 poem here.
Further, the addition of the indefinite article to 'little space' associ-
ates the echo specifically with *The Prelude* – a little space of time. In
Book X of Milton's *Paradise Lost*, however, Milton writes of how
Sin and Death in 'little space' bind the confines of Heaven and earth
and in turn Hell:

> with pinns of adamant
> And chains they made all fast, too fast they made
> And durable; and now in little space
> The confines met of empyréan Heav'n
> And of this world, and on the left hand Hell
> With long reach interposed.[84]

Tennyson might well have had both Milton and Wordsworth in mind
in writing this section, then: the speaker here is himself an embodi-
ment of Sin and Death, an agent of Satan momentarily climbing out
of his lonely Hell. But London becomes to the speaker of *The Prelude* its own kind of hell. Bloom avers that Wordsworth is involved
in a creative misreading of Milton in the 'Intimations' ode, suffering
what he terms a great defeat owing to the greatness of the precursor
poet.[85] The Wordsworthian echoes here could be viewed as a subver-
sion of Wordsworth's spiritual autobiography, with *Maud*'s speaker
progressing towards self-destruction rather than self-growth, involv-
ing Tennyson in a creative misreading of his precursor and enacting
a great defeat. Likewise, the Miltonic borrowing could be viewed as
an implicit misreading. Yet the echoes work on a local level, as the
speaker climbs that little bit nearer out of his lonely Hell, forming
in the process not so much a great defeat but a shifting intertextual
continuum that feeds into and supports a rare moment of speakerly
enchantment.[86]

The sections which begin with 'Cold and clear-cut face' (I. III)
and 'She came to the village church' (I. VIII) are linked in terms
of composition. Shatto describes how, in February–April 1855,
six sections, including these two, were composed after Tennyson
had read them aloud to Emily, his wife.[87] She confirms that 'Cold
and clear-cut face' 'is doubtless one of Emily's "tiny poems"'.[88]
As Shatto goes on, 'The addition develops the characterization
of Maud, and creates a coda for I ii and preface for I iv'.[89] 'She
came to the village church' develops 'both Maud's character
and the lovers' relationship and serves to prepare for I xi'.[90] The

sections are also linked to Wordsworth through their connection to Wordsworth's passion and 'STRANGE fits of passion' in particular. Shatto contends that

> What is noticeable about the entire group of added sections is that all but two (I iii and xxi) are narratives. The general effect of the additions is to develop characterization and heighten dramatic tension, propelling the movement of the first part of the sequence towards the climax in the garden.[91]

But if these sections are narratives, then they are also hugely indebted to Wordsworth's lyrics, encapsulating the lyric–narrative tension at work in the poem.

Another poem, contemporaneous with *The White Doe of Rylstone*, has a presence in Section I. IV. The speaker's 'little wood' (I. IV. iv. l. 125), where his father dashed himself down, becomes a 'dark wood', a wood of wild and dark thoughts, shaded by the ghost-inducing moon of line 506 of Section I. XIV. ii and forming a parallel to Maud's cultivated garden:

> I heard no sound where I stood
> But the rivulet on from the lawn
> Running down to my own dark wood;
> Or the voice of the long sea-wave as it swelled
> Now and then in the dim-gray dawn;
> But I looked, and round, all round the house I beheld
> The death-white curtain drawn;
> Felt a horror over me creep,
> Prickle my skin and catch my breath,
> Knew that the death-white curtain meant but sleep,
> Yet I shuddered and thought like a fool of the sleep of death.
> (I. XIV. iv. ll. 516–26)

With its resonances to Dante's opening to *The Inferno*, the dark wood is also a symbol of the speaker's condition, encapsulating his estrangement from the 'straight way' and his march to madness and murder ('In the middle of the journey of our life I [came / to] myself in a dark wood [where] / the straight way was lost').[92] But the dark wood also resonates with Wordsworth's sonnet, 'Composed while the author was engaged in writing a tract, occasioned by the Convention of Cintra' (1808, published 1815), another Wordsworthian poem concerned with political uprisings, this time Napoleon's invasion of Spain:

NOT 'mid the World's vain objects! that enslave
The free-born Soul, – that World whose vaunted skill
In selfish interest perverts the will,
Whose factions lead astray the wise and brave;
Not there! but in dark wood and rocky cave,
And hollow vale which foaming torrents fill
With omnipresent murmur as they rave
Down their steep beds, that never shall be still:
Here, mighty Nature! in this school sublime
I weigh the hopes and fears of suffering Spain;
For her consult the auguries of time,
And through the human heart explore my way,
And look and listen – gathering, whence I may,
Triumph, and thoughts no bondage can restrain.

Nature is generally unforgiving in *Maud*, but remains 'mighty' in Wordsworth. The speaker has become alienated from mighty nature in Tennyson, as the poet deconstructs the Wordsworthian sublime, but in describing the speaker as a dark wood Tennyson allows him to become Wordsworth's 'mighty' nature and therefore at odds with the estranged nature which *Maud* tracks. The speaker in Maud is unable to reach out to make the connection between self and world, mind and nature, yet ironically as Wordsworth's dark wood he retains this potentiality. The section charts how the river runs from the rivulet (a Romantic trope) into the speaker's dark wood, thereby feeding the imaginative process at work.[93] But in becoming mighty nature, Tennyson allows the speaker the means by which to transcend his imaginative incapacity and therefore, in part, his madness. In drawing on Wordsworth's language in this way, then, Tennyson reinstates the imaginative sublime in a poem which ostensibly ironises it, simultaneously offering the 'human heart', as in the 'Intimations' ode, as a conduit to imaginative redemption.

Maud also becomes a thing of nature – a pearl, noted for its associations with nobility – replacing the magisterial power in nature that has ostensibly been lost in the poem:

Here will I lie, while these long branches sway,
And you fair stars that crown a happy day
Go in and out as if at merry play,
Who am no more so all forlorn,
As when it seemed far better to be born
To labour and the mattock-hardened hand,
That nursed at ease and brought to understand

A sad astrology, the boundless plan
That makes you tyrants in your iron skies,
Innumerable, pitiless, passionless eyes,
Cold fires, yet with power to burn and brand
His nothingness into man.

But now shine on, and what care I,
Who in this stormy gulf have found a pearl
The countercharm of space and hollow sky,
And do accept my madness, and would die
To save from some slight shame one simple girl.

(I. XVIII. iv–v. ll. 627–43)

Tennyson's 'iron skies' here recall the 'iron' of Wordsworth's *Guilt and Sorrow or Incidents upon Salisbury Plain* (1842) in CVII, line 12, an allusion with which Tennyson plays in *In Memoriam*.[94] The section above is also reminiscent, however, of Wordsworth's 'Impromptu', composed in 1802 and republished in 1835:

The Sun has long been set:
The Stars are out by twos and threes;
The little Birds are piping yet
Among the bushes and trees;
There's a Cuckoo, and one or two thrushes,
And a noise of wind that rushes,
With a noise of water that gushes;
And the Cuckoo's sovereign cry
Fills all the hollow of the sky![95]

Echoes of Wordsworth's 'Impromptu' circulate in Tennyson. Stars that 'go in and out' in Tennyson 'are out by twos and threes' in Wordsworth. Tennyson finds in Maud the 'countercharm of space and hollow sky' to replace the cold pitilessness of tyrannical stars. In Wordsworth, by contrast, the sovereign cry of the cuckoo fills 'all the hollow of the sky'. But as in 'Impromptu', nature retains a magisterial power – the cuckoo's sovereignty remains undimmed. In Tennyson nature has become merely hollow, emptied of all meaning by a sad astrology, or the modern astronomy that speaks only of the materiality of the cosmos.[96] The speaker reaches for Maud to fill the vacancy a diminished nature creates, but, unwittingly, the poem offers the speaker an alternative means by which to fill the void.

Curiously, the speaker's bemusement about the strangeness of his own condition permeates the poem, as here:

Did I hear it half in a doze
   Long since, I know not where?
Did I dream it an hour ago,
   When asleep in this arm-chair?

Men were drinking together,
   Drinking and talking of me;
'Well, if it prove a girl, the boy
   Will have plenty: so let it be.'

Is it an echo of something
   Read with a boy's delight,
Viziers nodding together
   In some Arabian night?

Strange, that I hear two men,
   Somewhere, talking of me;
'Well, if it prove a girl, my boy
   Will have plenty: so let it be'.

          (I. VII. i–iv. ll. 285–300)

Is 'it' an echo of something heard, a dream, a story from the Arabian nights[97] – the speaker cannot locate the cause. This poem is also one of the 'tiny poems' added to *Maud* by Emily Tennyson. Wordsworth links all of these poems. In 'Strange, that I felt so gay' the speaker directly acknowledges how 'strange' his feelings are:

Strange, that I felt so gay,
Strange, that *I* tried today
To beguile her melancholy;
The Sultan, as we name him, –
She did not wish to blame him –
But he vext her and perplext her
With his worldly talk and folly:
Was it gentle to reprove her
For stealing out of view
From a little lazy lover
Who but claims her as his due?

          (I. XX. i. ll. 787–97)

And again here:

Strange, that the mind, when fraught
With a passion so intense
One would think that it well

Might drown all life in the eye,
That it should, by being so overwrought,
Suddenly strike on a sharper sense
For a shell, or a flower, little things
Which else would have been past by!
And now I remember, I,
When he lay dying there,
I noticed one of his many rings
(For he had many, poor worm) and thought
It is his mother's hair.

                                        (II. II. viii. ll. 106–18)

In each case, the speaker focuses on the strangeness of his situation. It is strange that two men should be talking of him; strange that he should feel gay and in mind to beguile Maud; strange that with a passion so intense the mind should settle on little things, like a shell or a flower. Pinch writes of how strangeness in 'STRANGE fits of passion' carries not only a sense of being odd, but a sense of being '"foreign"' or '"alien"',[98] claiming that the poem

> thus confirms that dilemmas about the proportions of a feeling are inseparable from questions about its origins, either within or without a person. These fond and wayward thoughts 'slide' into the head: an odd word here, where 'glide,' perhaps, might do (as in 'bright volumes of vapour through Lothbury glide'). 'Slide' imparts to these thoughts a more exteriorized, agentless quality, a viscous quality, like that of medicine sliding down a throat. It gives them the concrete character of things that exist in the world, and thus come from somewhere. Thus as personal and inward as this experience – and Wordsworth's account of it – seem, this fit of passion is an extrapersonal one.[99]

Maud's speaker also registers that his strange thoughts are extrapersonal, agentless somehow – they too, as in these examples, seem to slide into his head: they come from somewhere. The speaker, however, is unable to locate the origin of his feelings, unable to connect them to his father's death, or to the state of England – they seem foreign or alien; he has so 'dark a mind' (I. XV. l. 527) which he cannot fathom. The speaker's thoughts are 'alien', however, and unlocatable by the speaker, in that they stem from a 'literary' source – that is, in Wordsworth's 'STRANGE fits of passion'.

The speaker's bemusement at his own condition is also to be found in Part II of the poem, after Maud's brother's death:

Breton, not Briton; here
Like a shipwrecked man on a coast
Of ancient fable and fear –
Plagued with a flitting to and fro,
A disease, a hard mechanic ghost
That never came from on high
Nor ever arose from below,
But only moves with the moving eye,
Flying along the land and the main –
Why should it look like Maud?
Am I to be overawed
By what I cannot but know
Is a juggle born of the brain?

(II. II. v. ll. 78–90)

The hard mechanic ghost, the speaker wonders – is it a juggle born of the brain? Tennyson leaves the question open as to where this 'disease' comes from. The speaker, unlike the reader, is left wondering why such wayward thoughts have 'slid' into his head.

Echoes of Wordsworth's 'STRANGE fits of passion' are heard again, in Section II. V, where they close the section:

Dead, long dead,
Long dead!
And my heart is a handful of dust,
And the wheels go over my head,
And my bones are shaken with pain,
For into a shallow grave they are thrust,
Only a yard beneath the street,
And the hoofs of the horses beat, beat,
The hoofs of the horses beat,
Beat into my scalp and my brain,
With never an end to the stream of passing feet,
Driving, hurrying, marrying, burying,
Clamour and rumble, and ringing and clatter,
And here beneath it is all as bad,
For I thought the dead had peace, but it is not so;
To have no peace in the grave, is that not sad?
But up and down and to and fro,
Ever about me the dead men go;
And then to hear a dead man chatter
Is enough to drive one mad.

(II. V. i. ll. 239–58)

The horses' feet 'move on' in 'STRANGE fits of passion' – 'hoof after hoof / He raised, and never stopped' (ll. 21–2); they do not stop, as such, until they reach the fertile ground of Tennyson's poem.[100] Here, the steady movement of Wordsworth's horses descends into a relentless and chaotic beat, as the speaker hears the echo of Wordsworth's poem in his own head: the hoofs of the horses beat, beat at the back of his mind. Just as Tennyson 'completes' Wordsworth's 'A SLUMBER did my spirit seal' in the cold, clear-cut face section, here Tennyson seemingly 'completes' 'STRANGE fits of passion': the thoughts that slide into the semi-comic knight of 'STRANGE fits of passion' have turned him incontrovertibly mad, although the semi-comic elements from Wordsworth's poem remain. Yet Tennyson's borrowings from Wordsworth's 'STRANGE fits of passion' do not necessarily involve him in acts of self-saving caricature; rather, Wordsworth's 'caricature' feeds Tennyson's poem as much as it threatens it, allowing the later poet to achieve his dramatic-poetic effects, and the poem to fulfil its love–death trajectory.

'Far-off from the clamour of liars'

Maud, as has been noted, is reduced to a voice in the poem. Here in Part I, the voice is heard alone singing a 'passionate ballad and gay':

> A voice by the cedar tree
> In the meadow under the Hall!
> She is singing an air that is known to me,
> A passionate ballad gallant and gay,
> A martial song like a trumpet's call!
> Singing alone in the morning of life,
> In the happy morning of life and of May,
> Singing of men that in battle array,
> Ready in heart and ready in hand,
> March with banner and bugle and fife
> To the death, for their native land.
>
> Maud with her exquisite face,
> And wild voice pealing up to the sunny sky,
> And feet like sunny gems on an English green,
> Maud in the light of her youth and her grace,
> Singing of Death, and of Honour that cannot die,
> Till I well could weep for a time so sordid and mean,
> And myself so languid and base.

Silence, beautiful voice!
Be still, for you only trouble the mind
With a joy in which I cannot rejoice,
A glory I shall not find.
Still! I will hear you no more,
For your sweetness hardly leaves me a choice
But to move to the meadow and fall before
Her feet on the meadow grass, and adore,
Not her, who is neither courtly nor kind,
Not her, not her, but a voice.

(I. V. i–iii. ll. 162–89)

The section draws on a specific ballad here, one that is known to the poet if not to the speaker perhaps, and that is Wordsworth's 'The Solitary Reaper' (1807). Wordsworth's speaker observes an alienated and isolated figure, the Reaper, singing an air, a martial song, of men in battle array:

Behold her, single in the field,
Yon solitary Highland lass!
Reaping and singing by herself;
Stop here, or gently pass!
Alone she cuts and binds the grain,
And sings a melancholy strain;
O listen! for the Vale profound
Is overflowing with the sound.

No Nightingale did ever chaunt
More welcome notes to weary bands
Of Travellers in some shady haunt,
Among Arabian sands:
Such thrilling voice was never heard
In spring-time from the Cuckoo-bird,
Breaking the silence of the seas
Among the farthest Hebrides.

Will no one tell me what she sings?
Perhaps the plaintive numbers flow
For old, unhappy, far-off things,
And battles long ago:
Or is it some more humble lay,
Familiar matter of to-day?
Some natural sorrow, loss, or pain,
That has been, and may be again!

> Whate'er the theme, the Maiden sang
> As if her song could have no ending;
> I saw her singing at her work,
> And o'er the sickle bending; –
> I listened – motionless and still;
> And, as I mounted up the hill,
> The music in my heart I bore,
> Long after it was heard no more.

Echoes from, and coincidences with, Wordsworth's ballad resonate their way through the section, as Maud's 'voice' becomes the Reaper's 'voice', blending with the voice of the mythical Echo, which also permeates the section.[101] Tennyson's speaker watches Maud sing her ballad, just as Wordsworth's speaker watches the Reaper sing hers. The peasant Reaper becomes the courtly Maud and Wordsworth's meadow becomes Tennyson's English green, as Tennyson draws on and reworks the tropes of the earlier ballad. Wordsworth emphasises the Reaper's solitariness, writing 'Behold her, single in the field, / Yon solitary Highland lass! / Reaping and singing by herself' (III. ll. 1–3); Tennyson, too, makes a key point of Maud's solitariness, stressing how she is 'Singing alone in the morning of life, / In the happy morning of life and of May' (III. l. 6). The Reaper's melancholy at battles long ago is replaced with a Tennysonian joy in military might and masculine power, of honour that cannot die, an honour from which the speaker excludes himself through his languidness and baseness. Tennyson's speaker asks that the voice be silenced, echoing directly the phrases from the earlier poem: 'Be still, for you only trouble the mind / With a joy in which I cannot rejoice, / A glory I shall not find. / Still! I will hear you no more'. Wordsworth writes, 'I listened, motionless and still; / And, as I mounted up the hill, / The music in my heart I bore, / Long after it was heard no more'. Tennyson transposes the 'still' and 'no more' of Wordsworth's poem, transfiguring Wordsworth's sense of stillness and loss as he mounts the hill and loses the sound of the Reaper's voice into a demand for silence – 'Still! I will hear you no more'. Echo becomes communal here,[102] as Wordsworth's ballad, with its oral tradition, weaves its way through the section, allowing the speaker an escape from his solipsism, a process implicit in the borrowing of the 'Lucy' poems in the other sections of the poem, but brought to fruition here. Rhythm in the ballad tradition, a tradition in which Wordsworth actively shared, fosters 'a sense of community across time . . . bearing witness to a shared cultural identity'.[103] Wordsworth's balladic rhythm – iambic tetrameter – is shared in part with Tennyson's speaker too, heard, for instance, in the repetition of 'no more'. The presence of Wordsworth's ballad allows the speaker to escape or transcend the language of sensation, with its introspective 'return of the mind upon itself, and the habit of seeking relief in idiosyncrasies rather than community of interest',[104] forming an antidote to the 'potentially distorting effects of viewing the world from the perspective of unhealthy preoccupations with one's own feelings'.[105] The speaker is provided with an alternative form of community to the one offered by the marching rhythms of war. Wordsworth is claimed as more than a purely subjectivist poet, a poet who is 'never contemptuous of community', and for whom 'one's place within society [is] always important'.[106] Wordsworth himself recognises the communitarian qualities of his poetry, acknowledging the social utility of both poetry and passion and their ability to bind society together into a cohesive whole. He writes in the 'Preface to the Second Edition' of *Lyrical Ballads* (1802), for instance, of how 'the Poet binds together by passion and knowledge the vast empire of human society, as it is spread over the whole earth, and over all time'.[107] In drawing from Wordsworth's Reaper, then, Tennyson is both acknowledging the power of the ballad to escape the introspective return of the mind upon itself, and offering an escape from the solipsism that the language of sensation engenders and that *Maud* is ostensibly ironising. But the Reaper is caught in a cycle of loss, a loss that has been and may be felt again: the ballad as a form may offer communality, but the community of war of which the Reaper sings is inchoate with loss. Hers is a song of woe rather than war. Richard Cronin notices how the rhythms at the close of the poem are at odds with the speaker's commitment to war.[108] But that dissonance is evident here too – the Reaper is caught in a cycle of revisiting a continuing loss, whether this is of battles long ago or a more humble present lay, of sorrows which may come again. Her 'plaintive numbers' thus inflect and distort Tennyson's speaker's jingoistic commitment to war, undermining *Maud*'s song of chivalry and the speaker's commitment to being 'one with [his] kind' (III. VI. v. l. 58).

Wordsworth's 'The Solitary Reaper' continues to echo through the poem and the speaker's mind, however:

I wish I could hear again
The chivalrous battle-song
That she warbled alone in her joy!
I might persuade myself then
She would not do herself this great wrong,
To take a wanton dissolute boy
For a man and leader of men.

Ah God, for a man with heart, head, hand,
Like some of the simple great ones gone
For ever and ever by,
One still strong man in a blatant land,
Whatever they call him, what care I,
Aristocrat, democrat, autocrat – one
Who can rule and dare not lie.

And ah for a man to arise in me,
That the man I am may cease to be!

(I. X. iv–vi. ll. 382–97)

The speaker wishes he could hear again Maud's 'chivalrous battle-song'. Echoes of Wordsworth's 'The Solitary Reaper' continue, as Tennyson overwrites Wordsworth's loss with joy, describing how Maud warbled alone in her joy, picking up Wordsworth's association of the Reaper with the nightingale and cuckoo in 'warbled'. But the chivalrous battle-song continues to carry the Reaper's song of alienation and loss. The speaker draws on Maud's battle-song in an attempt to 'masculinise' or militarise himself – for a man to arise in him – but the presence of Wordsworth's Reaper colours the concept of masculinity and militarism with never-ending woe and far-off unhappy things.

The section is weighted with Wordsworthian overtones, as has been recognised by Shatto, who suggests that 'Like some of the simple great ones gone' draws from Wordsworth's 'Poems Dedicated to National Independence and Liberty', Sonnet XV, lines 1–4:

Great men have been among us; hands that penned
And tongues that uttered wisdom – better none:
The later Sidney, Marvel, Harrington,
Young Vane, and others who called Milton friend.[109]

But the section also resonates with Wordsworth's 'SHE dwelt among the untrodden ways' in the phrase 'And ah for a man to arise in me, / That the man I am may cease to be!' Tennyson's speaker's desire for masculinity – for a man to arise in him – is informed by Wordsworth's speaker's exhortation from that poem, 'But she is in her Grave, and, oh, / The difference to me' (I. ll. 11–12). As we saw in Chapter 3, the phrase 'and, oh, / The difference to me' signals a slippage, a move into the 'expressive power of inarticulacy', as Wordsworth's public voice falters beneath a private pressure:[110] inexpressibility becomes of value.

In *In Memoriam* Tennyson draws on Wordsworth's inarticulacy, acknowledging how poetic incapacity can itself become capacitating. Here Tennyson once more borrows Wordsworth's inarticulate articulacy, with Wordsworth's phrasing 'to' and 'me' reflected in the line 'And ah for a man to arise in me'. There is also an echo 'and, oh' in the 'And ah' of Tennyson's poem. Who that man could be remains, in a sense, inexpressible. Tennyson adds the additional line 'That the man I am may cease to be', borrowing again from 'SHE dwelt among the untrodden ways': 'She lived unknown, and few could know / When Lucy ceased to be' (I. ll. 9–10). The Lucy of Wordsworth's poem has ceased to be, but the speaker of Tennyson's poem wishes that the 'demasculinised' man he has become may cease to be; Maud might then take a wanton dissolute boy for a man and leader of men. But again, who that man is himself is inexpressible. Drawing on Wordsworth in this way allows Tennyson to collapse the difference between Wordsworth and himself as public poets, both of whom in a sense are grappling with their public voice. Any kind of competitive poetic model that might be at work is dissolved by the practical need for a public voice on Tennyson's part.

The Reaper's song is also heard in the 'O that 'twere possible' section of Part II, after the supposed 'death' of Maud:

'Tis a morning pure and sweet,
And a dewy splendour falls
On the little flower that clings
To the turrets and the walls;
'Tis a morning pure and sweet,
And the light and shadow fleet;
She is walking in the meadow,
And the woodland echo rings;
In a moment we shall meet;
She is singing in the meadow
And the rivulet at her feet
Ripples on in light and shadow
To the ballad that she sings.

Do I hear her sing as of old,
My bird with the shining head,
My own dove with the tender eye?
But there rings on a sudden a passionate cry,
There is some one dying or dead,
And a sullen thunder is rolled;
For a tumult shakes the city,

And I wake, my dream is fled;
In the shuddering dawn, behold,
Without knowledge, without pity,
By the curtains of my bed
That abiding phantom cold.

(II. IV. vi–vii. ll. 171–95)

Ricks draws attention to how 'a dewy splendour' derives from
Shelley, '*Witch of Atlas* 78, which goes on to describe "A lovely lady
garmented in light"'.[111] The writing of 'Oh that twere possible' pre-
dates that of Section I. IV, but the same allusions to Wordsworth's
Reaper run through its lines. Wordsworth's Reaper is here, in the
morning 'pure and sweet' and the 'bird' with the shining head. The
song is heard in a dream, but its effects continue. The presence of
the Reaper undermines the ballad which the speaker imagines or
dreams Maud is singing (the play of light and shadow as Maud sings
her ballad emphasises the loss Wordsworth's poem contains, but
which is denied in I. IV), but also confirms a sense of community,
positioning itself against the impersonality of the city in the same
section, the 'faces that one meets, / Hearts with no love for me' (II. IV.
xiii. ll. 233–4). Nonetheless, Wordsworth's Reaper and the ballad
that she sings act as an antidote to the impersonality of Tennyson's
'crowd confused and loud' (II. IV. x. ll. 211). If *Maud* expresses the
'Condition of England', then by borrowing from Wordsworth's ballad, the poem also expresses a desire for a return to a pre-Victorian
condition of England, a world 'Far-off from the clamour of liars'
(I. IV. ix. l. 152) and emotionless strangers. In drawing on the com-
munality/orality of the ballad form in this way, Tennyson affords
ballad a privileged position in relation to the narrative self, allowing
it to act as an implicit ordering process, holding together the sense of
self as (narrative) text.

'The shiver of dancing leaves'

In a specific section of the poem, lines 252–67 in Part I, the speaker
gives an account of his condition of alienation:

Living alone in an empty house,
Here half-hid in the gleaming wood,
Where I hear the dead at midday moan,
And the shrieking rush of the wainscot mouse,

And my own sad name in corners cried,
When the shiver of dancing leaves is thrown
About its echoing chambers wide,
Till a morbid hate and horror have grown
Of a world in which I have hardly mixt,
And a morbid eating lichen fixt
On a heart half-turned to stone.

(I. VI. viii. 257–67)

The passage is famous for its resemblance to 'Mariana', like 'The Lady of Shalott' one of Tennyson's early poems of sensation, in which the speaker is trapped within her own subjectivity and, to some extent, her language. Mariana, like *Maud*'s speaker, projects her consciousness on the objects around her; objects become blended with mood; feeling is disconnected from the ligature of thought. Here is Mariana:

All day within the dreamy house,
    The doors upon their hinges creaked;
The blue fly sung in the pane; the mouse
    Behind the mouldering wainscot shrieked,
Or from the crevice peered about.
    Old faces glimmered through the doors,
    Old footsteps trod the upper floors,
Old voices called her from without.
        She only said, 'My life is dreary,
            He cometh not', she said;
        She said, 'I am aweary, aweary,
            I would that I were dead!'

(ll. 61–72)

Both sections are evidence of Arthur Henry Hallam's 'vivid, picturesque delineation of objects' and 'the peculiar skill with which he holds all of them *fused* . . . in a medium of strong emotion':[112] in 'Mariana' 'the mouse / Behind the mouldering wainscot shrieked, / Or from the crevice peered about'; in *Maud*, the speaker describes the 'shrieking rush of the wainscot mouse, / And [his] own sad name in corners cried' – both objects in both poems are held in a medium of strong emotion.

But Wordsworth's language also forms a presence here, allowing Tennyson to ponder his role as a poet. In reaching out to Wordsworth's language of 'reflection',[113] Tennyson is able to question not only his designation as a poet of sensation, but also his ability to invent and sustain new poetic forms like the 'phases of passion' that constitute *Maud*. The speaker's 'dancing leaves', for instance, dance to the sound and rhythm of Wordsworth's 'The Green Linnet' (1807), where the dazzling bird, 'so like the dancing Leaves' (I. l. 34), induces unbounded joy in the speaker observing him. Tennyson, by contrast, makes his dancing leaves 'shiver', converting Wordsworthian joy into obsessive foreboding; the joy of imaginative connection is displaced by the despair of imaginative disconnection. In borrowing from Wordsworth's 'The Green Linnet', Tennyson aligns the text with a lyric in which 'the song or flight of the bird becomes an emblem of the poet's own voice, of his vocation, in the original sense of a "calling or summons", as a poet'.[114] The speaker's 'dancing leaves' thus become a metonym for Tennyson's analysis of his own '"calling or summons"' as a poet, including whether he can function as a dramatic artist without Wordsworth. The monodrama of *Maud* is never very far away from Wordsworth, and the borrowings from the earlier poems serve to underline this fact; Wordsworth's 'The Thorn', for instance, a poem that forms a prototype for the madness of Mariana's speaker, can also be read as an exploration of the erotic subconscious of its speaker, paving the way for Tennyson's exploration of the erotic unconscious of the speaker in *Maud*.[115] In both 'The Thorn' and *Maud* there are doubts as to the existence of the objects of the speakers' erotic attention – that is, Martha Ray and Maud herself – further underpinning the connections between the two poems.[116] The borrowings from Wordsworth crystallise the way in which Tennyson weaves a dramatic situation around 'a few very beautiful lyrics';[117] but more than this, they reveal the extent to which Tennyson relies on Wordsworth both to shape and structure the poem, raising the question of whether *Maud* could or would exist without its precursor, and playing into the compositional anxieties Tennyson is thought to have had surrounding the writing of the poem.

The inclusion of Wordsworth's language here allows Tennyson to reflect on his role as a poet, but also as Poet Laureate. The passage on Tennyson's poetic calling is linked to a later one in Part II of the poem, where the speaker draws attention to the differences between public and private language. The speaker says:

> See, there is one of us sobbing,
> No limit to his distress;
> And another, a lord of all things, praying
> To his own great self, as I guess;
> And another, a statesman there, betraying
> His party-secret, fool, to the press;

And yonder a vile physician, blabbing
The case of his patient – all for what?
To tickle the maggot born in an empty head,
And wheedle a world that loves him not,
For it is but a world of the dead.

Nothing but idiot gabble!
For the prophecy given of old
And then not understood,
Has come to pass as foretold;
Not let any man think for the public good,
But babble, merely for babble.
For I never whispered a private affair
Within the hearing of cat or mouse,
No, not to myself in the closet alone,
But I heard it shouted at once from the top of the house;
Everything came to be known.
Who told *him* we were there?

(II. V. iii–iv. ll. 268–90)

The speaker rehearses here Tennyson's own concern in the poem with private versus public speech, confirming that he does not speak of private affairs in public. But there is an overlap between Tennyson and his speaker through the connections to the earlier section, allowing Tennyson to link his concerns over his poetic calling with the issue of public versus private speech. Tennyson has borrowed Wordsworth's public voice in *Maud*, even when this voice is reduced to inarticulacy as in 'SHE dwelt among the untrodden ways' and its acknowledgement of inarticulacy: 'oh / The difference to me!' Tennyson is ready to substitute Wordsworth's public voice for his own in the poem, collapsing the difference – and any Bloomian rivalry – that might exist between poets, or indeed Poet Laureates. Further, Wordsworth's language is both the language of men and the language of reflection; in his use of Wordsworth's language, Tennyson collapses the difference or rivalry that Arthur Hallam sets up between Wordsworth's language of 'reflection' and Tennyson's language of 'sensation' in his essay on Tennyson's 1831 *Poems, Chiefly Lyrical*.[118]

Conclusion

Tennyson's revisionary borrowings 'reinvent' Wordsworth's 'Lucy' poems and, to some extent, 'The Preface to the Second Edition' of *Lyrical Ballads*. *Maud* grows out of 'The Preface', in its concern with passion, but Tennyson loosens the poem from Wordsworth's affiliation of passion with morality, communitarianism and sympathy: the speaker's passion in *Maud* leads to madness, distortion and murder, as well as a sense of community found in the abstract concept of war rather than in the community of men and women. But Wordsworth also creates thematic and structural links in the poem – the 'Lucy' poems underpin the trajectory of the later monologue, confirming *Maud*'s literary heritage and Maud's destiny; the ballad forms patterns of connectivity, underpinning Tennyson's narrative project but at the same time questioning its purpose. Tennyson might well have been attracted to the 'Lucy' poems for their innovation in language and metre and in their expression of passion; *Maud* also functions as an extenuation of the narrative complexity of *Lyrical Ballads*, where the intersection between narrator-speaker, poet and reader is constantly shifting. A complex poetics is at work, however, as Tennyson also draws on the genre-shifting aspects of *The White Doe of Rylstone*, with its move towards lyric. Wordsworth's echoing presence in the poem forms a community of poets, providing Tennyson with a link to his Wordsworthian past and consolidating his sense of continuity with what came before; through such continuity comes strength and the creation of a 'new' form. Strong poets do not always 'misprise' each other in acts of '*perverse, wilful revisionism*',[119] but borrow from one another in self-supporting acts of poetic survival, as here. Wordsworth supplies Tennyson with a public voice; yet he both accentuates and assuages Tennyson's poetic, compositional anxiety. The borrowings from Wordsworth cause Tennyson to reflect on the nature of his poetic status in a language which is itself reflective: can the later poet create something 'new' in a poem made up from a series of passions, or does Wordsworth cast too long a shadow for that? Or does Tennyson stand gratefully in Wordsworth's lengthening shadow, drawing from a poet on whom he must depend for support and without whom he cannot function? Tennyson lacks confidence with regard to his own poetic skill;[120] the later poet's borrowings from Wordsworth in *Maud* both allay and emphasise his compositional anxiety. Wordsworth offers comfort, security and the alleviation of anxiety rather than the perpetuation of it. Tennyson, meanwhile, validates Wordsworth's critical reputation, stabilising the 'Lucy' poems and their reception and steadying *The White Doe of Rylstone* after its rocky critical reception. But Tennyson's borrowings do not necessarily stabilise Wordsworth's poems themselves – *Maud* continues the instability of *Lyrical Ballads* rather than acting to stabilise its form. A complex pattern of borrowing is at work, creating complex effects, which cannot fully be explained by Bloom's antagonistic model. Tennyson borrows what he needs from Wordsworth, being shaped by and shaping Wordsworth in turn.

Tennyson again borrows from Wordsworth what he needs in 'Tithonus' (1860), the subject of the next chapter. The poem, written in 1833 in response to Arthur Hallam's death and repackaged as a monologue in 1860, returns to 'Tintern Abbey', not simply to rework its tropes, but to revise them, as the chapter will demonstrate.

Notes

1. Tennyson, *The Poems of Tennyson*, II, p. 514.
2. Tennyson, *The Poems of Tennyson*, II, p. 515.
3. Tennyson, *The Poems of Tennyson*, II, p. 517.
4. Eliot, *Selected Prose*, p. 241.
5. Eliot, *Selected Prose*, p. 242.
6. Christ, 'T. S. Eliot and the Victorians', p. 163.
7. Christ, 'T. S. Eliot and the Victorians', p. 164.
8. Tennyson, *The Poems of Tennyson*, II, p. 517.
9. Tennyson, *The Poems of Tennyson*, II, pp. 517–18.
10. Tennyson, *The Poems of Tennyson*, II, p. 518.
11. Tennyson, *The Poems of Tennyson*, II, pp. 515–16.
12. Cronin, 'The Spasmodics', p. 291.
13. Shatto, in *Tennyson's* Maud, p. 34.
14. Shatto, in *Tennyson's* Maud, p. 36.
15. Shatto, in *Tennyson's* Maud, p. 37.
16. Tennyson, *The Poems of Tennyson*, II, p. 517.
17. Shatto, in *Tennyson's* Maud, p. 35.
18. Tennyson, *The Poems of Tennyson*, II, p. 519.
19. Cronin, *Reading Victorian Poetry*, p. 76.
20. Shires, '*Maud*, Masculinity and Poetic Identity', p. 286.
21. Shires, '*Maud*, Masculinity and Poetic Identity', p. 270.
22. Shires, '*Maud*, Masculinity and Poetic Identity', p. 280.
23. Pease, '*Maud* and its Discontents', p. 104.
24. Pease, '*Maud* and its Discontents', p. 104.
25. Dransfield, 'The Morbid Meters of *Maud*', p. 286.
26. Hollander, 'The Anxiety of Influence'.
27. Bloom, *The Anxiety of Influence*, p. 25.
28. Tennyson, *The Poems of Tennyson*, II, pp. 527–8 (I. III. ll. 88–101). All further references to Tennyson's poems in the chapter are to this edition and appear parenthetically in the text.
29. The similarities to the early poems are noticed by both Shatto, in *Tennyson's* Maud, p. 174, and Ricks, in Tennyson, *The Poems of Tennyson*, II, p. 526, i 79.
30. Ricks, in Tennyson, *The Poems of Tennyson*, II, p. 526, i 79.

31. Susan Shatto describes how Tennyson acknowledges to his friend, James Henry Mangles, his admiration for Wordsworth's 'daffodils': 'T[ennyson] told Mangles that a critic had complained that Orion is never "low down in the west" at this time of year. Mangles records: "Of course, he meant that Orion was setting over a high hill. I said I thought daffodils were favourites of his. He said they were. He admired very much Wordsworth's daffodils"'. Shatto, in *Tennyson's* Maud, notes to pp. 51–5 and pp. 55–6, pp. 174–5.
32. Hartman, 'Wordsworth's "Lucy" poems', p. 134.
33. Hartman, 'Wordsworth's "Lucy" poems', p. 140.
34. Wordsworth, 'Preface to the Second Edition', p. 357.
35. Hartman, 'Wordsworth's "Lucy" poems', p. 135.
36. Hartman, 'Wordsworth's "Lucy" poems', p. 136.
37. Wordsworth, *The Poetical Works of William Wordsworth in Five Volumes*, I, p. 168. All future references to Wordsworth's poems appear parenthetically in the text and are to these volumes unless otherwise stated. References are given via volume and line number.
38. Tennyson, *The Poems of Tennyson*, II, p. 519, i 4.
39. Tennyson, *The Poems of Tennyson*, II, p. 519, i 4. Ricks here quotes from Buckler, *The Victorian Imagination*, p. 226.
40. O'Neill, '"Infinite Passion"', p. 185.
41. Shatto, in *Tennyson's* Maud, p. 178.
42. Coleridge, *The Complete Poetical Works*, I, ll. 97–9 (p. 367). I am grateful to Anthony Harding for drawing my attention to this connection.
43. Newlyn, *Coleridge, Wordsworth, and the Language of Allusion*, p. 62 and p. 62, n. 7.
44. Wordsworth, 'Preface to the Second Edition', p. 382.
45. See 'Note' to 'The Thorn', n.p.
46. O'Neill, '"Infinite Passion"', p. 175.
47. O'Neill, '"Infinite Passion"', pp. 175–6.
48. Goldsmith, 'Wordsworth's *Lyrical Ballads*, 1800', p. 207.
49. Goldsmith, 'Wordsworth's *Lyrical Ballads*, 1800', p. 207.
50. Robinson, '*Lyrical Ballads*, 1798', p. 177.
51. O'Neill, '"A Kind of an Excuse"', p. 55.
52. Hartman, *Wordsworth's Poetry 1787–1814*, p. 159.
53. See Chapter 3, n. 101.
54. O'Neill, 'The Romantic Bequest', pp. 229–30.
55. Bloom, *The Anxiety of Influence*, p. 14.
56. Bloom, *The Anxiety of Influence*, p. 14.
57. Armstrong, *Victorian Poetry*, p. 281.
58. See Langbaum, *The Poetry of Experience*, p. 58.
59. For more on the complex relationship between 'narrative, narrator and poet' in *Lyrical Ballads*, see Robinson, '*Lyrical Ballads*, 1798', pp. 178–80.
60. Wordsworth, 'Preface to the Second Edition', p. 357.
61. Pinch, *Strange Fits of Passion*, p. 108.

62. Pinch, *Strange Fits of Passion*, p. 108.
63. Pinch, *Strange Fits of Passion*, p. 108.
64. McDonald, *Sound Intentions*, p. 21.
65. McDonald, *Sound Intentions*, p. 21.
66. McDonald, *Sound Intentions*, p. 21.
67. Pinch, *Strange Fits of Passion*, p. 108.
68. Pinch, *Strange Fits of Passion*, p. 108.
69. Pinch, *Strange Fits of Passion*, p. 73.
70. Tennyson wrote to Arthur Gurney, 6 December 1855, saying: '"I wonder that you and others did not find out that all along the man was intended to have an hereditary vein of insanity, and that he falls foul on the swindling, on the times, because he feels that his father has been killed by the work of the lie, and that all through he fears the coming madness."' See Tennyson, *The Poems of Tennyson*, II, p. 516.
71. Pinch, 'Female Chatter', p. 840.
72. Berglund describes how 'Throughout *Maud*, structural elements, including meter, assonance, punctuation and rhyme, often oppose the sentiments of the anonymous narrator. Form and content conflict, and Tennyson uses form to illuminate, and undercut, content in order to expose the method of what he called his narrator's "morbid poetic soul"'. See '"Faultily Faultless"', p. 47.
73. Manning, 'The White Doe of Rylstone', p. 268.
74. Manning, 'The White Doe of Rylstone', p. 269.
75. Manning, 'The White Doe of Rylstone', p. 270.
76. Manning, 'The White Doe of Rylstone', pp. 270–1.
77. Danby proposes that *The White Doe* is 'in many ways . . . Wordsworth's strangest, and in some ways his profoundest, exercise of the spirit' and 'realizes a new co-adunation of his major meanings. Human, natural, and divine, are brought into a final relationship'. Danby, *The Simple Wordsworth*, p. 130, p. 141, quoted in Manning, 'The White Doe of Rylstone', p. 276.
78. O'Gorman, 'What Is Haunting Tennyson's *Maud* (1855)?', p. 302.
79. Manning describes how 'The solitary maid is re-tied to the earth by the Doe, and then, though at a distance, to the congregation at Bolton Priory'. See Manning, 'The White Doe of Rylstone', p. 280.
80. See Manning, 'The White Doe of Rylstone', p. 278. Reference to the new verse appears in the text and is to Manning.
81. Tennyson, *The Poems of Tennyson*, II, p. 541, i. 362–5.
82. Keats, *Selected Poems and Letters of John Keats*, l. 1 (p. 124).
83. Wordsworth, *The Prelude*, ll. 58–61 (p. 173).
84. Milton, *Paradise Lost*, X. ll. 318–22 (p. 226).
85. Bloom, *The Anxiety of Influence*, p. 10.
86. Sarah Annes Brown describes a 'shifting, intertextual continuum', whereby texts betray 'the sum of several previous moments of charged recognition'. While the moments may not be several here, they are dual. See Brown, *A Familiar Compound Ghost*, p. 183.

87. Shatto, in *Tennyson's* Maud, p. 23.
88. Shatto, in *Tennyson's* Maud, p. 23.
89. Shatto, in *Tennyson's* Maud, p. 23.
90. Shatto, in *Tennyson's* Maud, pp. 23–4.
91. Shatto, in *Tennyson's* Maud, p. 24.
92. Dante, *The Inferno of Dante Alighieri*, Canto I. ll. 1–3 (p. 3).
93. See Pease, '*Maud* and its Discontents', p. 111 for more on the rivulet as a Romantic trope for the imagination.
94. See Chapter 3, n. 22.
95. Wordsworth, *Poems, in Two Volumes*, II, ll. 1–9 (p. 41).
96. See *The Poems of Tennyson*, II, p. 554, i. 634.
97. Tennyson, *The Poems of Tennyson*, II, p. 537, i. 285–300.
98. Pinch, *Strange Fits of Passion*, p. 108.
99. Pinch, *Strange Fits of Passion*, p. 108.
100. Shatto notes the influence of Edgar Allan Poe in the writing of this section, particularly 'The Premature Burial'. See Shatto, in *Tennyson's* Maud, p. 19.
101. See *The Poems of Tennyson*, II, p. 519, i. 4.
102. Ricks, *Allusion to the Poets*, p. 201. Ricks calls allusion in Tennyson 'an honourable seeking of relief in community of interest', p. 201.
103. Barton, *Alfred Lord Tennyson's* In Memoriam, p. 15.
104. Hallam, 'On Some of the Characteristics of Modern Poetry', p. 105.
105. Dransfield, 'The Morbid Meters of *Maud*', p. 286.
106. Wu, *Wordsworth: An Inner Life*, p. 37.
107. Wordsworth, 'Preface to the Second Edition', p. 375.
108. Cronin, *Reading Victorian Poetry*, p. 77.
109. See Shatto, in *Tennyson's* Maud, pp. 189–90, from where the quotation is taken. Also see *Poems, in Two Volumes*, I, p. 141.
110. Perry, 'Elegy', p. 118.
111. Tennyson, *The Poems of Tennyson*, II, p. 573, n. ii. 172.
112. Hallam, 'On Some of the Characteristics of Modern Poetry', p. 109.
113. Hallam, 'On Some of the Characteristics of Modern Poetry', p. 93.
114. Sprinker, '"A Counterpoint of Dissonance"', p. 6.
115. Robinson, '*Lyrical Ballads*, 1798', p. 182, quoting Parrish, '"The Thorn"', pp. 153–63.
116. See Robinson, '*Lyrical Ballads*, 1798', p. 182, and Shatto, in *Tennyson's* Maud, p. 37.
117. Eliot, *Selected Prose*, p. 242.
118. Hallam, 'On Some of the Characteristics of Modern Poetry', p. 93.
119. Bloom, *The Anxiety of Influence*, Preface, p. xiii, p. 30.
120. See Ricks, *Allusion to the Poets*, p. 184; Decker, 'Tennyson's Limitations', p. 58.

Chapter 5

Tennyson's 'Tithonus' and the Revision of Wordsworth's 'Tintern Abbey'

In 1859 William Makepeace Thackeray petitioned Tennyson for a poem to be published in the 1860 edition of the *Cornhill Magazine*;[1] the poet turned to 'Tithon', a poem he first wrote in 1833 as a companion piece to 'Ulysses' after the sudden death of Arthur Henry Hallam,[2] reworking it in dramatic form and giving it the new title of 'Tithonus'. 'Tithonus' has been described as 'one of the most intense descriptions of sensation ever',[3] with its lush poetic effects and beguiling syntax seemingly justifying Hallam's classification of Tennyson in his 1831 essay as a poet of the sensational kind.[4] It recounts an episode from the marriage of the Trojan prince, Tithon, and the goddess of the dawn, Aurora or Eos, and is based on the *Homeric Hymn to Aphrodite*, which itself recounts Aphrodite's seduction of Anchises;[5] the poem traces the effects of eternal life without eternal youth, as Tithonus is doomed to grow old, and yet cannot die.[6] The form of the monologue allows Tennyson to explore an aspect of himself – in the case of 'Tithonus', grief – while simultaneously distancing himself from it; almost a fifth of Tennyson's poems are written in this way,[7] including, of course, 'Ulysses'.

Keats and Shelley influence the poem in a number of ways. Margaret A. Lourie describes how Aurora can 'recall *Hyperion*; her passionate embrace suggests Keatsian sexuality; and Tithonus shares something of Keats's attitude toward immortality in "Ode on a Grecian Urn"'.[8] Referring specifically to the 1833 version of the poem, however, Lourie notes 'how Shelley's presence also pervades [the] poem':[9] Shelley, 'the author of the "Hymn to Apollo," who set so many of his poetic revelations at dawn and whom Browning in *Pauline* would christen "Sun-treader," can scarcely be very deeply buried behind Tennyson's Aurora'.[10] Lourie also notes how Harold Bloom, E. D. H. Johnson and W. David Shaw 'adequately demonstrate what "Tithonus" owes to

Keats'.[11] She reiterates how, as 'Bloom rightly maintains, Tithonus is the belated Romantic poet, powerless either to escape his heritage or to rekindle its former fire'.[12] Bloom himself describes 'Tithonus' as 'an act of defense against the composite precursor, Keats-and-Wordsworth',[13] 'at once a narcissistic apotheosis and a powerful repressive reaction against the greatest poets ever to have attempted a humanized Sublime, an attempt made by way of a humanization of the ancient poetic lust for divination'.[14]

Wordsworth forms a presence in the poem too, most famously in its opening lines, which draw on 'The Simplon Pass' section of Wordsworth's *The Prelude* vi 624–5, published in 1860, with its woods that 'decay and fall'.[15] Christopher Ricks is prompted to claim that the replacement of the opening lines of the 1860 'Tithonus' – 'Ay me! Ay me!' – with 'The woods decay, the woods decay and fall' in the 1864 version of the poem 'suggests the influence of one of [Tennyson's] favourite passages of Wordsworth'.[16] 'Tintern Abbey' provides a thematic link in the poem: 'Tithonus', according to Seamus Perry, 'works a remarkable variation on the theme' of 'Tintern Abbey',[17] with Tithonus always the same 'yet dreadfully mutable',[18] continually reminded of his 'changefulness' by the goddess of the dawn's own return on her silver wheels.[19] Tennyson himself describes his 'profound admiration for "Tintern Abbey"',[20] citing the poem's influence in the writing of 'Tears, Idle Tears' (1847): '"This song came to me on the yellowing autumn-tide at Tintern Abbey, full for me of its bygone memories. It is the sense of the abiding in the transient"'.[21] Yet, his admiration for Wordsworth's poem was not unqualified; too much excessive repetition, he complains to Frederick Locker-Lampson, listing how the word '"again" occurs four times in the first fourteen lines' of Wordsworth's poem.[22] One might note that repetition is a trait to which Tennyson's poetry is not itself noticeably immune, however.[23] The later poet borrows Wordsworth's trope in many poems of his own, nonetheless, including 'Tears, Idle Tears', 'The Daisy' (1853), 'The Brook' (1855) and indeed 'Tithonus'.

This chapter maintains that 'Tithonus' does more than simply provide a remarkable variation on 'Tintern Abbey''s trope of recurrence, however, revising the connection between memory and nature underpinning Wordsworth's narrative of 'returning'. Sections LV and LVI of *In Memoriam* (1850) already make clear the poet's awareness of a nature 'careless of the single life' (LV. l. 8) and 'red in tooth and claw' (LVI. l. 15); in *Maud* (1855), 'nature is one with rapine, a harm no preacher can heal' (I. IV. iv. l. 123). The Wordsworthian correspondence between memory and nature as it appears in 'Tintern

Abbey' has loosened, a position to which Wordsworth himself moves in 'Elegiac Stanzas: Suggested by a Picture of Peele Castle, in a Storm, Painted by Sir George Beaumont' (1807; hereafter 'Elegiac Stanzas'). On revisiting the River Wye in *In Memoriam*, Tennyson's speaker can find only 'tears that cannot fall'.[24] As we saw in Chapter 3, Tennyson draws on Wordsworth both to soothe a terroristic nature and to express it. Yet, Tennyson's acknowledgement of an indifferent nature long precedes that of *In Memoriam*. Richard Cronin reveals how Tennyson did not find an easy connection between nature and the moral life: even as an undergraduate Tennyson was convinced that 'the existence of an intelligible First Cause could not be deducible from the phenomena of the universe'.[25] The poet, in a way Wordsworth is not, is attuned to the 'scientific' view that the 'world is subject to physical laws, which are assumed to be independent of human psychology'.[26] In revising Wordsworth's psychologised relationship with nature in 'Tithonus', then, Tennyson can thus seemingly release himself from an 'anachronistic' Wordsworthian narrative that is in the process of being superseded by the findings of nineteenth-century science and to which he is not fully committed.

The revision of Wordsworth's pantheistic nature is evident in the earlier 'Tithon', but its effects gain in intensity in the later monologue. The monologue as a form is already establishing a difference from Wordsworth in its rejection of Romantic universal subjectivity and its adoption of a fictional and performative persona. In the monologue, a silent addressee directly reverses the Romantic ideal of the poet's private, lyrical self-expression,[27] while the dialogic language of the speaker opens up the text to time and history. Thus in reworking Wordsworth's interaction between mind and nature, 'Tithonus' is consolidating a new poetic alongside revising what has become an anachronistic poetic trope. A similar process takes place in 'Ulysses'; in the 1842 poem Tennyson revises the concept of selfhood on which Wordsworthian transcendence is based, as well as the notion of the growth of the self through loss. The revisions in 'Tithonus' ostensibly free Tennyson's poem from the universal subjectivity of the lyric speaker, thereby ostensibly strengthening the strategies and performativity of the monologue. Yet, Tennyson's borrowings and echoes create effects that Tennyson cannot fully control, feeding, compromising, supporting, directing the poem, and, as in 'The Lady of Shalott', returning Tennyson to the language of reflection. In the 1842 'The Lady of Shalott' Tennyson's borrowings from Wordsworth allow him to expose the arbitrary division made by Hallam between the language of sensation and the language of reflection. Similarly, in 'Tithonus' Tennyson draws from the language of reflection while simultaneously employing the language of sensation, thereby dissolving the arbitrary separation of the two forms of poetry. Tennyson, according to Hallam in his review, is a poet of sensation rather than Wordsworthian reflection, whose 'fine organs',[28] like those of Shelley and Keats before him, 'trembled into emotion at colours, and sounds, and movements, unperceived or unregarded by duller temperaments'.[29] Tennyson's returns to Wordsworth's language of reflection therefore, where nature acts as the ground for 'philosophical understanding',[30] complicate the poet's use of a language of sensation in which nature is instead viewed purely as a source of aesthetic emotion.

The processes at work in the poem move beyond Harold Bloom's revisionist intra-poetic model, revealing how Bloom's revisionary ratios cannot fully explain the processes at work in Tennyson's poem; Bloom, as has been noted, considers there to be a 'powerful repressive reaction' against Wordsworth and Keats at work in 'Tithonus'; the 'hidden concern of the poem', he maintains, is 'Tennyson's own belatedness as a poet'.[31] But the chapter reveals how Tennyson's powerlessness to escape his Romantic heritage becomes in itself a form of power. The chapter, too, focuses on language and phrasing, rhythm and metre, the very surface or superficial level of poetic influence that Bloom rejects as the 'wearisome industry of source-hunting, of allusion-counting'.[32]

Wild Aurora

'Tithonus' works its poetic magic under 'Tintern Abbey''s 'quiet' sky,[33] in that 'quiet limit of the world' (l. 7) where spaces are 'ever-silent' (l. 9). In Wordsworth's poem, the speaker is nourished by nature under this quiet sky, with its 'green earth' (II. l. 106), and its 'waters, rolling from their mountain-springs' (II. l. 3). Nature provides a way for the speaker to 'see into the life of things' (II. l. 50), to gain 'a sense sublime / Of something far more deeply interfused' (II. ll. 96–7), whatever that 'something' is. Nature's 'beauteous forms' (II. l. 24), and the memory of those forms, when 'the picture of the mind revives again' (II. l. 61), evoke 'that blessed mood, / In which the burthen of the mystery, / In which the heavy and the weary weight / Of all this unintelligible world, / Is lightened' (II. ll. 38–42). This process, in turn a product 'Of eye, and ear, – both what they half create, / And what perceive' (II. ll. 107–8), is random, although the gleams of transcendence are always in danger of being 'half-extinguished' (II. l. 58). Dorothy, the speaker's auditrix, becomes the person to whom the experiences of the eye and ear are entrusted, the guardian of those memories that have the capacity to sustain the self: the speaker hopes to read his 'former pleasures' (II. l. 119) in the 'shooting lights' (II. l. 119) of her 'wild eyes' (II. l. 120).

The adjective 'wild' here has a particular significance, as 'wild' in Wordsworth's poem is overtly associated with both nature and the transcendent process to which it gives rise: nature in 'Tintern Abbey' is described as a 'wild secluded scene' (II. l. 6), which engenders 'wild ecstasies' (II. l. 139). Dorothy is linked to this 'wild' landscape, and its capacity to induce sublimity in the speaker, through her 'wild' eyes. As a result of her 'wildness', Dorothy becomes 'nature', as well as a future custodian of the sublime moments it precipitates, although her 'wildness' suggests that her role as protector is not a secure one.

In 'Tithonus', Tennyson's borrowings and echoes of the earlier poem assign a similar role to Aurora, in that she is the speaker's auditrix but also 'nature', though not simply in the sense of a pathetic fallacy as Shaw suggests.[34] Verbal echoes between 'Tithonus' and 'Tintern Abbey' underline the connections between both Aurora and nature and Aurora and Dorothy in the latter's capacity as 'nature'. Aurora's beauty is emphasised in 'Tithonus', evoked through the 'beauteous forms' (II. l. 24) of nature carried over from 'Tintern Abbey': the speaker confirms that she 'ever thus . . . grow[s] beautiful' (l. 43); her 'beauty' will be renewed 'morn by morn' (l. 74). Likewise, nature can impress with her 'silence' (II. l. 19) in 'Tintern Abbey'; Aurora lives in a realm of beautiful 'silence' (l. 44). Moreover, 'nature and the language of the sense' (II. l. 109) anchor the speaker's 'purest thoughts' (II. l. 110) in 'Tintern Abbey'; Tennyson's Aurora is described as having 'pure brows' (l. 35) and 'shoulders pure' (l. 35), immersing her in the language and epistemology of the earlier poem. It is from these 'pure' brows and 'pure' shoulders that the 'old mysterious glimmer' (l. 34) of imaginative transcendence steals for Tithonus, deepening the sense of Aurora as Wordsworth's 'nature' in the poem.

Interestingly, these connections are shared with the poem's earlier incarnation, 'Tithon', where Aurora's eyes are 'sweet'[35] and her brows and shoulders 'pure' (l. 31). Much is made of Aurora's beauty in the earlier poem, too: the speaker asks imploringly whether 'thy love, / Thy beauty [can] make amends, though even now, / Close over us, the silver star' (ll. 15–17), linking it, like the later version, specifically with 'Tintern Abbey'; similarly, at line 38 Tithon concludes that Aurora's sweetness and wildness ensure that she grows 'more beautiful' (l. 38). The similarities between Tennyson's two poems imply that the allusive connections with 'Tintern Abbey' start immediately after Hallam's death and come to fruition in the later poem, rather than beginning with the connections that occur in 'Tithonus'.

Darkness releases rather than conceals another connective link between 'Tintern Abbey', Aurora and nature. 'Tintern Abbey', like much of Wordsworth's poetry, contains darkness as well as light, as Keats notably recognises, writing of how Wordsworth's imagination in the poem is 'explorative of . . . dark passages'.[36] Nature is associated with darkness in 'Tintern Abbey', despite her power of being able to produce the light of transcendence in the speaker. She is Wordsworth's loving 'nurse' (II. l. 110), although her nurturing capability is underpinned by an incipient malevolence: the sycamore under which the speaker sits to contemplate his beloved nature's beauty is 'dark' (II. l. 10); the music he hears when looking on nature is 'still' and 'sad' (II. l. 92), and has the power to 'chasten and subdue' (II. l. 94). In 'Tithonus', nature's implicit malevolence in 'Tintern Abbey' is projected directly onto Aurora as 'nature' via the language borrowed from Wordsworth in the poem. She is associated with light and lucidity (l. 53), but her luminosity is offset by a corresponding sense of darkness: she moves in a 'dark' world; her wild team shake the 'darkness' (l. 41) from their loosened manes;[37] she bathes Tithonus in her 'rosy shadows' (l. 66). Moreover, she has the power to 'scare' (l. 46) Tithonus with her tears, to make him 'tremble' (l. 47) with the thought that the gods themselves cannot recall their gifts; her team 'beat' (l. 42) the twilight into flakes of fire. Ricks, in his gloss to the poem, confirms how the term 'beat' is traditionally associated with the dawn, and how Tennyson's phrasing is 'apparently also a reminiscence of Marston's *Antonio's Revenge* I. ii 120, i 107–8; "flakes of fire", "coursers of the morn / Beat up the light with their bright silver hooves"'.[38] Yet, the echoing 'beat' here is also a self-conscious reminder of the intertextual transference of Wordsworth's language and phrasing, and the echoing beat of Wordsworth's language and influence taking place in the poem.[39] These effects are intensified from the earlier 'Tithon', where Aurora's 'team' (l. 35) spread a 'rapid glow with loosened manes [and] / Fly, trampling twilight into flakes of fire' (ll. 36–7). Trampling implies wantonness, but beat denotes a mediated violence, complicating the violence inherent in the language of sensation.[40]

But if Aurora is linked to nature – as dark and potentially dangerous – in 'Tintern Abbey', then she is also linked to Dorothy in her role as nature; Dorothy, too, contains 'dark passages', although these remain, like nature's malevolence in general, implicit in Wordsworth's poem. Nature produces 'sensations sweet' (II. l. 28) in 'Tintern Abbey', and Dorothy's memory is 'as a dwelling-place / For all sweet sounds and harmonies' (II. ll. 142–3) that nature produces, linking Dorothy directly to nature; Aurora's 'sweet eyes brighten' (l. 38) close to Tithonus' eyes. But the association has 'darker' overtones through the specific use of the adjective 'wild' in both texts; just as Dorothy is described as having 'wild eyes', which link her to the 'wild secluded scene' (II. l. 6) of 'Tintern Abbey' and the 'wild ecstasies' (II. l. 139) it generates, so Aurora is associated with wildness: she has a 'wild team' (l. 39), as she does in the earlier 'Tithon' (l. 35). She is nature here, with the same capacity for sweetness and wildness as Dorothy, a duality neatly emblematised in whisperings that are not only 'sweet' but 'wild' (l. 61), and 'wild and airy' (l. 51) and 'more sweet' (l. 51) in the earlier version of the poem.

Malevolence is related to the way in which nature is eroticised in 'Tintern Abbey', as is Dorothy as 'nature' through her 'wildness', and this is a pattern Tennyson's borrowings replicate in 'Tithonus': the speaker in 'Tintern Abbey' describes nature as 'a feeling and a love' (II. l. 81), which produces 'aching joys' (II. l. 85) and 'dizzy raptures' (II. l. 86) that produce 'wild ecstasies' (II. l. 139) in him; it is 'the thing he loved' (II. l. 73). For Wordsworth, there is a 'moral act' of fidelity that occurs as a result of the mind's 'marriage' to nature.[41] 'Tintern Abbey' pivots this moral act in a nature that is 'The guide, the guardian of my heart, and soul / Of all my moral being' (II. ll. 111–12). However, 'Tintern Abbey' dislocates the speaker's moral connection with nature, as nature's eroticism signals another potential inconstancy, complementing her potential 'wildness'. This is a submerged effect, however, like that of wildness: nature is a lover who loves and then leaves, 'the thing he loved' (II. l. 73). In 'Tithonus', Aurora is objectified as erotic 'nature': it is her 'shoulders' (l. 35) which are pure, her 'eyes' which are sweet (l. 38), her 'cheek' which is reddened (l. 37). Tennyson's borrowings thus allow the erotic implications of Dorothy's 'wildness' to be made manifest in the later poem, as what is implicit in 'Tintern Abbey' becomes explicit in 'Tithonus': the 'wild' team 'love' (l. 40) Aurora, and are 'yearning' (l. 40) for her 'yoke' (l. 40); they shake their 'manes' (l. 41) like loosened hair. As with Aurora's malevolence, the effects gain in intensity from the earlier 'Tithon', where Aurora's 'bosom' (l. 32) is 'throbbing' (l. 32), but where the 'wild team' do not 'love' her, as they do in 'Tithonus' (l. 40), simply 'Spreading a rapid glow' (l. 36).

If Tennyson's allusions to 'Tintern Abbey' feed into Aurora's eroticism in 'Tithonus', however, then this eroticism is nevertheless streaked with the artificial, a disingenuousness suppressed or denied in Wordsworth's 'Tintern Abbey'. If Dorothy is 'wild' nature, then she is nature with its social inscription denied. Wordsworth is often criticised for 'greening' nature,[42] for portraying her as a purely benign force, and for failing to acknowledge that she is a 'construct' as much as she is an expression of natural forces. Saree Makdisi notes how, in Wordsworth's *An Evening Walk* (1793), 'the straight lines of the enclosure hedges are softened, and . . . transformed into graceful "*willowy* hedgerows," anticipating *Tintern Abbey*'s "hedge-rows, hardly hedge-rows, little lines / Of sportive wood run wild"'.[43] Aurora's erotic seduction of 'Tithonus' makes Wordsworth's artifice and manipulation of the natural world unambiguous, as Tennyson's borrowings allow her to become a fully sexualised and constructed 'nature'. It is the 'wild' Aurora of 'Tithonus', with her synthetic and malign wiles, who fulfils what is inherent in 'Tintern Abbey', in the reworking of the benign and moral nature of 'Tintern Abbey' that is taking place in the later poem.

Nature's own sounds are foregrounded in 'Tintern Abbey' and are synonymous with the transcendence they produce in the mind of the speaker: the mountain springs create a 'sweet inland murmur' (ll. l. 4); the 'sounding cataract' (ll. l. 77) haunts Wordsworth's speaker like a 'passion' (ll. l. 78). Dorothy is also associated with the sounds of transcendence in her role as nature; Wordsworth's speaker hears in her 'voice' (ll. l. 117) the language of his 'former heart' (ll. l. 118). She will become his 'voice' (ll. l. 149) as well as his eyes. Aurora, like Dorothy, is allied with the sounds as well as the sights of nature. Her eyes are 'tremulous' (l. 26), for instance. Ricks in his gloss to the poem suggests a raft of sources for the term 'tremulous eyes', such as:

> Keats, *I stood tip-toe* 146–7, on Cupid and Psyche: 'And how they kist each other's tremulous eyes: / The silver lamp, –'. Also Shelley, *Revolt of Islam* XII xiv 1–2: 'The warm tears burst in spite of faith and fear / From many a tremulous eye'.[44]

Ricks goes on to note how the phrase occurs in John Keble's bestseller, *The Christian Year* (1827), xviii.[45] The term tremulous also carries a sense of musically repeated notes, however, which blend with the existing sources to the poem, acting to combine the senses of sight and sound of 'Tintern Abbey': the musicality of 'tremulous' is reinforced by the violent 'beat' (l. 42) of Aurora's team, which has rhythmic, as well as the menacing, overtones. Matthew Campbell maintains that the sounds and echoes of nature are unrepresentable in Wordsworth, in that they remain '"The ghostly language of the ancient earth"',[46] but emphasises how Wordsworth's poetic rhythms allow the poet to sound the echoes of his experience through 'metrical variation'.[47] Campbell hears 'three unstressed syllables' in '"The ghostly language of the ancient earth"', for instance, which draw 'attention to the ways in which the reading voice is led away from iambic expectation and into a connection with a flexing of the vocal effects to which the poet wishes us to attend'.[48] As in *The Prelude*, from which Campbell's example is taken, nature's sounds are foregrounded in 'Tintern Abbey' and are synonymous with the transcendence they produce in the mind of the speaker. But from Campbell's standpoint, these sounds of nature are representable only through 'voiced sound' and the 'metrical variation' the poet employs to draw attention to his vocal effects. If Wordsworth seeks to 'voice' the sound of nature in the poem, then it is conceivable that he hears in Dorothy's 'voice' (ll. l. 117) 'The language of [his] former heart' (ll. l. 118). Here the three unstressed syllables in the second and third feet of the line break its iambic regularity and focus the reader's attention on the poet's 'metrical variation' and deliber-ate vocal effect. A similar metrical and vocal pattern is operative in 'Tithonus', as Aurora evokes the sounds and rhythm of Wordsworth's nature in 'Tintern Abbey' and the speaker's experience of it through metrical variety. Her 'tremulous eyes' (l. 26), with their freight of musi-cally repeated notes, mimic the sound and rhythmic representation of nature in the earlier poem, with the unstressed syllable in 'tremulous' focusing attention on the line's metrical variation and vocal effect, a variation already given prominence in the switch to the trochaic 'Shines' in its first foot ('Shines in those tremulous eyes that fill with tears'). However, where Dorothy's sonic alignments with nature will allegedly secure Wordsworth's future 'immortality', Aurora's evoke the 'strange song [Tithonus] heard Apollo sing / While Ilion like a mist rose into towers' (ll. 62–3). Drawing on Elaine Jordan's *Alfred Tennyson*, Aidan Day compares Aurora here to Shelley's Witch of Atlas – the spirit of poetry and daughter of Apollo – in the 1824 poem of the same name, and suggests that Tithonus discovers the gulf between himself and the goddess, thereby signalling Tennyson's own anti-Romantic frustration at the unbridgeable gulf between the transcendent and the human.[49] Ricks notices how these lines evoke Shelley's *To Constantia, Singing* 12: 'Wild, sweet, but uncommunica-bly strange'.[50] But sweet sounds not only become wild but also form a 'strange song' in Aurora's immortal world, as the musical accord that nature produces in the mind of the speaker in 'Tintern Abbey' becomes discordant, a discordance reflected in the (un)musicality of the line's insistent sibilants. If Wordsworth hopes to hear the voice of nature in Dorothy's 'voice' (ll. l. 148), then it is a voice of nature that nevertheless sings the sad music of humanity. It is left to 'Tithonus' to make this disconnection explicit, with an Ilion that rises into towers with the aid of 'Tintern Abbey''s 'misty mountain winds' (II. l. 137).

The sounds and rhythms of Wordsworth's nature also inflect Tennyson's celebrated poetic 'ear' for vowel sound and poetic rhythm.[51] The poetry of sensation privileges the power of sound over meaning, whereby the poet places 'an enormous faith in the representational power of sound', and where 'sounds, like objects . . . contain within themselves the potential for their own meaning'.[52] The Ilion section of 'Tithonus' is thought to characterise such poetry. Ricks describes the lines thus:

> In this subtle and persistent paradox of silence and sound, Tennyson found a thrust of relationship with his own fineness of musical verbalism that makes 'Tithonus' his most assuredly successful poem, at once quintessentially Tennysonian and yet with its Tennysonian felicities of sound made stronger and more poignant by its chill of silence, its desolated loss of that 'strange song' which had once animated its world.[53]

Yet the Ilion section registers Wordsworth's poetic experience of nature as much as it does Tennyson's musical verbalism. The desolated loss the poem locates is for the sweet and wild sounds of Wordsworth's 'former heart' that have become a 'strange song'. The language of 'sensation' becomes inflected by the language of 'reflection', which situates Wordsworth's 'philosophical' thought securely within the poem; here nature acts as the site of philosophical understanding rather than simply aesthetic emotion, compromising the quintessentially 'Tennysonian felicities of sound' and questioning Tennyson's commitment to the language of sensation.

In revising Wordsworth's nature, Tennyson nevertheless replicates Wordsworth's apparent gender bias: the female does not speak; she therefore has no 'existence'.[54] Dorothy has a 'voice' in 'Tintern Abbey' yet does not 'speak'; in 'Tithonus' Aurora is similarly reduced to a 'whisper'.

In 'days far-off'

If Tennyson reworks Wordsworth's nature in 'Tithonus', then Tithonus as Wordsworth's speaker undergoes a similar reconfiguration.

Tennyson's borrowed language works to question the process, and value, of the poem's 'abiding' self, that sense of self where the speaker 'discovers he is the same, but not the same, person that he was five years before'.[55] Tithonus speaks of a self that is able to reach moments of sublimity, but that self is a previous self in time. It is in 'days far-off' (l. 51) and 'with . . . other eyes' (l. 51) that Tithonus 'felt [his] blood / Glow with the glow' (ll. 55–6) of transcendence that Aurora as nature produces in him. This is a moment of Tinternesque sublimity, of a speaker looking back at a former self, as the poem echoes with the language of Wordsworth's poem to delineate Tithonus' experience. 'Felt my blood' (l. 55), for instance, echoes with the 'sensations sweet, / Felt in the blood, and felt along the heart' (II. ll. 28–9) that support the speaker of 'Tintern Abbey' in his 'hours of weariness' (II. l. 28), replicating the intimate connection between imagination and feeling that exists in Wordsworth. Wordsworth's images of 'blood' and 'heart' also resonate in the 'crimsoned' Aurora (l. 56), as she suffuses Tithonus with her glowing presence (l. 57). However, the replacement of Wordsworth's 'the' with 'my' in Tennyson's line directly attributes the feeling to Tithonus himself. The text's replacement of an iamb with a trochee in the first foot of the line – 'Glow with the glow' – also captures the rhythm of Wordsworth's speaker's pulsating sensations, while the slow pull of alliteration and assonance in the 'Glow with the glow that slowly crimsoned all' (l. 56) hints at how Tithonus' moment of transcendence is taking place out of ordinary time.

Tithonus himself does not, or cannot, continue to transcend time in the way that is offered in the moment of Wordsworthian sublimity; his sensations sweet do not pass into the 'purer mind' (II. l. 30) with 'tranquil restoration' (II. l. 31) as they do in 'Tintern Abbey'. Tellingly, the 'other eyes' to which Tithonus refers reveal that the moment of retrospective sublimity is potentially vitiated from within, and thus not worthy of being 'remembered', as the phrase contains echoes of *An Evening Walk*, which includes a speaker 'with other eyes' (I. l. 15), who looks back at his former ability to invest nature with significance, an ability he subsequently loses but recaptures. Unlike Wordsworth's speaker in the poem, however, Tithonus seems unable to recover his lost imaginative power, and remains trapped within the process of looking back 'with other eyes'. He fails to sublimate, and thus recover, his loss in the way that Wordsworth's speaker does, largely because the echoes at work prevent him from doing so. The double-set of 'days far-off' (l. 48 and l. 51) of which he speaks, for instance, echoes Wordsworth's 'The Solitary Reaper' (1807), which is predicated on the speaker's observation of the Reaper's perpetual revisiting of a sorrow:

> Will no one tell me what she sings?
> Perhaps the plaintive numbers flow
> For old, unhappy far-off things,
> And battles long ago:
> Or is it some more humble lay,
> Familiar matter of to-day?
> Some natural sorrow, loss, or pain,
> That has been, and may be again!
>
> Whate'er the theme, the Maiden sang
> As if her song could have no ending.
>
> (III. ll. 17–26)

These lines, in effect, work as a framing device, trapping the speaker within his own imaginative loss. Like the Reaper, Tithonus seems to be caught in a cycle of revisiting an imaginative vacuum, from which he wants to escape, but in which he inextricably looks to be bound. Rather than 'dreadfully mutable', Tennyson's revisions manoeuvre towards making Tithonus dreadfully immutable here.

Tithonus is trapped with his own failing imagination, and with his inconstant and discordant nature, Aurora. The 'warmer love' (l. 154) nature induces in Wordsworth's speaker in 'Tintern Abbey' becomes 'cold' and distant in 'Tithonus': in contrast to the 'shooting lights' (II. l. 119) of Dorothy's eyes, 'cold are all [Aurora's] lights' (l. 67), and 'cold' are Tithonus' 'wrinkled feet / Upon [her] glimmering thresholds' (ll. 67–8). In another echo with *An Evening Walk*, 'cold' Aurora's 'tears' (l. 45) evoke the 'cold cheek' (I. l. 339) and the 'shuddering tear [it] retains' (I. l. 339) after the speaker of that poem realises that his imaginative powers are momentarily lost to darkness. 'Glimmering', as either a verb or an adjective, specifies a 'faint or wavering light' (*OED*), but the word is also suggestive of *An Evening Walk*, where it, too, indicates a weakened or wavering imagination. In Wordsworth's poem, the speaker experiences a moment of transcendence, where 'music, stealing round the glimmering deeps / Charm'd the tall circle of th' enchanted steeps' (I. ll. 320–1). The mind's imaginative power appears to be subverted in the poem, although the loss remains couched rather than explicit, or is displaced onto a source other than the failing power of the mind itself. For instance, with the coming of night comes the loss of imagination, and 'Lost in the thicken'd darkness, glimmers hoar' (I. l. 329), prompting the speaker to exhort: 'Stay! pensive, sadly-pleasing visions, stay! / Ah no! as fades the vale, they fade away' (I. ll. 336–7). While the speaker acknowledges that the 'glimmers' are lost and the visions fading, he seemingly attributes this loss to the darkness rather than to the mind's failing powers. The present tense in 'glimmering', however, suggests that Tithonus cannot break free from his cycle of yearning and fading; nor can he seem to attribute his failing power to the 'darkness' that is Aurora. Additionally, 'the old mysterious glimmer' (l. 34) that steals from Aurora's 'pure' brows and 'shoulders' (ll. 36–7) for Tithonus evokes the 'burthen of the mystery' (l. 39) of the earlier poem, but whereas for the speaker of 'Tintern Abbey' the transcendence that nature provides acts as a powerful mystery, a pulse of warm sensational blood that feeds the purer mind, for Tithonus it acts only as an enervated glimmer that results in cold, wrinkled feet.

There seems to be no hope of escape from this post-'Tintern' world for Tithonus, no projections into or onto the future, but simply a perpetual present of loss and fading power, as Tennyson continues to rework the mind's connection with nature. Whereas the speaker of 'Tintern Abbey' finds the mind's transcendence of nature rewarding, as there will always ostensibly be 'food / For future years' (II. ll. 65–6), Tithonus is 'consumed' by the process of 'transcending'. The 'gloomy wood' (II. l. 79) sustains the speaker in 'Tintern Abbey': it is literally an 'appetite' (II. l. 81), a provision of spiritual nourishment, whereas the 'gloom' (l. 37) of the dark world has an obverse effect in 'Tithonus': Aurora's 'cheek begins to redden through the gloom' (l. 37), but gloom carries the sense of a loss of hope as well as a sense of darkness (*OED*), counterpointing the 'life and food / For future years' (II. ll. 65–6) that nourishes Wordsworth's speaker. In Wordsworth, 'to deny imagination its darker food, to seek and make it a "Shape all light," is to wish imagination away',[56] but in 'Tithonus', the food with which the imagination is fed connotes depletion rather than nourishment. Aurora's blush – itself transient, or perhaps duplicitous – cannot feed this loss of hope for Tithonus, as she functions as its cause, the heart of its darkness. She represents Wordsworth's speaker's repository of hope writ large, but can offer Tithonus only an etiolated present, tendering not the growth of the mind through darkness,[57] but merely perpetual and enervating stasis.

The speaker's circular return to his moments of sublimity in 'Tintern Abbey', those moments that nourish him in his loneliness, but which nevertheless echo with loss, are hyperbolised in Tithonus' circular return to his faded nature, Aurora. With Wordsworth, 'his mind circles and haunts a particular place until released into an emancipatory idea of Nature'.[58] Tithonus' mind circles, but cannot be released, as his 'nature' remains suffocatingly dark rather than emancipatory. Nature as woman becomes the destroyer rather than the creator, as the text works to sunder Wordsworth's 'covenant of mind and nature'.[59] In 'Tithonus', nature does not remain supine, a passive partner over which the mind can continue to have an ongoing and superior control, but is a wilful seductress and destroyer, with the power to tease and depress as well as to feed the mind. The moral and cooperative nature which sustains the speaker in 'Tintern Abbey' no longer exists, as Tennyson works to reveal her as a recalcitrant partner. Wordsworth comes to postulate a non-cooperative nature in the 1807 'Elegiac Stanzas', but 'Tithonus' specifically disassembles the imaginative promise of 'Tintern Abbey', confirming and consolidating the essential vacancy at its core, and laying bare the ruptured relationship between mind and nature – and the mind and itself – in the post-'Tintern' world Tennyson creates in the text.

The evidence of an imaginative self that exists prior in time is less potent in the 1833 'Tithon', from which the 1860 version is drawn. Tithon bemoans how he was once 'wooed' (l. 47) by Aurora's charms: 'Ay me! ay me! with what another heart, / By thy divine embraces circumfused, / Thy black curls burning into sunny rings / With thy change changed, I felt this wondrous glow' (ll. 41–4). He recognises that Aurora's 'change' is 'changed', her blackness dissipated, unlike in the later version, where it continues to depress and subdue. The 'wondrous glow' that ends line 44, however, while extended in its intensity via its enjambment, nevertheless lacks the connective beat to Wordsworth's 'Tintern Abbey' of 'Tithonus', suspended in splendid isolation as it is at the end of line. The connections to 'Tintern Abbey' gain in intensity in the later poem, where they also create a more persistent effect. 'Tithon', for instance, is suggestive of a self-expressive lyricism, where lines 11–15 assert a 'personal emotional state [that] is couched as a definitive statement of a universal condition, outside language',[60] although 'after the initial self-pitying lament, the passage seeks, through rhythmic regularity and repeated infinitives, to transcend the individual predicament, depicting an ahistorical condition of mythic suffering'.[61] 'Tithonus' supplants the strategies of the earlier poem, as it becomes the 'poetry of enactment',[62] replacing the lyrical and self-expressive with the performative and dramatic. Tennyson's reworking of Wordsworth's

narrative of recurrence ostensibly strengthens the form of the monologue, with its fictionalised self, as it distances it further from the
earlier poet's universal subjectivity. The Wordsworthian echoes and
associations in the poem simultaneously work to complicate its performative and rhetorical status, however, pulling it inexorably back
to the Wordsworthian lyricism and universalism it is formulated to
supplant. Tennyson's attempt to create a new poetic is thus compromised by the language of the very poet whose self-expressiveness
he is attempting to supplant. And yet, paradoxically, it is Wordsworth's language that enables the monologue to function best by
anchoring its dramatic experimentation, providing the linguistic
scaffolding from which the text can work its revisionary changes.
Herbert F. Tucker, Jr, reveals how the subdued lyric presence in the
monologue – 'what you cannot have and what you cannot forget'[63]
– frequently functions as a disruptive or irruptive force, breaking
through the dramatic narrative in discrete acts of transgression.
Tucker cites Browning's 'Fra Lippo Lippi' (1855) to illustrate the
disruptive lyrical patterns at work within the monologue, where
'*stornelli*', 'lyrical catches Englished in italics',[64] or transgressions
'into lyric' in Browning's 'My Last Duchess' (1842), break into the
'story'.[65] But the absorption of Wordsworth's language in Tennyson
refutes Tucker's transgressive pattern, as it is woven organically into
the poem. Wordsworth's narrative of the mind's interaction with
nature survives, despite its vitiated state, helping the poem to cohere
in its dramatic form. Tennyson might wish to free himself from
both Wordsworth's imaginative investment in nature and the earlier
poet's universal subjectivism, but he is nevertheless dependent on
both for his poetic and dramatic effects. Likewise, Tennyson's revisions do not liberate Tithonus from his cycle of endless return; they
do not release him to the ground. Rather, he is as trapped by his
'immutable' self as he is by the self that is forever changing.

Wordsworth has been called Tennyson's 'poetic father-figure',[66]
a phrase that itself invokes the language of Bloomian filiation, and
it is possible to read the revisionary process at work in 'Tithonus'
as fulfilling Bloom's defensive revisionary movements: the revision
of Wordsworth's nature, for instance, can be seen to comply with
Bloom's second revisionary ratio, *tessera*, where a poet 'antitheti-
cally' 'completes' his precursor, by 'so reading the parent-poem as to
retain its terms but to mean them in another sense, as though the precursor had failed to go far enough'.[67] Likewise, Tennyson's revision
of Tithonus' sense of the abiding in the transient could be seen to
comply with the first of Bloom's revisionary ratios, *clinamen*, which

'implies that the precursor poem went accurately up to a certain point, but then should have swerved, precisely in the direction that the new poem moves'.[68] Yet the poem's reliance on the language of Wordsworth's obsolete cycle of recurrence undermines Bloom's theory of revisionary relations. 'Tithonus''s revision of 'Tintern Abbey' reveals a sense of anxiety, but this appears not to be of the strong poet wanting to become his 'own Great Original',[69] but instead of the poet wanting to remain with his 'poetic father-figure', or at least to benefit from his overwhelming presence. The revisionary process at work may be working at a psychic level, but this is not at the level of deep impulse and defensiveness; it is also, importantly, working at surface level, at the level of language, cadence and rhythm. Both the psychic and linguistic patterning in the poem reveal Tennyson to be attempting to define himself in relation to Wordsworth, but nevertheless remaining dependent upon him. Bloom claims that the hidden concern of 'Tithonus' is Tennyson's own belatedness as a poet, 'his arrival on the scene *after the event*, after the triumph of poetry of "reflection" in Coleridge and Wordsworth, and of poetry of "sensation" in Shelley and Keats, to use a technical distinction invented by Hallam'.[70] Yet the powerful repressive action against the reflective poets, Coleridge and Keats, of which Bloom writes is not at work in 'Tithonus'; rather, Tennyson does not so much lament his belatedness but draw at will from Wordsworth's reflective language in the poem, aligning himself with its overwhelming 'triumph'. There is a return of the repressed here, an effect traceable through the very language that Bloom outlaws from his methodology. The effects of Tennyson's paternal dependency are profound, no more so than in relation to the monologue itself. In seeking to remain with Wordsworth, Tennyson seemingly cannot move on either from 'returning to things' or from the 'things' that themselves return,[71] despite the opportunity for 'emancipation' the monologue has afforded him through its objective status. The poet seems to retain a lingering regard for Wordsworth's spiritual and moral investment in nature, even while simultaneously confirming that this investment is in the process of being displaced by the laws of evolutionary science. The poem's reliance on these disassembled fragments also goes some way towards confirming both the monologue's inability to function independently of the language of its Romantic past and the facilitative role Wordsworth plays in a poetic form from which he has in theory been distanced.

The sense of the diminishing power of transcendence – a theme Wordsworth himself returns to in his 'Intimations' ode – openly preoccupies the Victorians, who begin to voice concerns that Wordsworthian imaginative transcendence has lost its power: Matthew Arnold's 'fading gleam' in 'Dover Beach' (1867), for instance, signals 'the extinction of Wordsworth's visionary project'.[72] 'Tithonus' takes this preoccupation to extremes, as both the mind and nature lose their power in the post-'Tintern' world that is created in the poem. The mask of the dramatic monologue should allow Tennyson to shield himself from the implications of the poem's critique, but the nature of the inscription renders him unable to do so, as his rewriting of the earlier poem is laid bare. Geoffrey H. Hartman, musing on 'nature-loss' in Wordsworth, suggests that

> though Wordsworth engages in 'Tintern Abbey' and elsewhere with the theme of loss and gain, he will not take an ultimate decision upon himself. On this issue there is vacillation rather than an authoritative resolution by means of visionary or poetic voice. 'Milton! England hath need of thee,' yet Wordsworth refused to be Milton on the matter of nature's ultimate importance to the life of the mind.
> He delays, in fact, rather than hastens a decision.[73]

'Tithonus' neither vacillates nor delays, laying bare the ruptured relationship between mind and nature, and the mind and itself, in the post-'Tintern' world imagined by Tennyson. The gleam might have faded for Tennyson, as it has for Arnold, but it is a gleam on which Tennyson and the poem nevertheless continue to depend. The dying light of the Wordsworthian imaginative process has revealed itself as too valuable and irresistible to be labelled 'extinct'.

'Resolution and Independence'

'Resolution and Independence' (1807) continues Wordsworth's preoccupation with the question of whether or not the failing imagination can be revivified. Tithonus has been granted immortality without immortal youth, but the echo of Wordsworth's 'Resolution and Independence' in the poem works to draw attention to how immortal age has not only wearied Tennyson's speaker, but deprived him of imaginative power. In 'Resolution and Independence', the speaker has the power to invest the Leech-Gatherer with imaginative significance, even if this is via a 'troubled imagination'.[74] Wordsworth writes on the nature of the imaginative process taking place in the poem as an explanation of the image of the Leech-Gatherer as a 'huge stone' (II. l. 57) that lies on 'top of an eminence' (II. l. 58) and as a 'sea-beast' (II. l. 62) sunning itself on rock or sand:

> In these images, the conferring, the abstracting, and the modifying powers of the Imagination, immediately and mediately acting, are all brought into conjunction. The Stone is endowed with something of the power of life to approximate it to the Sea-beast; and the Sea-beast stripped of some of its vital qualities to assimilate it to the stone; which intermediate image is thus treated for the purpose of bringing the original image, that of the stone, to a nearer resemblance to the figure and condition of the aged Man; who is divested of so much of the indications of life and motion as to bring him to the point where the two objects unite and coalesce in just comparison . . .
>
> Thus far of an endowing or modifying power: but the Imagination also shapes and *creates*; and how? By innumerable processes; and in none does it more delight than in that of consolidating numbers into unity, and dissolving and separating unity into number, – alternations proceeding from, and governed by, a sublime consciousness of the soul in her own mighty and almost divine powers.[75]

The Leech-Gatherer could be said to have no imaginative power, however; he functions as one of the unimaginative souls Wordsworth had in mind when writing the final version of *The Ruined Cottage* in 1804,[76] who are ineluctably separated from those invested with the power to transfigure their lives through the imagination.[77] He appears, instead, to be a conduit to imaginative power, curing the speaker of the descent into the 'de-sublimated' madness into which he has sunk.[78] Verbal connections abound between Tithonus and the Leech-Gatherer, which emphasise that Tithonus, like the Gatherer, has little or no imaginative power. Both 'roam': Tithonus, a 'white-haired shadow' (l. 8), roams 'like a dream / The ever-silent spaces of the East' (ll. 8–9); the Gatherer 'roamed' (II. l. 103), and paces 'About the weary moors continually, / Wandering about alone and silently' (II. ll. 130–1). The Leech-Gatherer is 'grey' (II. l. 56); Tithonus is a 'gray shadow' (l. 11).

But the Leech-Gatherer exists as one of the 'ordinary men' ('Resolution and Independence', II. l. 96), one of those, like the speaker of 'Tintern Abbey' and the speaker of 'Resolution and Independence', in fact, who has 'the power to die' ('Tithonus', l. 70). His 'measured phrase' (II. l. 95) may place him 'above the reach' (II. l. 95) of most, and he may be invested with mystical status by the speaker, but he remains mortal, nonetheless. Tithonus lacks the capacity to die, by contrast, and has the power only to roam. He is doubly doomed in this sense: doomed to roam without the ability to die, and doomed to live without imaginative power. Wordsworthian echoes foreground the reverse positions here of Tithonus and the Leech-Gatherer. In 'Tithonus', it is 'happy men' who have the power to die, like the 'ordinary men' (II. l. 96) of 'Resolution and Independence': Tithonus is excluded from this happy, ordinary race by the gift of unwanted immortality. The speaker of 'Resolution and Independence' is 'a happy Child of earth' (II. l. 31), as, ultimately, is the Leech-Gatherer, and was once 'as happy as a Boy' (II. l. 18) before his state of despondency. All are 'happy' in this way, except for Tithonus.

Moreover, the Leech-Gatherer might be seen as dying 'into the life of nature',[79] the very nature in which Tithonus craves to be immersed, but to which he is denied access. Tithonus cannot die into the life of Aurora as nature, as she does not provide the safety and comfort of Wordsworth's nature in 'Tintern Abbey'. 'Resolution and Independence' exemplifies a Wordsworthian 'faith in nature' that 'Tithonus' works to deny,[80] although echoes of Wordsworth's 'nature' resound through Tennyson's poem, nonetheless: in 'Resolution and Independence' the air after the storm is filled with the 'pleasant noise of waters' (II. l. 7) and the hare 'from the plashy earth / Raises a mist' (II. ll. 12–13); in 'Tithonus', the mists are 'Far-folded' (l. 10) and the air is 'soft' (l. 32). The liminality of the Leech-Gatherer, a natural, yet seemingly supernatural, being, 'not all alive nor dead' (II. l. 64), is also evoked in Tithonus' liminal state, on the edge of the world where he was born, but consigned to a perpetual after-life from which he wants to escape. The Leech-Gatherer is a part of nature, no more so perhaps than in the description of him in the lines Wordsworth picks out to illustrate the powers of the imagination, although he is thus in this sense also 'imagined' as a part of nature:

> As a huge Stone is sometimes seen to lie
> Couched on the bald top of an eminence;
> Wonder to all who do the same espy,
> By what means it could thither come, and whence;
> So that it seems a thing endued with sense:
> Like a Sea-beast crawled forth, that on a shelf
> Of rock or sand reposeth, there to sun itself;
>
> Such seemed this Man.
>
> (II. ll. 57–64)

Tithonus, too, was once part of nature, and is longing to be 'earth in earth' (l. 75), but is confined by the text to a state beyond nature. Tithonus, as speaker, is denied an act of imaginative revivification, such as the speaker of Wordsworth's poem experiences through the Leech-Gatherer as a part of nature; Aurora as nature does not stimulate his imaginative powers, but depletes them.

The latter effect gains emphasis through time changes in both 'Resolution and Independence' and 'Tithonus'. 'Tithonus' looks back to a time when he could 'Glow with the glow' (l. 56), replete with transcendent power, but such power belongs to his past, a past he appears doomed perpetually to revisit. In 'Resolution and Independence', the speaker acknowledges the differences between past and present selves: he 'was a Traveller then upon the moor' (II. l. 15) when he 'heard distant waters, roar' (II. l. 17). The time difference replicates itself in 'Tithonus' in the way in which Tithonus looks back on his former self, although Wordsworth's speaker's subsequent move into sublimity appears exhausted for him. Similarly, 'Resolution and Independence' functions as a 'dialogic' poem, albeit an implicit one,[81] as Wordsworth 'confronts and seeks to overcome the self that experiences chilling "thoughts"';[82] he also steps '"outside himself" while examining his imagination at work'.[83] Tennyson's speaker is also bifurcated in this way, as he seeks to absorb 'chilling "thoughts"' of his former imaginative self. This, combined with the sharing of linguistic phrases between the poems, confirms that if 'Tithonus' is reworking 'Tintern Abbey', then it does so, in part, via 'Resolution and Independence'. At the same time, the revisions in 'Tithonus' rework Wordsworth's own imaginative rewriting in 'Resolution and Independence', which, itself, acts as a corrective or 'answer' to 'Tintern Abbey''s doubts over the power of the imagination to continue to sustain itself. As a result, 'Tithonus' advertises its dependence on a Wordsworthian narrative that it simultaneously promotes as obsolete; and as with the revision of 'Tintern Abbey', Tennyson relies on the language of the earlier poem for his dramatic and poetic effects, subverting any Bloomian revisionary process that could be said to be taking place.

Conclusion

The Wordsworthian echoes in 'Tithonus' allow Tennyson to subvert 'Tintern Abbey''s exploration of the limits of imaginative reach: the synergy between mind and nature, and the mind and itself, breaks down, as Aurora becomes an attenuated version of nature/Dorothean nature and Tithonus a version of Wordsworth's speaker. Nonetheless, Wordsworth's language is vital to the monologue, a form expressly designed to transcend the limitations of universal Romantic subjectivity. The connection between nature and the moral life may well be unsustainable for a Tennyson rewriting the poem for a new audience in 1860 but its broken fragments still have a significant part to play in his poetics, as he recommits both himself and his speaker to Wordsworth's outworn poetic trope. Eighteen years after the publication of 'Ulysses', and the breaking of form through the development of the monologue, Tennyson still cannot break free from Wordsworth's influence. Ulysses goes in search of the lost Wordsworthian imagination; Tithonus dismantles the Wordsworthian correspondence between mind and nature, but cannot function without it. Tennyson creates a new Wordsworth for the Victorians, one whose influence is essential to the monologue, simultaneously 'completing' the monologic aspects of Wordsworth's 'Tintern Abbey'. Tennyson does not perform a powerful repressive action against one of the 'greatest poets ever to have attempted a humanized Sublime';[84] he does not lament his own belatedness at arriving 'on the scene *after the event*, after the triumph of poetry of "reflection"'.[85] Rather, the poet's inability to escape the Romantic burden of the past becomes empowering rather than disempowering, enabling both the poem and the poet to be; Tennyson, in writing the monologue, breaks form, yet Wordsworth's language and outworn epistemology are woven seamlessly into the poem. At the same time, 'Tithonus' shares in the 'triumph' of Wordsworth's language of reflection, just as it embraces the enervated gleam of the Wordsworthian sublime. But in so doing, the poem, like *Maud* before it, questions its own ability to function as a dramatic text and Tennyson's ability to function as a dramatic poet.

Tennyson turned once more to 'Tintern Abbey''s tropes in 'In the Valley of Cauteretz', written in 1861 and published in 1864, and in 'Enoch Arden', written likewise in 1861 and published in 1864. Tennyson draws on Wordsworth's trope of returning to the past in 'In the Valley of Cauteretz', which recalls a visit he and Hallam made to a valley in the Pyrenees in 1830.[86] The speaker recalls a self that is not itself, as 'two and thirty years were a mist that rolls away' (l. 6). The poem assigns the 'thy voice' of 'Tintern Abbey' to the stream that flashes white: 'All along the valley, stream that flashes white, / Deepening thy voice with the deepening of the night' (ll. 1–2). 'Thy' and 'voice' are separated yet joined by the adjective 'living' – the 'living air' (II. l. 99) of 'Tintern Abbey' – emphasising how it is the voice of the stream in the rocky valley that makes both the dead and a past self live once more in the present: 'For all along the valley, down thy rocky bed, / Thy living voice to me was as the voice of the dead' (ll. 7–8). In the light of Tennyson's acknowledgement of 'Tintern Abbey''s belatedness in 'Tithonus', the 'living voice' of 'Tintern Abbey' is indeed as the voice of the dead. Yet, as in 'Tithonus', Tennyson concludes that the dead voice of 'Tintern Abbey' is nevertheless a necessary and living one, with the ambiguity of simile – 'Thy living voice to me was as the voice of the dead' – concretised into metaphor: 'And all along the valley, by rock and cave and tree, / The voice of the dead was a living voice to me' (ll. 9–10).

'Enoch Arden' sees Tennyson return to the unpoetical language and subject matter of the early English 'Idyls'; the poem borrows from Wordsworth's *The Excursion* (1814), with its 'long-haired long-bearded solitary' (l. 633), and is freighted with the 'clusters', 'hazelwood' and 'nutters' of Wordsworth's 'Nutting' (1800).[87] 'Enoch Arden' also revisits Wordsworth's narrative of coming again, although returning ends in loss rather than deferral, as in 'Tintern Abbey', or a perpetuation of the narrative's enervated tropes as in 'Tithonus': when Enoch 'comes again' (l. 308), 'if he come again' (l. 300) – notice the direct echo of Tennyson's phrasing in 'Tithonus' here – Enoch finds 'neither light nor murmur' (l. 683): Dorothy's lighted eyes and voice find no place in this poem. It is only 'A bill of sale' that 'gleamed through the drizzle' (l. 684). 'Tintern Abbey''s 'dwelling-place' (II. l. 142), the 'mansion for all lovely forms' (II. l. 141), lies empty. The past is '"dead or dead to me"', as Enoch himself confirms, with the latter phrase echoing in its confirmation of irretrievability Wordsworth's 'SHE dwelt among the untrodden ways' (1800) and its 'And oh / The difference to me' (I. ll. 11–12). The dead past is balanced by a Wordsworthian nature that is also devoid of meaning: the 'dead leaf' (l. 674) can be nothing but a 'dead weight' (l. 674).

Notes

1. Tennyson, *The Poems of Tennyson*, II, p. 605.
2. Tennyson, *The Poems of Tennyson*, II, p. 606.
3. Pearsall, *Tennyson's Rapture*, p. 252.
4. See Hallam, 'On Some of the Characteristics of Modern Poetry', p. 107.
5. Pearsall, *Tennyson's Rapture*, p. 225.
6. Tennyson himself says of Tithonus that he '"was beloved by Aurora [goddess of the dawn], who gave him eternal life but not eternal youth. He grew old and infirm, and as he could not die, according to the legend, was turned into a grasshopper"'. See Tennyson, *The Poems of Tennyson*, II, p. 606.

7. Hughes, *The Manyfacèd Glass*, p. 1.
8. Lourie, 'Below the Thunders of the Upper Deep', p. 25.
9. Lourie, 'Below the Thunders of the Upper Deep', p. 25.
10. Lourie, 'Below the Thunders of the Upper Deep', p. 25.
11. Lourie, 'Below the Thunders of the Upper Deep', p. 25.
12. Lourie, 'Below the Thunders of the Upper Deep', p. 25.
13. Bloom, *Poetry and Repression*, p. 161.
14. Bloom, *Poetry and Repression*, pp. 165–6.
15. See Ricks, in Tennyson, *The Poems of Tennyson*, II, l. 1 (p. 607). All further references to this and the other Tennyson poems quoted in the chapter are to this edition and appear parenthetically in the text unless otherwise stated.
16. See Ricks, in Tennyson, *The Poems of Tennyson*, II, p. 607, 324, l. 1.
17. Perry, *Alfred Tennyson*, p. 52.
18. Perry, *Alfred Tennyson*, p. 52.
19. Perry, *Alfred Tennyson*, p. 52.
20. Page, *Tennyson: Interviews and Recollections*, p. 176, quoted in Perry, *Alfred Tennyson*, p. 45.
21. Tennyson, *The Poems of Tennyson*, II, p. 232, l. 21.
22. Tennyson, *Alfred Lord Tennyson: A Memoir*, II, p. 70.
23. Perry notes how repetition is one of Tennyson's 'own most distinctive poetic resources . . . but repeating the word "again", in particular, served him superbly well on several occasions'. See Perry, *Alfred Tennyson*, p. 46.
24. Rapf, '"Visionaries of Dereliction"', p. 377, n. 14.
25. Cronin, *Reading Victorian Poetry*, pp. 161–2.
26. Cronin, *Reading Victorian Poetry*, p. 161.
27. Martens, *Browning, Victorian Poetics and the Romantic Legacy*, p. 9.
28. Hallam, 'On Some of the Characteristics of Modern Poetry', p. 93.
29. Hallam, 'On Some of the Characteristics of Modern Poetry', pp. 93–4.
30. Christ, *Victorian and Modern Poetics*, p. 57.
31. Bloom, *Poetry and Repression*, p. 168.
32. Bloom, *The Anxiety of Influence*, p. 31.
33. Wordsworth, *The Poetical Works of William Wordsworth in Five Volumes*, II, l. 8 (p. 179). All subsequent references to Wordsworth's poems, including 'Tintern Abbey', that appear in the text are to these volumes unless otherwise stated. Each reference is given by volume and line number.
34. Shaw, *Tennyson's Style*, p. 89.
35. Tennyson, *The Poems of Tennyson*, I, l. 34 (p. 621). All future references to this poem appear parenthetically in the text.
36. Keats, *Selected Poems and Letters of Keats*, p. 52.
37. Lawrence Kramer comments on the way in which Victorian poets rewrite the close of 'Tintern Abbey', and how these rewritings tend to be 'erotic ones', as 'Tintern Abbey' is read 'as a model of human desire'. See Kramer, 'Victorian Sexuality and "Tintern Abbey"', p. 400.

38. Tennyson, *The Poems of Tennyson*, II, pp. 609–10, l. 42, 'noted by C. R. Forker, *Notes and Queries*, Dec. 1959'.
39. Hollander maintains that 'echo is a metaphor of, and for, alluding [that] does not depend on conscious intention'. See *The Figure of Echo*, p. 64.
40. Dillon, 'Canonical and Sensational', p. 96.
41. Hartman, 'Retrospect 1971', in *Wordsworth's Poetry 1787–1814*, p. xv.
42. Levinson, *Wordsworth's Great Period Poems*, pp. 24–39, quoted in Makdisi, *Romantic Imperialism*, p. 49.
43. Makdisi, *Romantic Imperialism*, p. 54.
44. Tennyson, *The Poems of Tennyson*, II, pp. 608–9, l. 26.
45. Tennyson, *The Poems of Tennyson*, II, pp. 608–9, l. 26.
46. Campbell, *Rhythm and Will in Victorian Poetry*, p. 36.
47. Campbell, *Rhythm and Will in Victorian Poetry*, p. 36.
48. Campbell, *Rhythm and Will in Victorian Poetry*, p. 36.
49. See Day, *Tennyson's Scepticism*, p. 46.
50. Tennyson, *The Poems of Tennyson*, II, p. 612, l. 62.
51. Eliot, *Selected Prose*, p. 239.
52. Christ, *Victorian and Modern Poetics*, pp. 61, 62.
53. Ricks, *Tennyson*, pp. 131–2.
54. Mellor, *Romanticism and Gender*, p. 19.
55. Perry, *Alfred Tennyson*, p. 47.
56. Hartman, *The Unremarkable Wordsworth*, p. 141.
57. Hartman, *The Unremarkable Wordsworth*, p. 139. See Hartman, *The Unremarkable Wordsworth*, p. 139 for more on the role of darkness in 'the growth of the mind – especially the poet's mind'.
58. Hartman, *The Unremarkable Wordsworth*, p. 137.
59. Hartman, *Wordsworth's Poetry 1787–1814*, p. 267.
60. Slinn, 'Dramatic Monologue', p. 86.
61. Slinn, 'Dramatic Monologue', p. 86.
62. Slinn, 'Dramatic Monologue', p. 86.
63. Tucker, 'Dramatic Monologue and the Overhearing of Lyric', p. 235.
64. Tucker, 'Dramatic Monologue and the Overhearing of Lyric', p. 232.
65. Tucker, 'Dramatic Monologue and the Overhearing of Lyric', p. 234.
66. Padel, 'Tennyson: Echo and Harmony', p. 327.
67. Bloom, *The Anxiety of Influence*, p. 14.
68. Bloom, *The Anxiety of Influence*, p. 14.
69. Bloom, *The Anxiety of Influence*, p. 64.
70. Bloom, *Poetry and Repression*, p. 168.
71. Perry, *Alfred Tennyson*, p. 46.
72. Rowlinson, 'Lyric', p. 68.
73. Hartman, *The Unremarkable Wordsworth*, p. 150.
74. O'Neill, '"A Kind of an Excuse"', p. 58.
75. 'Preface to the Edition published in 1815', pp. xxviii–xxix.
76. See Graham Davidson's comments on *The Ruined Cottage*, in 'Wordsworth's Wasteland or the Speargrass Redemption', pp. 79–82.

77. Davidson, 'Wordsworth's Wasteland or the Speargrass Redemption', pp. 79–82.
78. Thomas Weiskel suggests that Wordsworth is fully committed to de-sublimation in 'Resolution and Independence'. See Weiskel, *The Romantic Sublime*, p. 58.
79. Hartman, *Wordsworth's Poetry 1787–1814*, p. 202.
80. Hartman, *Wordsworth's Poetry 1787–1814*, p. 203.
81. O'Neill, '"A Kind of an Excuse"', p. 57.
82. O'Neill, '"A Kind of an Excuse"', p. 57.
83. O'Neill, *Romanticism and the Self-Conscious Poem*, p. 42.
84. Bloom, *Poetry and Repression*, pp. 165–6.
85. Bloom, *Poetry and Repression*, p. 168.
86. See Ricks, in Tennyson, *The Poems of Tennyson*, II, p. 617.
87. See Ricks, in Tennyson, *The Poems of Tennyson*, II, p. 627, 330, ll. 4–8.

Crossing the Wordsworthian Bar

Tennyson's 'Crossing the Bar' (1889) focalises the poet's own brand of faith as he approaches death and crosses the bar, turning home for the last time to the limitless deep:

> Sunset and evening star,
>   And one clear call for me!
> And may there be no moaning of the bar,
>   When I put out to sea,
>
> But such a tide as moving seems asleep,
>   Too full for sound and foam,
> When that which drew from out the boundless deep
>   Turns again home.
>
> Twilight and evening bell,
>   And after that the dark!
> And may there be no sadness of farewell,
>   When I embark;
>
> For though from out our bourne of Time and Place
>   The flood may bear me far,
> I hope to see my Pilot face to face
>   When I have crost the bar.[1]

The poem was written in October 1889 while Tennyson was crossing the Solent.[2] It came, Tennyson was to recall, '"in a moment"'.[3] It engages with familiar Tennysonian themes – death and what comes after it, the separation that comes with death – as well as with familiar Tennysonian tropes, such as the threshold (both between life and death and between day and evening), the 'boundless deep' and the sense of repletion or fullness (in a reminder of the feeding and sleeping hoard of 'Ulysses', the moving tide seems asleep, 'too full' for sound and foam).

Yet, in keeping with the pattern that this book has traced, the poem also echoes with Wordsworth's language and phrasing. In coming quickly to Tennyson, the poem reveals an automatic and instinctive recalling of Wordsworth; 'Crossing the Bar' has affiliations with both Wordsworth's *An Evening Walk* (1793) and 'Elegiac Stanzas' (1807), for instance. In *An Evening Walk*, the speaker describes how

> Hung o'er a cloud, above the steep that rears
> An edge all flame, the broad'ning sun appears;
> A long blue bar its aegis orb divides,
> And breaks the spreading of its golden tides;
> And now it touches on the purple steep
> That flings his shadow on the pictured deep.
> 'Cross the calm lake's blue shades the cliffs aspire
> With tow'rs and woods a 'prospect all on fire'.[4]

The earlier poem echoes through Tennyson's late lyric, as his speaker's auxiliary 'may' posits no moaning of the bar as he puts out to sea, but only the spreading of golden tides. *An Evening Walk* posits a 'pictured' deep which becomes 'boundless' with possibility in Tennyson.

The image of the 'deep' itself has deep significances for Tennyson throughout his career: *In Memoriam*, for instance, draws on the 'deep' significances in the 1807 'Elegiac Stanzas: Suggested by a Picture of Peele Castle, in a Storm, Painted by Sir George Beaumont' (hereafter 'Elegiac Stanzas'). 'Elegiac Stanzas' reveals Wordsworth as making his own accommodations with the God who is not named, accepting 'what is to be born [*sic*]',[5] while conceding that 'Not without hope we suffer and we mourn' (l. 60). Wordsworth too 'Turns again home'. But in turning, 'Crossing the Bar', like 'Elegiac Stanzas' before it, moves away from the self to embrace the many,[6] as 'my' becomes 'our', although 'our' soon returns to 'me' and 'I' and considerations of the self: 'For though from out our bourne of time and place / The flood may bear me far / I hope to see my Pilot face to face / When I have crost the bar'.

Tennyson's 'tide as moving seems asleep / Too full for sound or foam' also resonates with 'Elegiac Stanzas'. Writing as if his 'had been the Painter's hand' (l. 13) to 'express what then I saw' (l. 14), Wordsworth's speaker says of Peele Castle: 'A Picture had it been of lasting ease, / Elysian quiet, without toil or strife; / No motion but the moving tide, a breeze, / Or merely silent Nature's breathing life' (ll. 25–8). Wordsworth's 'moving tide' in Tennyson becomes a 'tide as moving seems asleep', as the barely susceptible 'motion' of the tide in 'Elegiac Stanzas' reaches stasis. Tennyson's speaker hopes to be carried home for one last time on his sleeping tide, as the stanza itself, in its wave-like rhythm, mimics the action of the tide itself, simultaneously confirming yet undermining the speaker's wishes.

That Tennyson should be carried on a moving, yet recalcitrant, tide of Wordsworth's language seems a fitting metaphor for the processes at work in his poetry that this book has traced. Tennyson's poetry has been fed, supported, clarified, complicated and directed by the Wordsworthian echoes it contains; redirected by it in some instances. The book has moved on from existing readings to offer a more complicated, nuanced view of Tennyson's relationship with Wordsworth's poetry and some of its key themes, such as the re-encountering of the self in time and the concept of sympathy; it has offered a more intricate view of Tennyson's dramatic experiments, the monologue and the monodrama, as well as a more complex view of Tennyson's own relationship with the poetry of sensation. Tennyson draws freely from Wordsworth's language, even in poems of sensation like 'The Lady of Shalott' (1832; revised 1842), *Maud* (1855) and 'Tithonus' (1860). Tennyson's borrowed language strengthens the 1842 version of 'The Lady of Shalott', but also complicates it. It tests Tennyson's designation as a poet of sensation, a status which he himself tests in later poems; 'Dora' (1842) and 'The Gardener's Daughter' (1842) are revealed as part of a Wordsworthian continuum. It also stabilises Tennyson's public voice, as he shares in the earlier poet's cultural status. Tennyson revises his predecessor, but is simultaneously revised by him, as he shares in a poetry less concerned with self and more concerned with general humanity. At the same time, Tennyson helps to stabilise Wordsworth's own poetic reputation. *Maud* develops Wordsworth's poetics and reveals its dependency on them, growing out of Wordsworth's 'The Preface', in its concern with passion, but distanced from Wordsworth's morality, communitarianism and sympathy. Wordsworth forms thematic and structural links in the poem – the 'Lucy' poems underpin the trajectory of the later monologue, for instance, confirming *Maud*'s literary heritage and Maud's destiny. *Maud* also functions as an extenuation of the narrative complexity of *Lyrical Ballads*, but also draws on the genre-shifting aspects of *The White Doe of Rylstone* (1815), with its move towards lyric. Wordsworthian ballad forms patterns of connectivity in the poem, helping the poem to cohere, but also diverts and redirects it. Wordsworth's echoing presence in the poem provides Tennyson with a link to his Wordsworthian past, consolidating his sense of continuity with what came before; through such continuity comes strength and the creation of a 'new' dramatic form. The borrowings from Wordsworth enable Tennyson to reflect on the nature of his poetic status in a language which is itself reflective, while simultaneously validating Wordsworth's critical reputation. In 'Tithonus' Tennyson breaks form, revising the Wordsworthian trope of the self in time, but cannot escape the influence of its attenuated gleam; rather, Wordsworth's enervated trope is integral to the functioning and cohesion of the monologue, questioning in turn the later poet's ability to write as a dramatic artist and his distance from Romantic subjectivity. Tennyson does not repress Wordsworth, nor his language of reflection, in acts of Bloomian repression or revisionism but is empowered by both; he does not lament his belatedness in these poems so much as embrace it.

Similarly, in 'Ulysses', Tennyson seemingly strengthens the form of the monologue, revising the universal subjectivity of the Wordsworthian speaker; and yet Wordsworth's presence in the monologue remains vital, a fact underlined by Ulysses' own search for that which the poem has itself defined as lost. In writing the poem as a monologue, Tennyson breaks form but cannot break his dependency on Wordsworth's subjectivity. Tennyson is less overwhelmed by Wordsworth here than overwhelmed by his absence. In *In Memoriam*, Tennyson again draws on Wordsworth to settle his public voice, but also to mitigate the vagaries of faith and science and to make his accommodations with them; he draws too on Wordsworth's pastoralism in support of the poem. Wordsworth's presence becomes an enabling one, allowing the later poet to stabilise the form of the elegy. Likewise, Tennyson validates and consolidates Wordsworth's own acknowledgement of the disjunction between mind and nature and the sad mechanic exercise that the pastoral elegy has become.

The book has worked at the level of language and phrasing, what Harold Bloom would consider the surface level.[7] But the surface reveals its own depths. Wordsworth's presence is enabling for Tennyson, allowing him to create, to revise, to position his poetry in relation to what came before; but in a reciprocal process, Tennyson is himself positioned and directed, supported and sometimes diverted. In echoing Wordsworth's language, Tennyson redefines his own status as both poet and post-Romantic poet. He also singularly questions Bloom's theory of anxiety-ridden psychic competition, with Wordsworth revealed as the lynchpin of Tennyson's poetry from 1842 to 1889. Tennyson is not flooded by Wordsworth's presence in this period so much as borne by it. Yet, at the same time, Tennyson redefines Wordsworth's status, reshaping the earlier poet for a new age, and complicating standard Victorian models of the prophetic or nutritive Wordsworth of Matthew Arnold's 'Memorial Verses, 1850'. Arnold in the 'Memorial Verses' laments the loss of Wordsworth's power to 'make us feel',[8] asking, 'But where will Europe's latter hour / Again find Wordsworth's healing power?' (ll. 62–3). Wordsworth's power to make us feel has been transfigured in *Maud*; the link between imagination and nature has been severed in 'Tithonus'. Yet, through Wordsworth, Tennyson helps the reader to feel in a new way; the gleam, though faded, has a new power. Wordsworth also has a healing power of a new kind, helping Tennyson to heal the wound in his poetic art; to heal his 'crisis' of faith, his 'crisis' of composition, sometimes his 'crisis' of form. Borrowing Wordsworth's language from 'Tintern Abbey', Arnold urges 'Rotha' to 'Keep fresh the grass upon [Wordsworth's] grave' (l. 71) with his own 'living wave!' (l. 72); 'Sing him thy best! for few or none / Hears thy voice right, now he is gone' (ll. 73–4). But Wordsworth has not gone; he remains a vital presence in Tennyson's poetry until the end of his career. Tennyson does not move away from Wordsworth as his career progresses, revealing himself just as reliant on the 'old Bard' in 1889 as he is in 1842.[9]

In looking back to Wordsworth, Tennyson nevertheless also looks forward. Tennyson's images of weaving and reaping are often read as prescient signifiers of poststructuralism and the instability or fluidity of the postmodern text.[10] Tennyson once described his own interpretive strategies, stating that '"I hate to be tied down to say '*This* means *that*,' because the thought within the image is much more than any one interpretation"'.[11] 'This' has not meant 'that' in the Tennyson poems featured in the book, as the poet's language and phrasing echoes and re-echoes with multiple meanings. Equally, Tennyson has not been tied down in his reading of Wordsworth. I began the book by stating that the reading of poetry is a creative as well as an imaginative act,[12] and this is as true of Tennyson's reading of Wordsworth as it is of my reading of Tennyson reading Wordsworth.

Stephen Gill suggests that Tennyson knew his own value, his own place as a poet, as Poet Laureate and as a Victorian cultural icon, and that his reverence for Wordsworth was not disabling to his own work; the Wordsworthian 'thick ankles' allow Tennyson better to know his own place, from this perspective.[13] Yet, as the book has shown, Wordsworth's thick ankles have not proved so unwieldy for Tennyson: Tennyson's engagement with Wordsworth's prosaic language is more vital than previously thought, giving the lie to Tennyson's glib parody, 'A Mr Wilkinson, a Clergyman'.[14] Tennyson does not know his own place as a poet, as Poet Laureate and as a Victorian cultural icon through Wordsworth's apparent weaknesses; rather, he reveals through his echoes and borrowings from the full range of Wordsworth's language and phrasing that his place is with the earlier poet. It is through Wordsworth that Tennyson is able to anchor himself as a poet, as Poet Laureate and as a Victorian cultural icon. If, as Arnold suggests, Tennyson overtakes Wordsworth in the public imagination from 1842,[15] then this is a transition that is supported and facilitated by Wordsworth himself.

Notes

1. Tennyson, *The Poems of Tennyson*, III (p. 253). All other references to the poem are to this volume and appear parenthetically in the text.
2. Tennyson, *The Poems of Tennyson*, III, p. 253.
3. Tennyson, *The Poems of Tennyson*, III, p. 253.
4. Wordsworth, *The Poetical Works of William Wordsworth in Five Volumes*, I, ll. 173–80 (p. 61). Other references to the poem are to this volume and appear parenthetically in the text.
5. Wordsworth, *Poems, in Two Volumes*, II, l. 58 (p. 144). Other references to the poem are to this volume and appear parenthetically in the text.
6. Ricks notices the movement towards the collective at the close of 'Crossing the Bar' too. See Ricks, *Tennyson*, pp. 314–15.
7. Bloom, *The Anxiety of Influence*, p. 31.
8. Arnold, 'Memorial Verses, April 1850', l. 67 (p. 188).
9. Tennyson, *Alfred Tennyson: A Memoir*, I, p. 210.
10. Stott, 'Introduction', p. 4.
11. Tennyson, *Alfred Lord Tennyson: A Memoir*, II, p. 127.
12. Iser, 'The Reading Process', p. 215.
13. Gill, *Wordsworth and the Victorians*, p. 195.
14. Tennyson, *Alfred Lord Tennyson: A Memoir*, I, p. 153.
15. Arnold, 'Wordsworth', p. 699.

Bibliography

Allen, Graham, *Intertextuality* (London: Routledge, 2000).

Allen, Peter, *The Cambridge Apostles: The Early Years* (Cambridge: Cambridge University Press, 1978).

Armstrong, Isobel, 'Tennyson's "The Lady of Shalott": Victorian Mythography and the Politics of Narcissism', in J. B. Bullen (ed.), *The Sun Is God: Painting, Literature and Mythology in the Nineteenth Century* (Oxford: Clarendon Press, 1989), pp. 48–107.

—, *Victorian Poetry: Poetry, Poetics and Politics* (London and New York: Routledge, 1993).

Arnold, Matthew, 'Memorial Verses, April 1850', in *Matthew Arnold: Poetry and Prose*, ed. John Bryson (London: Rupert Hart-Davis, [1850] 1954), pp. 187–9.

—, 'On Translating Homer', in *Matthew Arnold: Poetry and Prose*, ed. John Bryson (London: Rupert Hart-Davis, [1861] 1954), pp. 287–316.

—, 'Wordsworth', in 'Essays in Criticism', in *Matthew Arnold: Poetry and Prose*, ed. John Bryson (London: Rupert Hart-Davis, [1879] 1954), pp. 698–714.

Ball, Patricia M., 'Tennyson and the Romantics', *Victorian Poetry*, 1.1 (January 1963), pp. 7–16.

Barthes, Roland, *Image-Music-Text*, trans. Stephen Heath (London: Fontana, 1977).

Barton, Anna, *Alfred Lord Tennyson's* In Memoriam: *A Reading Guide* (Edinburgh: Edinburgh University Press, 2012).

Berglund, Lisa, '"Faultily Faultless": The Structure of Tennyson's *Maud*', *Victorian Poetry*, 27.1 (Spring 1989), pp. 45–59.

Bloom, Harold, *Poetry and Repression: Revisionism from Blake to Stevens* (New Haven, CT and London: Yale University Press, 1976).

—, *The Anxiety of Influence: A Theory of Poetry*, 2nd edn (New York and Oxford: Oxford University Press, 1997).

Brown, Sarah Annes, *A Familiar Compound Ghost: Allusion and the Uncanny* (Manchester and New York: Manchester University Press, 2012).

Bruns, Gerald, 'The Formal Nature of Victorian Thinking', *PMLA*, 90 (1977), pp. 404–18.

Bruster, Douglas, *Quoting Shakespeare: Form and Culture in Early Modern Drama* (Lincoln, NE: University of Nebraska Press, 2000).

Buckler, W. E., *The Victorian Imagination: Essays in Aesthetic Exploration* (Brighton: Harvester, 1980).

Byron, George Gordon, Lord, *The Poetical Works of Lord Byron*, ed. George Cumberlege (London: Oxford University Press, 1950).

Cameron, Sharon, *Impersonality: Seven Essays* (Chicago: University of Chicago Press, 2007).

Campbell, Matthew, *Rhythm and Will in Victorian Poetry* (Cambridge: Cambridge University Press, 1999).

Cavell, Stanley, *In Quest of the Ordinary: Lines of Skepticism and Romanticism* (Chicago and London: University of Chicago Press, 1994).

Chadwick, Joseph, 'A Blessing and a Curse: The Poetics of Privacy in Tennyson's "The Lady of Shalott"', in Herbert F. Tucker, Jr (ed.), *Critical Essays on Alfred Lord Tennyson* (New York: G. K. Hall & Co., 1983), pp. 83–9.

Chandler, James, 'Hallam, Tennyson, and the Poetry of Sensation: Aestheticist Allegories of a Counter-Public Sphere', *Studies in Romanticism*, 33.4 (Winter 1994), pp. 527–37.

Christ, Carol T., 'Introduction: Victorian Poetics', in Richard Cronin, Alison Chapman and Antony H. Harrison (eds), *A Companion to Victorian Poetry* (Malden, MA and Oxford: Blackwell, 2007), pp. 1–21.

—, 'The Feminine Subject in Victorian Poetry', *ELH*, 54.2 (Summer 1987), pp. 385–401.

—, 'T. S. Eliot and the Victorians', *Modern Philology*, 79.2 (November 1981), pp. 157–65.

—, *Victorian and Modern Poetics* (Chicago: University of Chicago Press, 1984).

Churton Collins, John, 'A New Study of Tennyson', *Cornhill Magazine*, 241 (January 1880), pp. 36–50. By permission of The Tennyson Research Centre.

Cole, Sarah Rose, 'The Recovery of Friendship: Male Love and Developmental Narrative in Tennyson's *In Memoriam*', *Victorian Poetry*, 50.1 (Spring 2012), pp. 43–66.

Coleridge, Samuel Taylor, *The Complete Poetical Works of Samuel Taylor Coleridge*, including *Poems* and *Versions of Poems* now published for the first time, ed. with textual and bibliographical notes by Ernest Hartley Coleridge, 2 vols (Oxford: Oxford University Press, 1912), I.

Croker, John Wilson, 'John Wilson Croker on Alfred Tennyson – from Spring 1833', <http://www.quarterly-review.org/poem-by-alfred-tennyson-review-from-spring-1833/> (last accessed 31 July 2017).

Cronin, Richard, 'Edward Lear and Tennyson's Nonsense', in Robert Douglas-Fairhurst and Seamus Perry (eds), *Tennyson among the Poets: Bicentenary Essays* (Oxford: Oxford University Press, 2009), pp. 259–75.

—, *Reading Victorian Poetry* (Chichester and Malden, MA: Wiley-Blackwell, 2012).

—, *Romantic Victorians: English Literature, 1824–1840* (Basingstoke: Palgrave, 2002).

—, 'The Spasmodics', in Richard Cronin, Alison Chapman and Antony H. Harrison (eds), *A Companion to Victorian Poetry* (Malden, MA and Oxford: Blackwell, 2007), pp. 291–304.

Danby, John F., *The Simple Wordsworth: Studies in the Poems 1797–1807* (London: Routledge & Kegan Paul, 1960).

Dante Alighieri, *The Inferno of Dante Alighieri*, ed. Israel Gollancz (London: J. M. Dent, [1320] 1903).

Davidson, Graham, 'Wordsworth's Wasteland or the Speargrass Redemption', *Romanticism*, 20.1 (2014), pp. 73–83.

Day, Aidan, *Romanticism* (London and New York: Routledge, 1996).

—, *Tennyson's Scepticism* (Basingstoke: Palgrave Macmillan, 2005).

Decker, Christopher, 'Tennyson's Limitations', in Robert Douglas-Fairhurst and Seamus Perry (eds), *Tennyson among the Poets: Bicentenary Essays* (Oxford: Oxford University Press, 2009), pp. 57–75.

Dillon, Steven C., 'Canonical and Sensational: Arthur Hallam and Tennyson's 1830 *Poems*', *Victorian Poetry*, 30.2 (Summer 1992), pp. 95–108.

Douglas-Fairhurst, Robert, 'Introduction', in Robert Douglas-Fairhurst and Seamus Perry (eds), *Tennyson among the Poets: Bicentenary Essays* (Oxford: Oxford University Press, 2009), pp. 1–13.

—, 'Tennyson', in Michael O'Neill (ed.), *The Cambridge History of English Poetry* (Cambridge: Cambridge University Press, 2004), pp. 596–616.

—, *Victorian Afterlives: The Shaping of Influence in Nineteenth-Century Literature* (Oxford: Oxford University Press, 2004).

Dransfield, Scott, 'The Morbid Meters of *Maud*', *Victorian Poetry*, 46.3 (Fall 2008), pp. 279–97.

Eliot, T. S., *Collected Poems: 1909–1962* (London: Faber and Faber, 1974).

—, *Selected Prose of T. S. Eliot*, ed. and with an introduction by Frank Kermode (London: Faber and Faber, 1975).

Ellmann, Maud, 'Introduction', in Sigmund Freud, *On Murder, Mourning and Melancholia*, trans. Shaun Whiteside (London: Penguin, [1917] 2005), pp. vii–xxvii.

Freud, Sigmund, 'Mourning and Melancholia', in *On Murder, Mourning and Melancholia*, trans. Shaun Whiteside, with an introduction by Maud Ellmann (London: Penguin, [1917] 2005), pp. 203–18.

Gill, Stephen, *Wordsworth and the Victorians* (Oxford: Clarendon Press, 1998).

Goldsmith, Jason N., 'Wordsworth's *Lyrical Ballads*, 1800', in Richard Gravil and Daniel Robinson (eds), *The Oxford Handbook of William Wordsworth* (Oxford: Oxford University Press, 2015), pp. 204–20.

Gravil, Richard, 'Introduction', in Richard Gravil and Daniel Robinson (eds), *The Oxford Handbook of William Wordsworth* (Oxford: Oxford University Press, 2015), pp. 1–13.

Gray, Thomas, *The Complete Poems of Thomas Gray: English, Latin and Greek*, ed. H. W. Starr and J. R. Hendrickson (Oxford: Clarendon Press, 1966).

Hallam, Arthur Henry, 'On Some of the Characteristics of Modern Poetry, and on the Lyrical Poems of Alfred Tennyson', in Richard Le Gallienne (ed.), *The Poems of Arthur Henry Hallam: Together With His Essay on the Lyrical Poems of Alfred Tennyson* (London: Elkin Mathews & John Lane, [1831] 1893), pp. 87–139.

—, *The Poems of Arthur Henry Hallam: Together With His Essay on the Lyrical Poems of Alfred Tennyson*, ed. and with an introduction by Richard Le Gallienne (London: Elkin Mathews & John Lane, [1831] 1893).

Harris, Daniel A., 'Personification in "Tithonus"', in Herbert F. Tucker, Jr (ed.), *Critical Essays on Alfred Lord Tennyson* (New York: G. K. Hall & Co., 1993), pp. 100–24.

Hartman, Geoffrey H., 'Retrospect 1971', in *Wordsworth's Poetry 1787–1814*, 1964 edition, with the addition of the essay 'Retrospect 1971' (New Haven, CT and London: Yale University Press, 1971), pp. xi–xx.

—, *The Unremarkable Wordsworth*, foreword by Donald G. Marshall (London: Methuen, 1987).

—, *Wordsworth's Poetry 1787–1814*, 1964 edition, with the addition of the essay 'Retrospect 1971' (New Haven, CT and London: Yale University Press, 1971).

Hartman, Herbert, 'Wordsworth's "Lucy" Poems: Notes and Marginalia', *PMLA*, 49.1 (March 1934), pp. 134–42.

Hinds, Stephen, *Allusion and Intertext: Dynamics of Appropriation in Roman Poetry* (Cambridge: Cambridge University Press, 1998).

Hollander, John, 'The Anxiety of Influence', *New York Times* (4 March 1973), <http://www.nytimes.com/books/98/11/01/specials/bloom-influence.html> (last accessed July 2017).

—, *The Figure of Echo: A Mode of Allusion in Milton and After* (Berkeley, CA and London: University of California Press, 1981).

Hopkins, Gerard Manley, *The Poetical Works of Gerard Manley Hopkins*, ed. Norman H. Mackenzie (Oxford: Clarendon Press, 1990).

Hsiao, Irene, 'Calculating Loss in Tennyson's *In Memoriam*', *Victorian Poetry*, 47.1 (Spring 2009), pp. 173–96.

Hughes, Linda K., *The Manyfacèd Glass: Tennyson's Monologues* (Athens, OH: Ohio University Press, 1987).

Iser, Wolfgang, 'The Reading Process: A Phenomenological Approach', in David Lodge (ed.), *Modern Criticism and Theory: A Reader* (London and New York: Longman, 1988), pp. 212–28.

Jordan, Elaine, *Alfred Tennyson* (Cambridge: Cambridge University Press, 1988).

Jump, John D. (ed.) *Tennyson: The Critical Heritage* (London: Routledge & Kegan Paul, 1967).

Kant, Immanuel, *Critique of Pure Reason*, trans. Norman Kemp Smith (London: Macmillan, [1781] 1929).

Keats, John, *Selected Poems and Letters of John Keats*, ed. and with an introduction and commentary by Robert Gittings (London: Heinemann, 1966).

Keble, John, 'The Third Sunday after Epiphany', in *The Christian Year: Thoughts in Verse for the Sundays and Holydays Throughout the Year* (London and New York: Longmans, Green and Co., [1827] 1898), pp. 38–41.

Kennedy, Ian H. C., '*In Memoriam* and the Tradition of Pastoral Elegy', *Victorian Poetry*, 15.4 (1977), pp. 351–66.

Kramer, Lawrence, 'Victorian Poetry/Oedipal Politics: *In Memoriam* and Other Instances', *Victorian Poetry*, 29.4 (Winter 1991), pp. 351–63.

—, 'Victorian Sexuality and "Tintern Abbey"', *Victorian Poetry*, 24.4 (Winter 1986), pp. 399–410.

Kristeva, Julia, *Desire in Language: A Semiotic Approach to Literature and Art*, ed. Leon S. Roudiez, trans. Thomas Gora, Alice Jardine and Leon S. Roudiez (New York: Columbia University Press, 1980).

Landow, George P., 'Rainbows: Problematic Images of Problematic Nature' (July 2007), <http://www.victorianweb.org/art/crisis/crisis3c.httr> (last accessed 16 April 2013).

Langbaum, Robert Woodrow, *The Poetry of Experience: The Dramatic Monologue in Modern Literary Tradition* (London: Chatto and Windus, 1957).

Larkin, Peter, *Wordsworth and Coleridge: Promising Losses* (New York: Palgrave Macmillan, 2012).

Leighton, Angela, *On Form: Poetry, Aestheticism and the Legacy of a Word* (Oxford: Oxford University Press, 2007).

Levinson, Marjorie, *Wordsworth's Great Period Poems* (Cambridge: Cambridge University Press, 1986).

Lourie, Margaret A., 'Below the Thunders of the Upper Deep: Tennyson as Romantic Revisionist', *Studies in Romanticism*, 18.1, Victorian Romanticism II (Spring 1979), pp. 3–27.

McDonald, Peter, *Sound Intentions: The Workings of Rhyme in Nineteenth-Century Poetry* (Oxford: Oxford University Press, 2012).

—, 'Tennyson's Dying Fall', in Robert Douglas-Fairhurst and Seamus Perry (eds), *Tennyson Among the Poets: Bicentenary Essays* (Oxford: Oxford University Press, 2009), pp. 14–38.

McGann, Jerome J., *The Romantic Ideology: A Critical Investigation* (Chicago and London: Chicago University Press, 1983).

Makdisi, Saree, *Romantic Imperialism: Universal Empire and the Culture of Modernity* (Cambridge: Cambridge University Press, 1998).

Maltby, Paul, *The Visionary Moment: A Postmodern Critique* (Albany, NY: State University of New York Press, 2002).

Manning, Peter J., '*The White Doe of Rylstone* and Later Narrative Poems', in Richard Gravil and Daniel Robinson (eds), *The Oxford Handbook of William Wordsworth* (Oxford: Oxford University Press, 2015), pp. 268–88.

Martens, Britta, *Browning, Victorian Poetics and the Romantic Legacy: Challenging the Personal Voice* (Farnham: Ashgate, 2011).

Mellor, Anne K., *Romanticism and Gender* (New York and London: Routledge, 1993).

Mermin, Dorothy, 'The Damsel, the Knight, and the Victorian Woman Poet', *Critical Inquiry*, 13.1 (1 October 1986), pp. 64–80.

Mill, John Stuart, 'Thoughts on Poetry and its Varieties', in John M. Robson and Jack Stillinger (eds), *Collected Works of John Stuart Mill: Autobiography and Literary Essays*, 33 vols (Toronto: University of Toronto Press; London: Routledge & Kegan Paul, [1833] 1963–91), I, pp. 341–65.

Milton, John, *Paradise Lost*, edited with an introduction and notes by John Leonard (London and New York: Penguin, [1667] 2003).

Newlyn, Lucy, *Coleridge, Wordsworth, and the Language of Allusion* (Oxford: Clarendon Press, 1986).

—, 'Foreword', in Damian Walford Davies and Richard Marggraf Turley (eds), *The Monstrous Debt: Modalities of Romantic Influence in Twentieth-Century Literature* (Detroit, MI: Wayne State University Press, 2006), pp. vii–xiii.

Nichols, Ashton, *The Poetics of Epiphany: Nineteenth-Century Origins of the Modern Literary Moment* (Tuscaloosa, AL: University of Alabama Press, 1987).

O'Donnell, Angela G., 'Tennyson's "English Idyls": Studies in Poetic Decorum', *Studies in Philology*, 85.1 (Winter 1988), pp. 125–44.

O'Gorman, Francis, 'What Is Haunting Tennyson's *Maud* (1855)?', *Victorian Poetry*, 48.3 (Fall 2010), pp. 293–312.

O'Neill, Michael, '"A Kind of an Excuse": Shelley and Wordsworth Revisited', in Ashley Chantler, Michael Davies and Philip Shaw (eds), *Literature and Authenticity, 1780–1900: Essays in Honour of Vincent Newey* (Farnham: Ashgate, 2011), pp. 51–65.

—, '"Infinite Passion": Variations on a Romantic Topic in Robert Browning, Emily Brontë, Swinburne, Hopkins, Wilde and Dowson', in Andrew Radford and Mark Sandy (eds), *Romantic Echoes in the Victorian Era* (Aldershot and Burlington, VT: Ashgate, 2008), pp. 175–89.

—, 'The Romantic Bequest: Arnold and Others', in Matthew Bevis (ed.), *The Oxford Handbook of Victorian Poetry* (Oxford: Oxford University Press, 2013), pp. 217–34.

—, *Romanticism and the Self-Conscious Poem* (Oxford: Clarendon Press, 1997).

—, *The All-Sustaining Air: Romantic Legacies and Renewals in British, American, and Irish Poetry since 1900* (Oxford: Oxford University Press, 2007).

—, 'The Wheels of Being: Tennyson and Shelley', in Robert Douglas-Fairhurst and Seamus Perry (eds), *Tennyson among the Poets: Bicentenary Essays* (Oxford: Oxford University Press, 2009), pp. 181–98.

—, 'Yeats, Stevens, Rich, Bishop: Responses to Romantic Poetry', in Damian Walford Davies and Richard Marggraf Turley (eds), *The Monstrous*

Debt: Modalities of Romantic Influence in Twentieth-Century Literature (Detroit, MI: Wayne State University Press, 2006), pp. 143–62.

O'Neill, Michael and Paige Tovey, 'Shelley and the English Tradition: Spenser and Pope', in Michael O'Neill and Anthony Howe (eds), with the Assistance of Madeleine Callaghan, *The Oxford Handbook of Percy Bysshe Shelley* (Oxford: Oxford University Press, 2012), pp. 494–512.

Padel, Ruth, 'Tennyson: Echo and Harmony, Music and Thought', in Matthew Bevis (ed.), *The Oxford Handbook of Victorian Poetry* (Oxford: Oxford University Press, 2013), pp. 323–36.

Page, Norman, *Tennyson: Interviews and Recollections* (London: Macmillan, 1983).

Parrish, Stephen Maxwell, '"The Thorn": Wordsworth's Dramatic Monologue', *ELH*, 24 (1957), pp. 153–63.

Pearsall, Cornelia, *Tennyson's Rapture: Transformation in the Victorian Dramatic Monologue* (Oxford: Oxford University Press, 2008).

Pease, Allison, '*Maud* and its Discontents', *Criticism: A Quarterly for Literature and the Arts*, 36.1 (Winter 1994), pp. 101–18.

Perry, Seamus, *Alfred Tennyson* (Tavistock: Northcote House, 2005).

—, 'Betjeman's Tennyson', in Robert Douglas-Fairhurst and Seamus Perry (eds), *Tennyson among the Poets: Bicentenary Essays* (Oxford: Oxford University Press, 2009), pp. 409–26.

—, 'Elegy', in Richard Cronin, Alison Chapman and Anthony H. Harrison (eds), *A Companion to Victorian Poetry* (Malden, MA and Oxford: Blackwell Publishing, 2007), pp. 115–33.

—, 'Two Voices: Tennyson and Wordsworth', *Tennyson Research Bulletin*, 8.1 (2003), pp. 11–27.

Peterson, Linda H., 'Domestic and Idyllic', in Richard Cronin, Alison Chapman and Anthony H. Harrison (eds), *A Companion to Victorian Poetry* (Malden, MA and Oxford: Blackwell Publishing, 2007), pp. 42–58.

Pinch, Adela, 'Female Chatter: Meter, Masochism and the *Lyrical Ballads*', *ELH*, 55.4 (Winter 1988), pp. 835–52.

—, *Strange Fits of Passion: Epistemologies of Emotion, Hume to Austen* (Stanford, CA: Stanford University Press, 1996).

Plasa, Carl, '"Cracked from Side to Side": Sexual Politics in "The Lady of Shalott"', *Victorian Poetry*, 30.3–4 (Autumn–Winter 1992), pp. 247–63.

Psomiades, Kathy, '"The Lady of Shalott" and the Critical Fortunes of Victorian Poetry', in Joseph Bristow (ed.), *The Cambridge Companion to Victorian Poetry* (Cambridge: Cambridge University Press, 2005), pp. 25–45.

Rader, R. W., *Tennyson's 'Maud': The Biographical Genesis* (Berkeley, CA and London: University of California Press, 1963).

Radford, Andrew and Mark Sandy (eds), *Romantic Echoes in the Victorian Era* (Aldershot and Burlington, VT: Ashgate, 2008).

Rapf, Joanna E., '"Visionaries of Dereliction": Wordsworth and Tennyson', *Victorian Poetry*, 24.4 (Winter 1986), pp. 373–85.

Ricks, Christopher, *Allusion to the Poets* (Oxford: Oxford University Press, 2002).

—, 'Preface', in Robert Douglas-Fairhurst and Seamus Perry (eds), *Tennyson among the Poets: Bicentenary Essays* (Oxford: Oxford University Press, 2009).

—, *Tennyson* (London and Basingstoke: Macmillan, 1972).

Robinson, Daniel, '*Lyrical Ballads*, 1798', in Richard Gravil and Daniel Robinson (eds), *The Oxford Handbook of William Wordsworth* (Oxford: Oxford University Press, 2015), pp. 168–85.

Rowlinson, Matthew, *An Introduction to* In Memoriam, <http:// www. academia.edu>_(last accessed 3 March 2014).

—, 'Lyric', in Richard Cronin, Alison Chapman and Anthony H. Harrison (eds), *A Companion to Victorian Poetry* (Malden, MA: Blackwell, 2002), pp. 59–79.

—, *Tennyson's Fixations: Psychoanalysis and the Topics of the Early Poetry* (Charlottesville, VA and London: University Press of Virginia, 1994).

Ruskin, John, *The Works of John Ruskin*, ed. E. T. Cook and Alexander Wedderburn, 39 vols (London: George Allen; New York: Longmans, Green, 1903–12), XXXVI.

Sacks, Peter M., *The English Elegy: Studies in the Genre from Spenser to Yeats* (Baltimore, MD and London: Johns Hopkins University Press, 1985).

Sanford Russell, Beatrice, 'How to Exist Where You Are: A Lesson in Lotos-Eating', *Victorian Poetry*, 53.4 (Winter 2015), pp. 375–99.

Shaw, W. David, 'Poetry and Religion', in Richard Cronin, Alison Chapman and Anthony H. Harrison (eds), *A Companion to Victorian Poetry* (Malden, MA and Oxford: Blackwell Publishing, 2007), pp. 457–74.

—, *Tennyson's Style* (Ithaca, NY and London: Cornell University Press, 1976).

Shelley, Percy Bysshe, *The Complete Works of Percy Bysshe Shelley*, ed. Thomas Hutchinson (London: Oxford University Press, 1905).

Shires, Linda M., '*Maud*, Masculinity and Poetic Identity', *Criticism: A Quarterly for Literature and the Arts*, 29.3 (Summer 1987), pp. 269–90.

—, 'Patriarchy, Dead Men and Tennyson's *Idylls of the King*', *Victorian Poetry*, 30.3–4, Centennial of Alfred, Lord Tennyson: 1809–1892 (Autumn–Winter 1992), pp. 401–19.

Simonsen, Peter, *Wordsworth and Word-Preserving Arts: Typographic Inscription, Ekphrasis, and Posterity in the Later Work* (Basingstoke: Palgrave Macmillan, 2007).

Sinfield, Alan, *Alfred Tennyson* (Oxford: Blackwell, 1986).

—, *The Language of Tennyson's 'In Memoriam'* (Oxford: Blackwell, 1971).

Slinn, E. Warwick, 'Dramatic Monologue', in Richard Cronin, Alison Chapman and Anthony H. Harrison (eds), *A Companion to Victorian Poetry* (Malden, MA and Oxford: Blackwell Publishing, 2007), pp. 80–98.

Sprinker, Michael, "A Counterpoint of Dissonance": *The Aesthetics and Poetry of Gerard Manley Hopkins* (Baltimore, MD and London: Johns Hopkins University Press, 1980).

Starzyk, Lawrence, 'If Mine Had Been the Painter's Hand': *The Indeterminate in Nineteenth-Century Poetry and Painting* (New York: Peter Lang, 1999).

Stevenson, Lionel, 'The "High-Born" Maiden Symbol in Tennyson', in John Killham (ed.), *Critical Essays on the Poetry of Tennyson* (London: Routledge & Kegan Paul, 1960), pp. 126–36.

Stott, Rebecca, 'Introduction', in Rebecca Scott (ed.), *Tennyson* (Harlow: Longman, 1996), pp. 1–23.

Sullivan, Michael J., 'Tennyson and *The Golden Treasury*: A Rediscovered Copy', *Literary Imagination*, 18.3 (2016), pp. 230–8.

Sylvia, Richard A., 'Reading Tennyson's *Ballads and Other Poems* in Context', *The Journal of the Midwest Modern Language Association*, 23.1 (Spring 1990), pp. 27–44.

Tennyson, Alfred, Lord, *In Memoriam*, ed. Susan Shatto and Marion Shaw (Oxford: Clarendon Press, [1850] 1982).

—, '*In Memoriam*, Introduction by the Editor', in Hallam, Lord Tennyson (ed.), annotated by Alfred, Lord Tennyson, *The Works of Tennyson*, 9 vols (London: Macmillan Eversley, 1907–8), III, pp. 194–224.

—, 'Notes' to *In Memoriam*, in Hallam, Lord Tennyson (ed.), annotated by Alfred, Lord Tennyson, *The Works of Tennyson*, 9 vols (London: Macmillan Eversley, 1907–8), III, pp. 224–65.

—, *Poems*, with autograph notes and corrections (London: Moxon, 1833). By permission of the Syndics of the Fitzwilliam Museum, Cambridge.

—, *Tennyson's* Maud: *A Definitive Edition*, edited with introduction and commentary by Susan Shatto (London: The Athlone Press, [1855] 1986).

—, *The Letters of Alfred Lord Tennyson: Volume I, 1821–1850*, ed. Cecil Y. Lang and Edgar F. Shannon, Jr, (Oxford: Clarendon Press, 1982).

—, *The Poems of Tennyson in Three Volumes*, ed. Christopher Ricks, 2nd edn (Harlow: Longman, 1987).

Tennyson, Hallam, *Alfred Lord Tennyson: A Memoir by His Son*, 2 vols (London: Macmillan, 1897).

Tucker, Herbert F., Jr, 'Dramatic Monologue and the Overhearing of Lyric', in Chaviva Hosek and Patricia Parker (eds), *Lyric Poetry: Beyond the New Criticism* (Ithaca, NY: Cornell University Press, 1985), pp. 226–43.

—, 'Epiphany and Browning: Character Made Manifest', *PMLA*, 107 (October 1992), pp. 1208–21.

—, *Tennyson and the Doom of Romanticism* (Cambridge, MA and London: Harvard University Press, 1988).

Weinfield, Henry, '"Of Happy Men That Have the Power to Die": Tennyson's "Tithonus"', *Victorian Poetry*, 47.2 (2009), pp. 355–78.

Weiskel, Thomas, *The Romantic Sublime: Studies in the Structure and Psychology of Transcendence* (Baltimore, MD and London: Johns Hopkins University Press, 1976).

Wheeler, Michael, *Heaven, Hell, and the Victorians* (Cambridge: Cambridge University Press, 1994).

Wordsworth, William, *Early Poems and Fragments, 1785–1797 by William Wordsworth*, ed. Carol Landon and Jared Curtis (Ithaca, NY: Cornell University Press, 1997).

—, 'Essay, Supplementary to the Preface', in *The Poetical Works of William Wordsworth in Five Volumes* (London: Longman, Rees, Orme, Brown, and Green, 1827), II, pp. 357–91.

—, *Last Poems, 1821–1850 by William Wordsworth*, ed. Jared Curtis, with associate editors Apryl Lea Denny-Ferris and Jillian Heydt-Stevenson (Ithaca, NY: Cornell University Press, 1999).

—, *Lyrical Ballads, with Other Poems, in Two Volumes*, 2nd edn (London: Longman and Rees, 1800).

—, 'Note' to 'The Thorn', *Lyrical Ballads, with Other Poems, in Two Volumes*, 2nd edn (London: Longman and Rees, 1800), I, n.p.

—, *Poems, Chiefly of Early and Late Years; Including The Borderers, a Tragedy* (London: Edward Moxon, 1842).

—, *Poems, in Two Volumes* (London: Longman, 1807).

—, 'Preface to the Edition Published in 1815, in Two Octavo Volumes', in *The Poetical Works of William Wordsworth in Five Volumes* (London: Longman, Rees, Orme, Brown, and Green, 1827), I, pp. ix–xliv.

—, 'Preface to the Second Edition of Several of the Foregoing Poems, Published with an Additional Volume, under the Title of "Lyrical Ballads"', in *The Poetical Works of William Wordsworth in Five Volumes* (London: Longman, Rees, Orme, Brown, and Green, 1827), IV, pp. 357–89.

—, *The Miscellaneous Poems of William Wordsworth: In Four Volumes* (London: Longman, Hurst, Rees, Orme, and Brown, 1820), III.

—, *The Poetical Works of William Wordsworth*, edited from the manuscripts, with textual and critical notes by E. de Selincourt, 5 vols (Oxford: Clarendon Press, 1940).

—, *The Poetical Works of William Wordsworth in Five Volumes* (London: Longman, Rees, Orme, Brown, and Green, 1827).

—, *The Prelude; or, Growth of a Poet's Mind: An Autobiographical Poem* (London: Edward Moxon, 1850).

—, 'The Romantic Poets: Nutting by William Wordsworth' (2010), <http:// www.guardian.com/books/booksblog2010> (last accessed 5 March 2014).

—, *Yarrow Revisited; and Other Poems* (London: Longman, Rees, Orme, Brown, Green, & Longman and Edward Moxon, 1835).

Wu, Duncan, *Wordsworth: An Inner Life* (Oxford and Malden, MA: Blackwell, 2002).

Index